The Ritz Brothers

ALSO BY ROY LIEBMAN
AND FROM MCFARLAND

Broadway Actors in Films, 1894–2015 (2017)

*Silent Film Performers: An Annotated Bibliography
of Published, Unpublished and Archival Sources for More Than
350 Actors and Actresses* (1996; paperback 2012)

Vitaphone Films: A Catalogue of the Features and Shorts
(2003; paperback 2010)

The Wampas Baby Stars: A Biographical Dictionary, 1922–1934
(2000; paperback 2009)

*From Silents to Sound: A Biographical
Encyclopedia of Performers Who Made the Transition
to Talking Pictures* (1998; paperback 2009)

Musical Groups in the Movies, 1929–1970 (2009)

The Ritz Brothers

*The Films, Television Shows
and Other Career Highlights
of the Famous Comedy Trio*

Roy Liebman

McFarland & Company, Inc., Publishers
Jefferson, North Carolina

ISBN (print) 978-1-4766-8136-8
ISBN (ebook) 978-1-4766-4318-2

LIBRARY OF CONGRESS AND BRITISH LIBRARY
CATALOGUING DATA ARE AVAILABLE

Library of Congress Control Number 2021027817

© 2021 Roy Liebman. All rights reserved

No part of this book may be reproduced or transmitted in any form or by any means, electronic or mechanical, including photocopying or recording, or by any information storage and retrieval system, without permission in writing from the publisher.

Front cover image: Al, Harry, and Jimmy hope their hillbilly disguises will fool the real mountain people, the ever-feudin' Hatfields (movie still from *Kentucky Moonshine*, 1938).

Printed in the United States of America

*McFarland & Company, Inc., Publishers
Box 611, Jefferson, North Carolina 28640
www.mcfarlandpub.com*

For my family: Janine Liebman, Marissa Foss, Hannah Tragesser, Russell Foss and certain other (four-legged) family members who kept me close company during the wonderful experience of writing this book.

Acknowledgments

The assistance of the staff at the Cinematic Arts Library, University of Southern California, is much appreciated, especially the advice of the omni-knowledgeable Edward (Ned) Comstock. His help was, as always, invaluable … as the thousands of researchers who came before and after me will attest.

Also, a thank you to the people at Twentieth Century–Fox who many years ago had the foresight to preserve their invaluable archives for posterity. If only *every* studio of fabled Old Hollywood had done the same!

Table of Contents

Acknowledgments	vi
Preface	1
Introduction	7
An Overview	11
On Broadway	26
The Films	30
The Features	43
Sing, Baby, Sing (1936)	43
One in a Million (1936)	47
On the Avenue (1937)	52
You Can't Have Everything (1937)	57
Life Begins in College (1937)	63
The Goldwyn Follies (1938)	71
Kentucky Moonshine (1938)	78
Straight, Place and Show (1938)	85
The Three Musketeers (1939)	90
The Gorilla (1939)	96
Pack Up Your Troubles (1939)	103
Argentine Nights (1940)	108
Behind the Eight Ball (1942)	115
Hi'Ya Chum (1943)	119
Never a Dull Moment (1943)	122
Blazing Stewardesses (1975)	125

Table of Contents

Cameo Appearances ... 130
   Ali Baba Goes to Town (1937) ... 130
   Take It or Leave It (1944) ... 135
   Won Ton Ton, the Dog Who Saved Hollywood (1976) ... 139
   Silent Movie (1976) ... 144

The Short Subjects ... 148
   Hotel Anchovy (1934) ... 148
   Broadway Highlights #6: High Spots of the Main Stem (1936) ... 152
   Cinema Circus (1937) ... 153
   Screen Snapshots (1938–1955) ... 155
   Hollywood Hobbies (1939) ... 159
   Meet the Stars, #6: Stars at Play (1941) ... 162
   Show-Business at War (1943) ... 163
   Brooklyn Goes to Las Vegas (1956) ... 165

Live Television ... 167

Archival Appearances: Films and Television ... 178
   The Sound of Laughter (1963) ... 178
   Hollywood and the Stars: The Funny Men (1963) ... 179
   Hollywood: The Gift of Laughter (1982) ... 180
   Classic Comedy Teams (1986) ... 183
   20th Century–Fox: The First Fifty Years (1997) ... 184
   Hidden Hollywood II: More Treasures from the 20th Century–Fox Vaults (1999) ... 186
   Don Ameche: Hollywood's Class Act (1999) ... 187

Modern-Day Commentators; or, "We Don't Get No Respect" ... 189

Appendix One: The Ritz Brothers' Co-Stars ... 195
Appendix Two: Ritz Brothers Miscellany ... 205
Appendix Three: Versions of The Three Musketeers ... 207
Bibliography ... 209
Index ... 213

Preface

This may be the first full-length book to be written about the Ritz Brothers comedy team: Al, Jimmy and Harry Ritz. In 1958, Walter Ames announced that he was planning to write a book to be called *Don't Holla* (an often-used Harry Ritz line). In the 1960s, Harry claimed that he was writing an autobiography titled *From Rags to Ritzes*. Perhaps it was just the idea of that title which appealed to him. The noted and often controversial film critic Pauline Kael, a Ritz admirer, reportedly wanted to write a book on the team. Apparently none of these came to fruition.

This is not a biography of the Ritz Brothers but it does offer some biographical data about them and the Joachim family from which they sprang. It is primarily an account of the films, both features and short subjects, that the Ritzes made between the mid–1930s and the mid–1970s, and their television appearances. It also provides glimpses into other aspects of their working lives.

From 1949 to the late 1970s, the Ritzes were seen live on a relatively small number of TV shows. (They kept these to a minimum in order to not use up all their material.) On a few of the early shows, they did perform whole routines that gave viewers a good idea of their vaudeville and nightclub acts. A few of these live TV appearances have survived and provide a look at some routines that may not have appeared in their films.

The Ritzes also made radio appearances. One announcement in 1937 said that the brothers and co-star Ethel Merman had made "audition recordings" for radio. It may be that they mainly limited their broadcasts to interviews about upcoming films, but publicity about their radio appearances is scarce except for the *Hollywood Hotel* program.

An account of their career is certainly merited because in their 50-plus years of performing in vaudeville, the stage, movies, TV and nightclubs, they sang, danced, acted and joked their way to considerable fame. Some of their work is becoming more accessible via film festivals and television, and in filmclips and full films on Internet sites.

The Ritzes aren't even well-known by a large number of people in their fifties or even sixties. When the Ritz Brothers are mentioned today, the reaction is often, "Well, I know the name, but I don't know anything about them," or "I never heard of them. Who are they?" Other comedy teams of that era, like the once popular Bert Wheeler and Robert Woolsey, have also faded from modern-day memory, while the Ritzes' contemporaries the Marx Brothers and the Three Stooges have never left the public consciousness.

In 1936, the Ritzes made their feature film debut in *Sing, Baby, Sing*. Soon they were as well-known to moviegoers as they were to vaudeville audiences. "Not exactly stars," opined the *Independent Exhibitors Film Bulletin*, "the value of this trio of madcap clowns should not be underestimated by exhibitors." The fan magazine *Silver Screen* enthused: "The Ritz Brothers insanities are just as necessary to the screen as the genius of a [Charles] Laughton, the Marx Brothers and Eddie Cantor."

In 1937, the fan magazine *Modern Screen* concurred: "Nowadays putting on the Ritz means stealing a picture. Ritz stands for whirlwind action, belly laughs and standing room only. [They] ran up a record by making three pictures in five months."

Nowadays many who do become familiar with their comedy dislike them; in fact, they express their strong dislike with words like "hate." They are often unfavorably compared to the Marx Brothers, one detractor calling them "cut-rate Marx Brothers clones."

Over the years, many books have been written about comedy teams; in some, the Ritz Brothers rate a full chapter, in others a few paragraphs. (Some of these books are cited in the bibliography.) In these books, evaluations of the Ritzes' place in the comedy pantheon include one or more of the usual caveats. These include: "They may have been funny, but…" (there is usually a "but") "they were too similar to each other"; "…Harry was so dominant that the other two were practically his stooges"; "…they could not carry an entire film"; "…they were too slapstick and unsubtle"; "…they were just third-rate imitators of the Marx Brothers."

An excerpt from a review of their debut starring film, *Life Begins in College* (1937): "Clearly the thing to do with the Ritz Brothers is not to try to explain them. In no time at all, they have shot up from vaudeville stage and nightclub floor to a screen eminence." There was an explanation: They had already honed their multiple talents for more than ten years. Like every other comic and comedy team, they had their admirers and detractors. A 1953 article did try to explain them:

> The majority of modern men and women are human time bombs looking for places to explode. Most of their psychosomatic problems arise because they emit only quiet pops rather than loud bangs. Perhaps these Ritz Brothers are better oriented [i.e., adjusted] than the audiences who laugh at their mad antics.

The Ritz Brothers certainly did know how to emit loud bangs!

It may also be interesting to cite books in which they are *not* mentioned. In the scholarly *Jewish Humor: A Serious Study* (2017), written by a Columbia University professor of Yiddish language, literature and culture, the Marx Brothers and the Three Stooges are mentioned, as is every Jewish comedian who openly acknowledged his debt to the Ritz Brothers. There is no mention of the brothers themselves, not even as a footnote. When a serious scholar overlooks you, it is obscurity indeed.

The author appreciates the art of the Ritz Brothers; such disparagements as "cut-rate Marx Brothers clones" seem unfairly critical. They not only had the comedy string to their bow; they were excellent dancers and could put over a song with verve. It is not the author's intention to "restore" their reputation or to convince their detractors, of which there seem to be many. Their work will have to speak for itself.

Comedy is very subjective: Either you appreciate the kind that the Ritz Brothers purveyed, or you do not, or you could not care less one way or the other. The author does agree with many of the legendary comedians of the last few decades who considered them to be masters of the art of comedy.

That said, in 2011 a blog site took a poll of almost 6000 self-described movie buffs: "Who's Your Favorite Pre–1965 Movie Comedy Team?" Presumably there was a list of the teams to choose from. Beloved perennials Stan Laurel and Oliver Hardy vied with Bud Abbott and Lou Costello for the top spot, and the two teams finished far ahead of the others.

This was the result for the runners-up: the Marx Brothers, the Three Stooges, Bob Hope and Bing Crosby, Dean Martin and Jerry Lewis, the "Our Gang" kids, the Bowery Boys, Bert Wheeler and Robert Woolsey, Ole Olsen and Chic Johnson ... and last and apparently least in the opinion of those taking the poll, Al, Jimmy and Harry, the Ritz Brothers. These results could be partially due to the greater contemporary visibility of the higher rated teams. The films of all but the final three are much more widely available, so they are simply better known. Another obvious conclusion might be that the lowest-rated teams were just not considered as funny.

Among those with a much more extreme reaction was Italian dictator Benito Mussolini and his fascist regime. In the late 1930s, he threatened to ban the films of both the Ritzes and the Marx Brothers as being a "menace to public safety." It might be suspected that this was more a reaction to their being *Jewish* comedians, since he eventually followed Hitler's lead on curtailing Jewish life in Italy and then did much worse.

It could also be that both teams were comic anarchists and this was anathema to the rulers of tightly regimented countries. Mussolini's reaction to the

Three Stooges, if he knew of them, is not recorded but the same could be said about them. A few of their short comedies actually satirized the Hitler regime.

The major emphasis of this book is on the film work of the Ritz Brothers. There is a substantial body of reviews and opinions available from both the time the films played and from today's viewers. The section "Modern-Day Commentators; or, 'We Don't Get No Respect'" is devoted to the reactions of 21st-century viewers.

For many of the Ritzes' 1930s and '40s films, I've included the reviews of film critics and also the comments of small town and rural theater managers. The latter's comments mainly concentrated on audience satisfaction and profits, if any. *Motion Picture Herald* ran their reactions in the section "What the Picture Did for Me."

Reviews from (say) *The Hollywood Reporter*, *Variety* and *Film Daily*, and Hollywood newspapers like the *Los Angeles Examiner*, could sometimes be a bit more effusive about major-studio films than the films may have merited. A certain symbiotic relationship existed between them and the studios. Fan magazines obviously also fall in this category.

This was at a time when every small town had at least one movie theater. In those days of block booking theaters had to take the "B" films in order to get the "A" headliners. One bad season could lead to theaters closing. This was the Great Depression. Small-town theater owners were not necessarily interested in the artistic pros and cons of a film. Their concern was chiefly whether people came, did they like the film?, did their patrons want to see the same actors again?, did the film make a little profit?

Some of these little towns may not even exist any longer. Their modest theaters very often had grandiose names patterned after those of the big cities like the Princess, the Palace, the Strand, the Paramount, etc., and no doubt were often the center of the towns' social lives. Their opinions mattered as much as those who lived in big cities and could patronize the actual grand movie palaces.

The Book

The inclusion of the brief overview of the Ritz Brothers' five decades in show business is not in any way intended to be comprehensive. In the current absence of a full-length Ritz Brothers biography, it is included to provide a flavor of their career beyond movies and TV. Perhaps a full-fledged biography will someday fill in some blanks, particularly about their many vaudeville, nightclub and theater appearances.

The entries for the feature films and short subjects are preceded by an extensive introductory essay on the Ritzes' film career. It serves to link the films together with information not included in entries for the individual films. Most of those entries provide background on the films' production history and plots, and information about the casts. Contemporaneous release and even some modern-day critiques are quoted.

It is instructive to know some of what went on behind the scenes while the movies were being produced: changing ideas about casting, writers, plotlines, publicity. (This historical information is not available for a few Ritz films because many studios discarded their old production paperwork, or don't make it available to researchers.) There's also a detailed listing of all the Ritzes' known TV appearances.

A comprehensive study of the Ritz *oeuvre* is long overdue. There should be some recognition given to a comedy team that was very famous in their time and has too often been overlooked since. The fervent testimony of some of the most well-regarded comics of the modern era should tell us that.

Introduction

The era of the great, predominantly male American movie comedy teams eventually came to an end. Cheech Marin and Tommy Chong, with their drug-infused humor, could have been the last notable one, and even they (with their hip 1980s shtick) seem old-fashioned now. Changing tastes have made this true of most of the popular teams of the past.

There are exceptions like Stan Laurel and Oliver Hardy, whose endearing humanity seems eternal, and the Marx Brothers, whose anarchic antics continue to strike a chord. Because the Marxes and the Ritzes were trios active at the same time, there were inevitable comparisons. Whether or not they are fair is for viewers to decide.

Some well-known teams may have been popular on radio and/or television, or in live appearances, but have not had much presence in the cinema. They include talents like the Smothers Brothers, Dan Rowan and Dick Martin, Marty Allen and Steve Rossi, Bob Elliott and Ray Goulding, Mike Nichols and Elaine May, Penn Jillette and Raymond Teller, etc. Some of the lesser lights who were roughly contemporaneous with the Ritzes (Lum and Abner of radio fame, Wally Brown and Alan Carney) always languished in undistinguished bottom-of-the-bill fare.

Comedy teams were audience favorites when the broad ethnic Irish humor of Edward "Ned" Harrigan and Tony Hart (*née* Cannon) wowed Broadway in the 1870s and 1880s. A bit later, the Rogers Brothers (Gus and Max Solomon) competed with—and were unabashed imitators of—the legendary "Dutch" comedians Lew Weber and Joe Fields, as were the team of Clarence Kolb (later a presence in Hollywood movies) and Max Dill. A little later, Ed Gallagher and Al Shean, the Marx Brothers' uncle, found considerable success. Then there was Amos and Andy. There was an actual Black duo from the turn of the twentieth century, the talented Bert Williams and George Walker. A bit later, Flournoy Miller and Aubrey Lyles carried on their tradition.

In the 1870s, James McIntyre and Thomas Heath, in the minstrel tradition, put on blackface and spoke in what they considered to be Black dialect. Many years later the Duncan Sisters, Rosetta and Vivian, did the same.

Perhaps such acts could be said to have begun as early as the foolish Justices Silence and Shallow in Shakespeare's *Henry IV, Part Two*, or in his plays *A Midsummer Night's Dream* and *Two Gentlemen of Verona*. No doubt the rollicking ancient Roman comedies and the *commedia dell'arte* spawned their share as well. Possibly even two or three cavemen did an "act" in the gloom of prehistoric caves.

On a lengthy stretch of the once legendary (and now super-touristy) Hollywood Boulevard, and a small part of Vine Street, runs the Hollywood Walk of Fame. Every year, millions of out-of-town and out-of-country visitors tread this grimy precinct, jostling each other, food vendors, itinerant entertainers and bizarrely costumed (and sometimes belligerent) "superheroes." Phones pointed downward, they eagerly seek out the stars of their favorites.

The Walk passes gaudily decorated old-time movie palaces like Sid Grauman's Chinese and Egyptian Theaters, the El Capitan and the Pantages, which now mostly features stage musicals. When they were still working at Fox in 1937, the Ritzes put their hands and feet into wet cement in the famous forecourt of the Chinese. What was unusual, but perhaps typical for them, is that they were wearing old-fashioned bathing suits and Harry put one bare foot into the cement. For good measure, they planted smooches on Sid Grauman.

Among the newer attractions on the Walk are buildings which house Ripley's Believe It or Not, the Museum of Illusions, Madame Tussaud's Wax Museum, the Guinness Book of Records and the Hollywood Wax Museum. The Hollywood/Highland entertainment complex features kitschy décor modeled after the faux–Babylonian opulence featured in the 1916 D.W. Griffith film *Intolerance*.

Directly opposite the Museum of Selfies (only in Hollywood!), a cracked brass and pink star (or salmon or coral, depending on who's describing it) is set into the charcoal black speckled terrazzo sidewalk at 6756 Hollywood Boulevard. This is in the vicinity of small shops selling cheap souvenirs and several fast-food franchises. This star honors the three manic Ritz Brothers. It is said to be the 1860th star to have been dedicated.

Some members of leading comedy teams have separate stars; for instance, Bud Abbott and Lou Costello, Dean Martin and Jerry Lewis, Stan Laurel and Oliver Hardy, George Burns and Gracie Allen, and Charles Correll and Freeman Gosden (AKA Amos and Andy). Interestingly, only Groucho Marx has a star; his brothers Chico, Harpo and Zeppo appear nowhere on the Walk.

If Marie Dressler and Polly Moran could be considered a team, they too have separate stars, as do Thelma Todd and Patsy Kelly. ZaSu Pitts, who also teamed with Todd in comedy shorts, has a star too. The mixed-sex duo of Mickey Mouse and Minnie Mouse have not been overlooked either.

The Ritz Brothers are figuratively crowded together on a single star, as are such luminaries as Fibber McGee and Molly, the Three Stooges and the Dead End Kids. There are many teams missing from the Walk, including Bert Wheeler and Robert Woolsey, Ole Olsen and Chic Johnson, Bobby Clark and Paul McCullough, blackface comics Moran and Mack (AKA the Two Black Crows), Willie and Eugene Howard, Joe Smith and Charlie Dale, and silent comics "Ham" and "Bud" (Lloyd Hamilton and Bud Duncan).

The Ritzes' star is set directly between those of entertainment powerhouses Bob Hope (who has a total of four stars) and Fred Astaire. All found great popularity in their careers in movies and on the stage. Yet how many of the millions passing by will ever stop to pose and take a picture of the Ritz Brothers' star? How many would even recognize their name, much less their accomplishments? Hope and Astaire were alive and professionally active when they were memorialized in 1960, the inaugural year of the Walk. The Brothers waited more than 25 years. They were inducted in 1986, and their star was set in November 1987 after all had passed away.

In October 1996, a star for the Brothers was set into the Palm Springs Walk of Stars at 123 North Palm Canyon Drive, one of the Springs' main thoroughfares. The stars with brass palm trees in the middle are known as golden palm stars. That dusky pink walk was initiated in 1992. Palm Springs was the hideaway for numerous celebrities beginning in the 1920s.

At the peak of the Ritz Brothers' career, some critics did not find their frenetic antics funny. Audiences generally did because they needed to laugh during the long years of the Great Depression and of World War II. Now that some of the Ritzes' Fox and Universal films are more accessible, some modern-day critics and lay viewers also do not "get" them. They perhaps also do not get the social-historic context in which the Ritzes' popularity blossomed.

While the Brothers were still performing in clubs in 1961, a newspaper columnist opined: "Subtle they're not … new they're not … but [they are] funny." Some of the greatest comedians of our time agreed, including heavyweights Mel Brooks, Jerry Lewis, Sid Caesar and Milton Berle. They acknowledged drawing much of their comic inspiration from the Brothers, especially the whirly-eyed whirlwind who was Harry Ritz.

Some suggested that Al and Jimmy merely existed to set up shtick for Harry, that the trio was more appropriately called Harry Ritz and Brothers, or other variations of that putdown. The fact is that they were all talented men who danced, sang and created comedy chaos equally well (or not so well, depending on the viewer) and undoubtedly had learned much from each other in the decades of their partnership—their *equal* partnership. If Harry seemed to be the star, it was because his older brothers presumably felt it was best for the act's success.

Perhaps to satirize those who shared the view of their lesser status, Harry's brothers performed a song called "The Man in the Middle." Its lyrics included the lines:

> The guy in the middle is the funny one
> The other two ... Are just a pair of bums

A joke which supposedly went around many years ago was that the definition of a rotten agent was one who handled two Ritz Brothers, but not Harry.

Among the comedy bits which the Ritzes may have originated are Danny Kaye's "git gat gittle" rapid-fire songs; Jerry Lewis' side looks while ostensibly looking at something in front of him, and his uncomprehending stare; and Milton Berle's ankle walk. The list is no doubt much longer.

The rainy 1986 ceremony for the Ritz Brothers' Hollywood Walk of Fame induction was attended by comics Red Buttons and Jan Murray, the latter quoted as saying that the rain was "tears from heaven." The petition drive to install the star was sponsored by Milton Berle, Phyllis Diller and the Hollywood Friars Club.

The great majority of the stars on the Walk are for show business folk, in front of or behind the scenes, who may have been popular or well-known once, but who are now lost in the mists of obscurity. It is time to look more closely at the legacy of the three Ritz Brothers. They should not languish unseen among those long-forgotten on the Hollywood Walk of Fame.

An Overview

A Biographical Note

The Family Joachim/Ritz

First they were Abraham, Samuel and Harry, the Joachim brothers. Then they were Al, Jimmy and Harry, the Ritz Brothers. The true story of how they chose their professional surname is speculation so long after the fact. Their own accounts varied with the telling: The name was taken from a passing laundry truck, the famous hotel, the iconic salty cracker. One of the versions related by Al in a 1937 interview was that he looked out an office building window and spotted the Ritz Laundry across the street: "The name sounded classy to us, so we all went Ritzy."

The Ritz Brothers are generally credited with popularizing the expression "putting on the ritz" years before Irving Berlin wrote the song "Puttin' on the Ritz" in 1929. By 1927, they had incorporated a routine called "Putting on the Ritz" into their Collegians act.

According to Harry, their real surname was pronounced "Joe-ACK-him." That simply did not have the snappy sound of show business success about it.

The boys who were to become the Ritz Brothers were born in Newark, in Essex County, New Jersey. (Harry later joked he had been born in a log cabin.) The first-born Joachim scion was George Aaron (1896–1970), who was later reported to have acted as a part-time business manager for his brothers. Then came William (1897 or 1898–1927). The future Ritz Brothers were composed of third-born Abraham Leib, born on August 27, 1901; Samuel on October 5, 1904, and Harry on May 22, 1907. Some sources state that Harry was legally named Herschel, but this does not jibe with official birth and census records. It is most likely that Herschel was a family nickname; Herschel and its diminutives Hersch, Hesh and Heshey are common nicknames for Harry and Harold in Jewish families.

The only Joachim daughter, Gertrude (1911 or 1912–1986), completed the family; she was the first and only one to be born in Brooklyn, New York. The family is listed in the 1900 U.S. census as renting on Montgomery Street, in the 1905 New Jersey State Census as renting on Bruce Street, and in the 1910 U.S. census as renting on Belmont Avenue. These addresses were all in Newark, New Jersey. The family's move to Brooklyn must have therefore taken place sometime between 1910 and 1912.

One of their Brooklyn residences was on South 2nd Street in the Williamsburg section, now a desirable, regentrified area. In those days, shabby tenements were home to an admixture of immigrant Orthodox Jews, poor African Americans and, some time later, Puerto Ricans. Yiddish (which was the Joachims' first language, according to the census) and Spanish was heard on those mean streets.

Census records also indicate that widowed grandfather Morris Joachim (1843–1910) was living with the family during their years in Newark. He immigrated in 1887 so he probably brought his son Max over to the United States. Max and Pauline were the proud parents of this sizable (six kids) clan.

Max's birth date is usually given as December 1871. His gravestone in Mount Carmel Cemetery in Queens, New York, states that he died on January 4, 1939, at the age of 68. Austria is given as his birth place; it would then have been the Austro-Hungarian Empire. At least one genealogical source specifically narrows his birthplace to Rzeszow, Podkarpackie, Poland, and gives his birth date as May 1872.

Max probably immigrated in 1888, although the 1920 census lists an unlikely 1882 as the year. He and Pauline were married in February 1891 according to New Jersey census records. The 1900 U.S. census indicates that the marriage took place in 1896, but that seems unlikely; it was in late August 1896 that son George was born. If it is the earlier date, it would mean that their first child was born after five years of marriage.

If their generally accepted birthdates are correct, Max would have been 19 and Pauline 16 going on 17 when they wed. Early marriages were by no means uncommon then. Discrepancies in vital statistics occur frequently due to misreading of the handwritten census data, poor enumerator training, or misunderstandings because of heavy immigrant accents. The 1910 census records list Max's occupation as a hatter. The 1920 records list him as a "finisher" (of hats) then working in hotels.

Pauline's birth date is generally given as May 1874 in Jadów, Poland, which would have made her 61 at her death in November 1935. But her tombstone in Mount Carmel Cemetery gives her age as 62. In the nineteenth century, it was not uncommon for people from poorer backgrounds not to know the exact place of their birth or even the actual year of their birth.

It is well-known that authorities who processed immigrants at their points of entry into the U.S. often could not spell Eastern European names correctly. The name Joachim does seem to have the ring of accuracy. It is variously translated from the Hebrew as "raised by Yahweh," "God has granted (a son)" and "established by God."

The Biblical *Apocrypha* says that Saint Joachim was the husband of Saint Anne and thus the father of the Virgin Mary. Pauline's original surname can be found with several alternate spellings, including Bernstein, Brownstein, Broustein and Bronstein. As was also common, the senior Joachims' first names might have been Anglicized from their original Yiddish names.

The handwritten, often illegible scrawls of census takers in the nineteenth and early twentieth centuries made it inevitable that much of their information would be impossible to decipher correctly. Numerous mistakes were made. The Federal, New Jersey and New York State census records concerning the Joachim family illustrate this all-too common problem. The family's surname is variously transcribed from handwritten to official printed census records as Joachem, Jachim, Jonchins and Grashim. The children's first names are variously transcribed as Banlinal (Abraham), Janies (Samuel) (perhaps based on a misreading of Samuel as James), Garold (perhaps based on an assumption that Harry was really Harold) and Gestrude (Gertrude).

It is stated in show business accounts of the Ritz Brothers that the senior Joachim made sure they finished high school. If true, this was by no means a small accomplishment. It was much more the norm in a family of lower economic means that a year (or less) of high school was considered sufficient, and that children would go to work full-time to help support the family.

In interviews and even on some census forms, the Ritz Brothers always maintained that they had all graduated from an unnamed high school. However, in a 1937 *Picture Play* magazine interview, the Brothers said that they had attended P.S. 16 and had only gone as far in their education as graduation from P.S. 50. This presumably meant eighth grade. The two older Ritzes had then gone out to work, Al in a shoe store and Jimmy in a mail order house.

This story has the ring of truth to it. P.S. 16 is located in Williamsburg where they lived. P.S. 50, built in 1915 and now a junior high school, is on South 3rd Street in Williamsburg. The Joachims lived on South 2nd Street. The same article seems to contain a mixture of considerable truth and a bit of artistic license so the extent of their schooling should remain a bit of a mystery. If they did not graduate from high school, it was certainly no mark of shame in that era.

The tragic death of second-oldest son William on April 28, 1927, no doubt brought much sorrow to the close-knit Joachim family. He was the first of the siblings to pass away, at age 29 or 30. He is most probably the William

Joachim who New Jersey census records indicate was married in that state in 1917.

A 1917–18 draft registration card lists William as living (probably after his marriage) on Pulaski Street in Brooklyn. That is in the Bedford-Stuyvesant area, then probably a mostly white working class neighborhood. His wife's first name is listed on different official records as either Selma or Edna, again probably because of census enumerators' poor handwriting.

Although census records state he was born in 1897, William's death certificate gives his birth date as February 1898. His occupation is listed as traffic manager for a chemical company. He was then living with his wife on Keap Street in the Williamsburg section of Brooklyn. The cause of death is given as chronic nephritis and pencarditis, a swelling or irritation of the membrane surrounding the heart. He is buried at Mount Zion Cemetery in Queens, New York. In an interview ten years later, the Ritzes alluded to William without mentioning his name. They told of how their savings went toward paying a sibling's medical expenses but it was in vain.

Al Ritz (*née* Abraham Joachim) married Brooklyn-born Antoinette Calamari (1904–1992) in 1927. "Annette" had been his dance partner in vaudeville under the name Annette Nelson. They did not have any children. When people would comment about how hard the Ritz Brothers worked, she quoted Al as saying, "We can't work any other way." And yes, Al died "in harness" doing what he so obviously loved. After a brief hospitalization, he passed away on December 22, 1965, of an apparent heart attack at a time the trio was performing at the Roosevelt Hotel in New Orleans. He was 64.

After Al's death, Annette said, "They were truly three who were like one. Harry and Jimmy took it very hard. It was Al who pushed Harry to the forefront when they started…. Jimmy was just lost without Al." When Jimmy and Harry worked as a duo, they finished each performance with the tribute "Thank you from the *three* of us" as a spotlight represented the absent oldest brother. The plaque on Al's niche in the Hall of David Mausoleum in the Hollywood Forever Cemetery, shared with his devoted Annette, reads: "Al Joachim Ritz, Beloved Husband and Brother, 1901–1965." There is a Star of David at the top of the plaque.

In April 1938, Jimmy Ritz (née Samuel Joachim) married actress Ruth Hilliard (1916–1997). A former Broadway chorus girl, she made several movies in the 1930s; most of her parts were minor and uncredited. Jimmy had told her they would not be married until she abandoned her career. In 1953, after Jimmy and Ruth divorced, he married Judy Lee (née Judith Levy) (1931–?). They had a daughter, Allison (1955–1999). Judy filed for divorce in 1959. At that time, Jimmy's weekly earnings were estimated to be about $10,000.

On November 17, 1985, Jimmy died of heart disease at 81. The brass plaque on his niche in the Hollywood Forever Cemetery reads simply: "Beloved Dad, Jimmy Ritz, 1904–1985." He is the only one of the three Ritz Brothers not to have his surname on his plaque.

As seems appropriate, at least in Hollywood, films are often shown at the Hollywood Forever Cemetery and they draw substantial numbers of movie buffs. Jewish Heritage tours of the Cemetery highlight the fact that it is the final resting place of the Ritz Brothers *and* murdered gangster Benjamin "Bugsy" Siegel.

Harry Ritz (née Harry Joachim) was secretly married in September 1936 to photographer's model Charlotte Greenfield (1914–1939), the daughter of Hungarian immigrants. While attending her father's funeral, she reportedly caught a chill that turned into pneumonia. She passed away in a New York hotel at the age of 25 in October 1939. This added a level of tragedy at the time when the Brothers were making their acrimonious departure from Fox.

In 1942, Harry married Wife #2, actress Betty May Heath (c. 1922–?). They were divorced in 1944. His next marriage, to Betty Kellow (later Roday) (1925–1999), came in 1945. They had four children before they were divorced. Harry married his fourth wife Naomi Leon (born c. 1936) in 1965 and they had two children. Harry Ritz's children were Michael (born 1946), Philip (1949–1997), Robert (born 1951), Michelle (born 1952), Melinda and Janna. It seems likely that Michael was named for Max and Philip for Pauline.

During the final month of Harry's life, a local (San Diego) chapter (called a "tent") of the international Laurel and Hardy fan club The Sons of the Desert wanted to present him with a lifetime achievement award. His wife Naomi said, "He's never cared much about awards. All he wants to do is make people laugh. But it will be good for him to be around people who appreciate him. When the talk turns to the Ritz Brothers, he comes alive."

Harry had been suffering for some time from various ailments, and according to Naomi was coping with profound depression when he died of pneumonia in San Diego at age 78 on March 29, 1986. Because of the fragile state of his health, he had not been informed about Jimmy's death. He is interred near his brothers in Hollywood Forever Cemetery.

In death as in life, Harry's plaque has the most to say. It bears the words: "Harry Joachim Ritz. Beloved Husband, Father, Entertainer, 1907–1986." The word "Entertainer" had now sadly replaced the word "Brother." Their younger sister Gertrude Joachim Soll, the last of the six siblings, died in June 1986, just three months later.

At the 1986 dedication of the Ritz Brothers star on Hollywood Boulevard, Harry's eldest son Michael Ritz commented about his father and uncles:

"They were exceptionally tight-knit and devoted. They had to be together, in my father's eyes, to be effective.... They were brothers in comedy and reality." This was not hyperbole. At the times when any brother was offered solo jobs, he always insisted it was all of them or none of them. After Al's death, it was Jimmy and him or neither one. He always signed autographs "Harry Ritz (of the Ritz Bros)."

The Beginnings, 1925–1935

The Ritz Brothers' career spanned the years from 1925 to 1978. They performed in probably thousands of vaudeville, theater and nightclub shows during this time, so a detailed listing of these would be virtually impossible. Their appearances on Broadway, in the movies and on television are detailed in separate sections. The following sections provide a brief glimpse of the Ritzes' career in other areas.

In 1925, Al, Jimmy and Harry became an official vaudeville act as synchronized "eccentric" dancers. (They later joked they had done their first trio act on a basketball court.) Al had already led the way into vaudeville as a ballroom dancer with his partner (and wife-to-be) Annette Nelson (Calamari). Becoming a professional dancer had apparently always been his goal; all the Ritzes boasted of being natural dancers.

Al probably learned much from watching other dancers do their acts. He pursued his goal in dance contests and was said to have opened a dance school at age 18. Jimmy had been part of an act called The Solly Sisters and Jimmy Ritz, and young Harry had also dipped his oar into vaudeville waters when he was about 17. In an interview, Al claimed to have replaced George Burns in an act that was then renamed Lorraine and Ritz.

In the publicity campaign for their first starring film, 1937's *Life Begins in College*, it was claimed that the trio had been taught to dance by "Old Max," their father! According to the article, Max "was an actor and dancer who taught his sons to dance the moment they could walk, and kept up their training in physical endurance and tricks of the trade until they went on the stage themselves." At other times, they claimed that Max was a vaudeville performer or a saloonkeeper. Joachim had been a hatter.

In September 1925, the newly minted act was welcomed by *Variety*: "Al, Jimmy and Harry Ritz have been around but not together, this being their initial try in trio." The venue where their professional debut took place has been reported as either the College Inn or Fox's Folly Theatre, both in Brooklyn. Some sources claim that Jimmy Durante was their pianist.

The idea for their act, according to the brothers, came from the popular comic strip "Harold Teen." They imitated that callow college boy by wearing baggy white pants, beanies and oversized bow ties. This idea then morphed into their longer-term act, known as The Collegians.

From the very beginning, the brothers' brand of comedy was marked by nonstop, anything-for-a-laugh, frenetic energy. Not for nothing would the words "zany" and "antics" be applied to them with great frequency. When they were forced to rein in their exuberance in the movies or on television they would still show some, if not all, of their boundless Ritz-ness. The nightclub floor and theater stage was always to be their natural habitat.

Comedian Jan Murray later eulogized them as "tumult" comedians who ran around a lot, rolled their eyes, made loud noises, and joked about homosexuals, well-endowed women and other risqué targets. "They were masters of movement, and in addition to dances so extraordinarily well-timed that the three of them looked like they were sewn together, they were capable of a dozen comic walks and runs."

Although the Ritz Brothers always considered themselves an ensemble act, Harry was soon the "man in the middle," and considered to be the really funny one. He could roll his eyes, contort his body and do manic walks better than anyone. Al and Jimmy took to mock-complaining about their younger brother, saying the act should be called Harry Ritz and Brothers.

If they had been genuinely unhappy about Harry's dominance, it would have been aired in private. In public, the Brothers were an inseparable team, and teamwork was what mattered to them. They lived by the motto "All for one and one for all." To counter the common observation that they looked just alike, Al and Jimmy vowed they would wear monogrammed shirts to make it easier to tell them apart. They themselves joked that if they had not been together for a while, they had to ask each other's names.

Their rise was remarkably rapid: The Ritzes soon became well-paid headliners. As with most vaudeville performers, they continued to do the same basic act that had made them successful. By November 1925, they were already on Broadway in the musical comedy *Florida Girl*, which was not a success. Their Collegians persona was part of the plot. It is the only Broadway show for which there is firm verification that the Brothers were in the opening night cast. They may have been added to casts of other shows after the first nights.

A 1926 review described the blue-eyed brothers as "three blonde youths of one stature." In the 1940 census, Jimmy gave his height as 5'8", which would have made Al about 5'6". Harry was just about the same size as Jimmy.

The Ritzes soon broadened their dance act to include comedy and singing. This version of their act immediately clicked with the public and they continued doing it for several years. A description of the trio said they were dressed in "vivid red, green and yellow costumes." These colors seemed to suit them. They were still featuring them in the 1932 stage show in which they were dressed like "Roman senators." They would mine the material they had developed in their vaudeville days for the rest of their careers.

A 1926 review enthused: "The Ritz Brothers, the original collegiates [sic], are well-named. The stage was decorated with college pennants, and before the boys appeared a college yell in the distance announced the character of their act." Another 1926 review said: "The Ritz Brothers, besides proving artistically foolish, a condition which many vaudevillians strive to typify but few manage to make the grade, put on a batch of eccentric dancing that brought down the house." Apparently, the word "foolish" was a complimentary one in this case.

The enthusiastic reviews kept coming. In June 1926: "The nifty trio lashed into the original collegiate rah-rah number for an opener, then ran into a breathless potpourri of mad dancing and boyish burlesque [possibly including a Mickey Mouse imitation]. The white and red rose bit still yielded laughs." The latter may have referred to a feature of their act described in a later review as the "nance" which got "a load of laughs": This was presumably the part of the act where they assumed effeminate mannerisms. Irrepressible Harry carried this onto movie sets as well. When introduced to a young male cast member, he greeted him by saying, "Aren't you handsome? La-de-dah. Gather around, boys." The three Ritzes then joined hands and began to dance around the young actor, who claimed to take it in a spirit of fun.

In 1931, *Variety* took them to task for "going overboard on the pansy material, much overdrawn." They did continue to feature "nance" material in their act, and in many of their films they dressed in women's clothing. In the mid–1930s, *Variety*'s complaint was the brothers were incorporating too much Yiddish into their routines.

Even into the 1960s, Harry still believed that what he called the "faygeleh" material was funny, claiming he "killed" the audience at the Palace Theatre with it. ("Faygeleh" means little bird in Yiddish and is used to describe gay men.) Its resemblance to the pejorative word "fag" is linguistically a coincidence, but he continued to tell what he called "fag jokes" with appropriate (or inappropriate) gestures.

They were still going strong into 1927. "The Ritz Brothers scored heavily in the applause. These singing comedians have a good line of songs and their comedy antics are the collegiate bits that go over so well." Another review read: "The Ritz Brothers, the three peppy collegiate headliners, run amok with their ditties and fooling. Fresh and breezy, they entertain royally. Harmony is always good and the clowning is nicely balanced."

The same year, they literally did "put on the Ritz" by devising an act of that name. It was described as a comedy in a college atmosphere when they performed it at the Loew's Grand Theatre in Atlanta. In a much later interview, they acknowledged that by 1927 they were already experiencing weeks-long layoffs and financial problems. "Vaudeville was gone; nightclubs couldn't pay our salaries."

An August 1928 *Variety* ad read: "Al-Jim-Harry, Ritz Brothers, 'The Original Collegiates: Imitated, But Not Duplicated.'" Another ad that touted the Ritzes publicized other vaudeville acts of the day as well. The list of these now seems like a melancholy tolling of the bell for the long-forgotten acts that peopled vaudeville stages. It included Earl and Bell, "Twinkling Topical Tunes"; George Dewey Washington, "The Golden Voice from the Golden South"; Bee Sarche, "The Little Princess of Syncopation"; Johnny Mills and Tim Shea, "Always Working and Spreading Laughs"; "Booker's Best Bet: Bob, Bob, and Bobbie"; Tommy Wonder and Sisters, and "California Bluebirds." Many were called to vaudeville, but few were chosen; the Ritz Brothers resided among those chosen.

By 1929, the brothers were still being praised for their vigorous dancing. One reviewer wrote, "The Ritz Brothers are the hit and talk of the show. Their collegiate act is funny, crude, vulgar, fast and furious…. They have a riot of an act without the repulsive crudity." It was apparently all right to be just plain crude and vulgar.

In 1929, they played the crown jewel of vaudeville, New York's Palace Theatre. One of the ads touting their act read:

> R Stands for Ritz
> I for Imitated
> Tho' They Cop Our Stuff
> Zero's What They're Rated

Let's hope that their patter was better in the act. On the bill with them that week of March 24, 1929, were such well-known names as bandleader-composer Vincent Lopez, "Irish" comic Roger Imhof and the Polish shimmy girl Gilda Gray.

As early as 1926, success had encouraged the Ritzes to flex their muscles when they thought they had been slighted. It was announced that they had "left the Interstate Circuit in a huff at San Antonio, withdrawing from the bill after their second performance." The Interstate Theatre Circuit was mainly located in large Texas cities, and eventually expanded to Birmingham, Little Rock and Shreveport. It boasted of featuring only high-class, family-oriented acts. The Circuit pioneered the use of air conditioning in the summer so performances could take place all year around.

A couple of years later, the Ritzes "walked out suddenly from the 'Take a Chance' tour with the Publix Theatres and came to New York." Established in 1925, Publix was operating more than 1200 theaters in the U.S. and Canada by 1930. It was eventually subsumed into Paramount Pictures.

A year later, while playing the Palace Theatre in Chicago, the Ritzes complained about getting second place in the ads and took out their own ad in another paper. Some time in the late 1920s, they were sued and lost a judgment by default for breach of contract. The powerful Schuberts were said to be deeply unhappy with them. These assertions of the Ritzes' clout, though not always successful, were a foreshadowing of their walkout from Twentieth Century–Fox in 1939 over their unhappiness with the script for *The Gorilla*.

By the early 1930s, vaudeville had gone into a steep decline because of competition from the talkies and radio—and also the effects of the Great Depression. The Ritz Brothers dropped the Collegians act and successfully continued their careers in nightclubs and on theater stages.

Before the film was shown, they came out in vividly colored togas and performed their "Dr. Jekyll and Mr. Hyde" number, later used in their 1936 feature debut *Sing, Baby, Sing*. They then proceeded to imitate in rapid succession Clark Gable, John Barrymore, John Gilbert, Emil Jannings and Mae Murray. The toga bit was reused in their 1942 film *Behind the Eight Ball*.

In 1934, the Brothers entertained New York City's newly elected Mayor Fiorello La Guardia. A newspaper account read: "First good laugh that [the mayor] has had since he took office was handed to him by the three Ritz Brothers in their hilarious antics at the A.M.P.A. Naked Truth dinner." (This was an affair given for charity; A.M.P.A. was the American Motion Picture Association.) The Brothers were characterized on the list of performers as "The Trio of Buffoonery." Among the many other entertainers that star-studded evening were George Jessel, Jack Benny and Mary Livingston, Rudy Vallee, and film personalities Gloria Swanson, Mae Murray and Dorothy Mackaill.

That same year, while they were still a very successful draw in clubs and other venues, the Ritz Brothers' film career began modestly with the two-reel comedy *Hotel Anchovy*. The next chapter of the Ritz saga had begun.

The Middle Years, 1936–1955

During the years from 1936 to 1943, the Ritz Brothers appeared in feature films for Twentieth Century–Fox and Universal and in short subjects. They also pursued their real passion of performing before live audiences. They had a restless need to appear in venues where they could cast off the restraints of scripts, directors and Darryl Zanuck–like producers, and hear the sound of appreciative laughter.

In a 1937 interview, the Brothers gave their version of how they were signed by Fox. Studio head Darryl F. Zanuck had seen them perform in the Clover Club and liked their work. The Ritzes expected they would be offered a contract but then nothing happened. It was not until they did a later gig attended by Zanuck that he supposedly said: "I like those mugs, go get 'em."

According to a 1936 story about their first feature *Sing, Baby, Sing*, "The Ritz Brothers are so favored at Fox that they will probably be cast in as many pictures as possible." The same story reported that their on-set antics included climbing up into soundstage rafters, thereby disrupting the day's shooting. Zanuck was (for now) tolerant of such behavior and must have felt his judgment was vindicated with such reviews as that in the *Los Angeles Times*: It said, "The Ritz Brothers just about steal the picture."

In 1938, the brothers were said to be sorting through offers totaling $150,000 for additional vaudeville appearances. They had received $15,000 for one week of vaudeville shows in Chicago, supposedly the highest amount ever paid for a vaudeville act in that city.

In 1939, the Ritzes did a vaudeville tour that *Billboard* summarized with the familiar adjective "zany." Actually, it was "zany heckling," but instead of the audience doing it to them, they did it to the audience. At one point they climbed into the orchestra pit and confronted the front rows of onlookers. They also did their *Snow White* parody with two of them playing dwarfs and the other the Wicked Witch.

They also visited San Francisco at least twice in '39. Once was for the annual celebrity baseball game they seemed to relish. Their teammates included fellow actors Joe E. Brown, Keye Luke, Jane Withers, oater stars Buck Jones and Roy Rogers and many others. Their second visit that year was for a gig at the Golden Gate Theatre.

The brothers were also slated to appear at the Golden Gate International Exposition on San Francisco's Treasure Island. They were reportedly offered $50,000 for a two-week stand at the New York's World Fair in 1939.

When their movie career ended after *Never a Dull Moment* in 1943, they devoted themselves full-time to their primary audiences and toured military facilities. It was publicized that they did as many as seven performances a day at "offshore bases."

During a 1944 show at New York's Latin Quarter, they did a soft shoe dance and then stripped down to their shorts and socks. At another Latin Quarter show the following year, it was announced that when their engagement ended, they would audition for a new radio show to be called *Ritz Hotel*. Like many of their other projects, it fell through. In 1945, impresario Mike Todd claimed to be interested in having the Ritz Brothers return to the cinema with a project to be titled *Hotel Ritz*.

Towards the end of the war, the Brothers bought property on Wilshire Boulevard for an office building to be erected once the war ended. In 1946, it was reported that they might star in a film as brothers who embark on a series of screwball adventures after hibernating in the Rocky Mountains. This apparent updating of the Rip Van Winkle legend did not go anywhere.

The Ritz Brothers always claimed to be among the first big acts when the Mob opened Las Vegas hotels in the mid–1940s. One of them was Bugsy Siegel's pet project, the Flamingo. According to the Ritzes, they were the first Vegas act to be paid as much as $25,000 a week. Harry always said positive things about mob figures like Siegel and Moe Dalitz, contending that Vegas was never the same without them. He praised the murderous Siegel, calling him "a nice guy, good-looking boy."

In 1947, a nightclub act reunited them with their former co-star Jane Withers at a time when her movie career was coming to an end. (This was a reversal of their last teaming in 1939's *Pack Up Your Troubles* when it was the Ritzes' movie career that was on the decline.) That year they followed Danny Kaye in an engagement. He had commanded seat prices of $7.50 and $12.50, a good deal of money at the time. When their engagement began, the Ritzes demanded that tickets be reduced to their old prices out of loyalty to their audiences.

In 1948, they were writing (or they had ghostwritten *for* them) a column called—what else?—"Puttin' on the Ritz." It ran in a small handful of Midwest and Western newspapers. Upon the 1948 re-release of their 1940 Universal film *Argentine Nights*, Columbia Pictures boss Harry Cohn expressed interest in starring the Brothers in a new film. Also that year, there was an idea floated about them co-starring with Bud Abbott and Lou Costello in a story about the Hatfield-McCoy feud. The brothers had already done a similar story, *Kentucky Moonshine*; Abbott and Costello later did one, 1951's *Comin' Round the Mountain*.

In 1949, the Ritzes made their television debut on the Ed Sullivan variety show, then called *Toast of the Town*. They were apprehensive about using up too much of their material in that medium, so they tended to limit their appearances. Even so through the years that followed there were ideas floated about possible starring TV vehicles for the Brothers.

Harry was vocal about the constraints of television: "They want everything held to five or six minutes. How can I do that when my entrance alone, with *me* laughing at *me*, takes five minutes?" The brothers would have derived satisfaction from knowing that some shows, the western spoof *F Troop* for example, used many of their bits and sometimes entire routines.

When "Red Hot Mama" Sophie Tucker opened at Ciro's nightclub in Hollywood in 1950, the popular comedy team of Dean Martin and Jerry Lewis joined her on the floor, as did two of the Ritzes. The expected pandemonium ensued. Lewis later acknowledged that he owed a lot to Harry Ritz as a mentor.

Al, Jimmy and Harry were still going strong performing in clubs in 1952. From a review: "There isn't much of anything they don't do. They clown, sing, dance and generally go at such a breakneck pace that a virtual state of emergency exists. Harry Ritz is the fulcrum of the comedy with a rubber kisser and pieces of physical business that have been widely copied over the years."

In 1952, it was reported that they had signed a package deal with silent comedy veteran Mack Sennett to do a film called *Galloping Geese*, set in Los Angeles. It was meant to help Sennett make a comeback. Apparently there was no interest expressed in the old silent film veteran.

In 1953, big-time talent agent Abner (Abby) Greshler, who was credited with teaming Martin and Lewis, acquired some silent comedies from a European distributor. He proposed to do a film called *Past Performances*, with the Ritz Brothers providing the narration as well as doing song numbers and providing comedy interludes.

That same year, it was announced that the brothers were readying a Broadway musical comedy to be called *The Three Vaqueros* (shades of *Argentine Nights?*). It was to be co-written by Sid Kuller, who had written much of their movie special material. The Ritzes also announced they were planning to produce a "series of telefilms."

In 1954, a *Variety* headline read "Ritz Brothers Prepping a Series of Shindigs Celebrating 25 Years in Show Biz." In reality it had been 29 years since the inception of their act in 1925. It seemed they now wanted their initial appearances in big-time vaudeville from about 1929 to be the "real" beginning of their careers.

To prove that some plot ideas—whether good, bad or indifferent—never die, in 1954 yet another Hatfield-McCoy story was touted to star the Ritz Brothers, the Marx Brothers and comic Lou Holtz. In 1955, it was reported that the Ritzes were under consideration to host a "new format" CBS show. This may be the same proposed show that a 1954 article cited as featuring satires of well-known TV programs to be called *The Ritz Blitz*, or possibly the show in a circus setting to be called *Sawdust Serenade*. Aside from occasional TV appearances and film cameos, the remaining years of the Ritz Brothers' career would be spent entertaining enthusiastic but aging live audiences.

The Final Performing Years, 1956–1978

During the last couple of decades of their performing lives, the Ritz Brothers devoted most of their time to the clubs and hotels where they always been the most fulfilled ... and where they were supposedly paid $20,000 a week. They continued to draw crowds at venues in New York, Chicago, Miami, Las Vegas, New Orleans and other big cities. They still always went all-out in their shows, their energy never seeming to flag.

It is likely that most of their audiences were in an older demographic, and had the Ritzes continued performing, their audiences would inevitably diminish. Like many comics of their generation, they were not necessarily attuned to changing tastes in humor. What was deemed funny in previous decades might prove offensive in more politically correct times. The brothers were never afraid to push the envelope.

After Harry and Jimmy performed on the cruise ship *Fair Wind* Harry Ritz said, "We knocked the people dead. They weren't young, between 50 and 65, but they remembered us." Unspoken, but no doubt on their minds, was what would happen when they were not as well remembered.

They were still doing well when comic Jan Murray booked a club date in Miami. The Ritz Brothers were appearing across the street; in mock despair, Murray said the competition was just too great. He was to be one of the driving forces behind getting the Ritzes their star on Hollywood Boulevard's Walk of Fame in 1986, the year that Harry passed away.

In 1956, the Ritz Brothers announced that they had a pending deal with Allied Artists president Steve Broidy to make two major musical productions for that company. One of them was to be about three racetrack touts and the daughter of a stable owner. (This has echoes of their 1938 feature *Straight, Place and Show*.) That same year, it was planned that they would tour Europe and the Middle East as unofficial goodwill ambassadors for the State Department.

In 1958, the Ritzes celebrated what was publicized as their thirtieth year in show biz (the *Los Angeles Times* ran the headline "Ritz Brothers Feted on 30th Year as Show Team"). It was in reality their thirty-third year as a team. They now claimed they had made their debut at Brooklyn's Fox Folly Theatre in 1928 and not 1925. They jokingly said that they were also celebrating their 1218th fight. "Fights clear the air," declared Harry. "We keep score on ours. That way, one of us can start something if we fall behind on our quota." Al added, "Naturally the first donnybrook was over billing. All three of us couldn't be top-billed." Jimmy chimed in: "So we called ourselves the Ritz Brothers, and we've been fighting ever since over which one should be top-billed if we weren't brothers."

Another of their unsuccessful business ventures was their effort in 1955 to obtain a license for a new Las Vegas–based television station that would air movies 24 hours a day.

In 1959, it was reported that the Ritzes planned to star in a musical comedy in Los Angeles, the plot of which would involve Russian peasants and a score utilizing folk music. In 1960, they were signed for a never-made film called *Hope Deferred* in which they were to portray French cabbies. Both of these latter-day ventures would certainly have provided an opportunity to showcase their talent for ersatz foreign accents.

In 1962, an intriguing item ran in the *TV Radio Mirror*: "The Ritz Brothers hope to give the Three Stooges competition next season on TV." Like most of the ideas for TV shows of their own, this did not come to pass. That year, Al Ritz was hospitalized for severe nervous exhaustion due to overwork, bearing out his aforementioned observation "We can't work any other way" when questioned about the maximum effort the brothers always seemed to put into their performances.

In August 1966, at the opening of Caesar's Palace in Las Vegas, Jimmy and Harry were on hand to christen Nero's Nook, a 250-seat lounge with a reflecting pool. The undeniable fact was that after Al's death the previous December, the heart had largely gone out of the close-knit act. After appropriate mourning, Jimmy and Harry did soldier on for a while, and then Jimmy announced his semi-retirement.

In 1975 and 1976, Jimmy and Harry had cameos in *Blazing Stewardesses* and *Won Ton Ton, the Dog Who Saved Hollywood*. Neither film was worthy of their talents. Harry claimed that when he received the *Won Ton Ton* script, he was so incensed by what was planned for them that he threw the script in the director's face. This was may have been hyperbole but it demonstrates his continuing protectiveness of the Ritz image.

Harry claimed that he had auditioned for both the part that George Burns played in *The Sunshine Boys* and the Meyer Lansky role in *The Godfather II*, ultimately played by Lee Strasberg. Harry did do a cameo in Mel Brooks' *Silent Movie* in 1976. His retirement came in the late 1970s when illness was already upon him. The great days of the Ritz Brothers had drawn to a close.

On Broadway

There are sources which state that the Ritz Brothers made several Broadway appearances, including in *Earl Carroll's Vanities*, *Casino Varieties* and *Continental Varieties*. However, none of the opening night cast listings for these shows include the Ritz Brothers. According to the Institute of the American Musical, *Broadway World*, *Playbill* and the Internet Broadway Database, the only Main Stem show in which they were original cast members was *Florida Girl*, also an Earl Carroll show.

It is always possible that they were added to Broadway show casts after the shows opened. The brothers themselves claimed they were in other shows and that is certainly possible. They may have worked in out-of-town road productions of shows, like those on the Schubert Circuit. They did perform at vaudeville's most prestigious venue on Broadway, the Palace Theatre.

Florida Girl *(1925)*

The History

One of the major scandals of the 1920s was the mid-decade Florida land boom. The state became the scene of frenzied real estate speculation because much of its land was undeveloped and inexpensive. People in the middle class had become better off after the end of the Great War. They doubtless dreamed of being able to winter in warm climates just as the rich had always been able to do. Between 1920 and 1925, Miami more than doubled its population, from 30,000 to 75,000.

Getting credit was easy in those days of false hyper-prosperity. It was estimated that there were some 25,000 Florida real estate agents offering land. People would buy land only to sell it at a profit to someone else. Where there is a boom based on speculation, there will be a bust. Even though many areas of

Florida had had some previously unusable land filled in, much of the land sold during the boom turned out to be swampy and unfit for building.

About a year after the frenzied buying spree began, two major hurricanes decimated parts of the state; the land boom went bust. Some of the cities that saw population growth did manage to prosper; other developments were (literally) built on shaky ground. A string of failed settlements littered the landscape. It would be a while before Florida became a haven for much of middle class America, as hundreds of condominium communities attest.

Prohibition was the genesis for some Broadway musicals; the Florida land boom would also generate its share. The first of these was *Florida Girl*, which opened at New York's Lyric Theatre on November 2, 1925. The show's working title was *Oh, You!* There had been earlier shows titled *Oh, Boy!* and *Oh, Lady, Lady!* so that title may have been an attempt to cash in on previous hit shows. The Prohibition musical *Oh, Kay!* was to open in 1926.

There had been earlier shows that took place in Florida, prior to the land boom. These included Eddie Cantor's hit *Kid Boots* and the Jerome Kern musical *Sitting Pretty*. It seems obvious that *Florida Girl* was set in Florida merely to take advantage of the publicity surrounding the land boom. Plot-wise it could easily have taken place anywhere. The show was built around popular musical and operetta star Vivienne Segal.

The Show

Under the personal direction of Earl Carroll. Produced by Earl Carroll. Book and lyrics by William A. Grew, Benjamin Hapgood Burt and Paul Porter. Music: Milton Suskind. Staging: Frederick Stanhope. Choreography: David Bennett. Scenic design: Karl O. Amend and Willy Pogany. Costume design: John E. Stone. Opened on November 2, 1925. 40 performances.

Cast: Vivienne Segal (Daphne), The Ritz Brothers (Harry Aristotle, Al Socrates, Jimmy Plato), Lester Allen (Sandy, the detective), James S. Barrett (Horace Egan), Irving Beebe (Henry Elkins), Nellie Breen (Betty), Parker Fennelly (Mike), William Foran (Hop Morgan), Chester Fredericks (Gregory), Jack Norton (Wilmer Bantam), Arthur Bryson (Chocolate), Nina Penn (Wee Toy).

Synopsis: Followed by gangsters Al, Jimmy and Harry, innocent Daphne leaves a train in Coral Gables, Florida, and her shoes are stolen. It turns out that purloined diamonds have been hidden in the heel of one of them. Soon she and her boyfriend Henry, the police and private detective Sandy are all frantically searching for the jewels. One of the plot complications is that they must be recovered before midnight.

Sandy uses a variety of disguises to try to trap the thieves. Wilmer Bantam is so upset that his black toupee turns white from fright. In the midst of the action, chorus girls frolic in diaphanous costumes and tight-fitting bellbottom trousers. The Ritz Brothers in their Collegians persona clown and dance in their inimitable style. In the musical comedy tradition, all ends happily by the conclusion of the second act.

* * *

Because *The Cocoanuts*, the new Marx Brothers musical, was scheduled to open at the Lyric Theatre early in December 1925, it was decided that *Florida Girl* would move to the 44th Street Theatre. The show closed after 40 performances, presumably because ticket sales were not great, and/or because of competition from the similarly themed Marx Brothers musical.

Florida Girl's songs included "Travel, Travel, Travel," "Lady of My Heart," "Daphne," "Smile On," "Trouble," "Oranges," "Venetian Skies" and "Oh, You!" (the original title of the show). One of the dance numbers was the sprightly "Chinky China Charleston," which the Ritzes performed with a character named Wee Toy. It was the only Broadway show of music composer Milton Suskind.

Nineteen twenty-five was the year the Ritz Brothers formed their enduring partnership; Harry was just 18. At that point, they were primarily a dance team. One critic drew attention to their "terpsichorean gyrations" as the clowning thugs Al Socrates, Jimmy Plato and Harry Aristotle. They also performed two songs solo in the first act: "The Collegians," which was the name of their vaudeville and stage act for the next several years, and "Into Society."

Although this show was not a success, it was barely a blip in the career of Vivienne Segal. She had already been on Broadway for ten years and went on to star in the musicals *The Desert Song*, *The Chocolate Soldier* and *No, No, Nanette*. Her most praised performance came toward the end of her storied career, playing the older woman in love with the heel Joey (Gene Kelly) in the Rodgers and Hart musical *Pal Joey*. Thirty years old at the time of *Florida Girl*, she lived to the ripe old age of 95.

The man with the color-changing toupee was played by Jack Norton, who later appeared in countless movies, usually doing his falling-down-drunk act. Parker Fennelly became well-known on the radio as one of the "Allen's Alley" regulars on *The Fred Allen Show*. He played Titus Moody, whose tagline was "Howdy, Bub!" For most of the other cast members, show business obscurity was to be their lot.

Tip-Toes was another show that opened in December 1925 and was set in Florida. It had the advantage of a George and Ira Gershwin score, a book co-written by Guy Bolton, and a star in Jeanette MacDonald. This show, too, had a plot that could have been set anywhere, but it ran for almost 200 performances.

The Florida-themed show that proved to be the most successful was the four Marx Brothers' second Broadway show *The Cocoanuts*. It had the benefit of Irving Berlin's music and George S. Kaufman's book. Opening the day after *Florida Girl* closed, *The Cocoanuts* ran well into the summer of 1926 and had a brief revival the following year. The only show to directly deal with the Florida land boom, it co-starred the perennial Marx Brothers' foil, stately Margaret Dumont. In its similarity to *Florida Girl*, its plot also involved the theft of a valuable jewel.

The Chico Marx character was named Willie the Wop, a sobriquet apparently a bit more acceptable in those days. Zeppo was called Jamison, a name he carried into the movies. The show ran for more than 270 performances and was the basis of the Marx Brothers' first feature film in 1929. Schlemmer, Groucho's surname in the show, was changed to Hammer in the film.

Florida Girl Reviews

"Boresome, tedious, uninspired, brazenly plugging production that masquerades as entertainment…. A bust that should fold up soon." *Variety*.

"The best dancing show on Broadway." *Minneapolis Star*.

"[The plot is] utterly illogical, but completely, amusingly suited to musical comedy." *Time Magazine*.

The Films

An Introduction

This section provides an overview of the Ritz Brothers' film career from 1934 to 1976. It presents a considerable amount of linking information that is not provided in the entries for their individual films. The entry for each film supplies the in-depth detail about that specific film.

The First Film

HOTEL ANCHOVY (1934)

The Ritz Brothers had been performing in vaudeville for about nine years, part of that time in an act called The Collegians, when they were signed by Educational Pictures. The company's motto was "The Spice of the Program." The Ritzes' first film was the 1934 two-reel comedy *Hotel Anchovy,* shot at Educational's studio in Astoria, Queens.

Under the guidance of old silent comedy pro Al Christie, the 17-minute film presents the brothers as new employees in a failing hotel. Their leading lady was the fading Doris Hill, who began in silent films. This short was successful enough to encourage Educational to offer the trio a six-picture deal.

Eldest brother Al Ritz was quoted as saying that they would not accept such a deal. It was reported at about the same time that Warner Brothers wanted to sign the Ritzes to make two shorts or even a series of shorts. This offer was also turned down.

The Ritzes returned to live performing, probably awaiting a major studio offer. In 1936, they were signed by Twentieth Century–Fox to appear in films as a specialty act. If the brothers were indeed signed by Fox while performing in a Hollywood club, accounts vary about *what* club and who saw them as potential feature film material. The club may have been the Clover Club, or perhaps the Trocadero, where co-star Tony Martin was supposedly discovered. Perhaps it was just the Ritz Brothers' reputation as manic merrymakers that interested the studio. At this time, Fox did not have its own resident comedy team.

In 1937, columnist Ed Sullivan claimed he had been instrumental in persuading Darryl Zanuck to sign them. Sullivan said,

> The Ritz Brothers must have proved to the little Swiss genius of celluloid [Zanuck] that vaudeville audiences know their stuff. For two years I tried to get anyone and everyone interested in the Ritz frères.... Show after show they tied up the proceedings in a knot. Audiences yelled at their comedy, howled at their facial grimaces. I knew that would be the same reaction of any audience that would be exposed to their inanities.

The Twentieth Century–Fox Features

Sing, Baby Sing (1936)

The first of their features was 1936's *Sing, Baby, Sing*, in which the brothers (seventh billed) do a version of their Jekyll and Hyde stage number. They were given a generous amount of screen time to prove their movie chops, and prove it they did to that exacting taskmaster Darryl F. Zanuck, Fox's production chief.

The film is a musical comedy about a drunken actor who was obviously and openly acknowledged to be John Barrymore. Barrymore was then in the news for being pursued by an obsessed fan—who would now be called a stalker—across the entire country. The Ritz Brothers were adjudged to be a success in their first feature.

One in a Million (1936)

The Brothers' next was *One in a Million*, Olympic skating champion Sonja Henie's film debut. She was not a real actress, but the kind of novelty Hollywood always sought, as she naturally garnered a great amount of publicity. The Ritzes moved one notch up in the credits, billed sixth between Jean Hersholt and Arline Judge. Their big number "The Horror Boys of Hollywood" is not too dissimilar from the Jekyll and Hyde number of their previous picture.

On the Avenue (1937)

Of the four Fox musicals in which the Ritz Brothers do specialty acts, *On the Avenue* appears to have the most cachet with modern-day audiences. It is probably the one that is most revived at film festivals. The fact that Irving Berlin composed the songs is obviously a strong factor. Its backstage plot is not the greatest of selling points.

Billed now in the fourth spot, the Ritzes are reunited with *Sing, Baby, Sing* leading lady Alice Faye. "He Ain't Got Rhythm," performed as part of the film's Broadway revue, is their big set piece. They also get to do one of their signature parody numbers, this time spoofing Alice Faye. Dick Powell was borrowed from Warner Brothers to play the male lead.

You Can't Have Everything (1937)

In 1937's *You Can't Have Everything*, Al, Harry and Jimmy look chagrined that a café customer (played by an unidentified bit player) is letting them know that they really can't have everything. It was their last Fox film as specialty performers before they got promoted to "B" picture stardom.

This is the last Fox film in which the Brothers were only specialty performers. They are billed second after Alice Faye (again) and before the rising Don Ameche. Its far-fetched premise about Edgar Allan Poe's great-granddaughter, a playwright, is the hook on which to hang the musical numbers. Gypsy Rose Lee made her film debut in this movie under her real name.

The Ritz specialty "Long Underwear" was perhaps their weakest. However, the cumulative success of their first four features may have been the cause of their being given the starring roles in their very own (albeit much less lavish) programmers.

Life Begins in College (1937)

It is not known with certainty what led Darryl Zanuck to give the Ritzes their own starring vehicles. It appears to have been almost accidental. It is also not known what the Ritz Brothers' feelings were; presumably they were happy about it. The decision seems to have been made with some haste, driven by Zanuck's desire to have a fast follow-up to the football story *Pigskin Parade*.

During much of the planning for this film, the Ritzes were not even considered for roles in it. A football story was patched together and Al, Jimmy and Harry were selected to be the nominal stars; a strong supporting cast backed them up. The original idea was to call it *Pigskin Parade of 1937*.

In those less politically correct days, much of the humor was based on what modern-day audiences would now consider to be racial stereotyping, if not downright racism, about Native Americans.

Some time in 1937, it was reported that Zanuck was so pleased with the Ritz Brothers that he offered them a new contract calling for three pictures a year at $100,000 each. In 1938, columnist Hedda Hopper ran an item debunking the rumor that the Brothers were planning to launch careers separate from each other. Their new contract was to include the proviso that they would always remain as a team. The "rumor" sounds like something that might have been generated by the Ritzes themselves, to put Zanuck on the spot. He had considered casting them separately but they would not hear of it.

THE GOLDWYN FOLLIES (1938)

In 1938, the Ritz Brothers did their final feature film specialties when they were loaned out to Goldwyn Studios for *The Goldwyn Follies*. Featuring an array of talent, including George Gershwin's final movie music, this should have been a prestige assignment. It turned out to be a financial failure and it does not reflect too well on the second-billed Ritzes. Over the decades, it has had its very checkered reputation somewhat re-evaluated, but the Ritz Brothers' main number "Here, Pussy, Pussy" still seems quite bizarre. They are also made to imitate a well-known Marx Brothers routine, probably the last thing they wished to do.

KENTUCKY MOONSHINE (1938)

In this musical programmer, the brothers play ersatz hillbillies. It marked their return to "B" level stardom. The film milks the already shopworn plot of city slickers unknowingly getting into the middle of a mountain feud. Another plotline that was becoming old even then was the demanding radio show sponsor who wants to find great new acts for his show. Reviews were mixed but generally positive and the supporting cast, which includes Slim Summerville and Tony Martin, is a plus. It is as hoary as the false beards the Ritzes wear.

While filming this movie, the Ritzes brought older brother George into the limelight. George, described as being in the mercantile business in New

Orleans, had supposedly been accused by friends of cashing in on his resemblance to the famous Ritz Brothers by claiming kinship. Because his surname was Joachim, his neighbors were sure he was just trying to drum up business. He asked his brothers to prove he was related and they supposedly had a studio lawyer draft an affidavit attesting he was indeed their brother. They also gave him permission to "act as screwy as he pleases if it helps his business." Of course, all of this is part of an elaborate Ritz gag.

STRAIGHT, PLACE AND SHOW (1938)

A racing story, *Straight, Place and Show* came to the screen two years after it was first proposed for Eddie Cantor. The Ritzes inherited the story and again have some good support including Ethel Merman and Richard Arlen. Running only a bit more than an hour, its convoluted plot is studded with musical numbers. The brothers improbably play racehorse owners and jockeys. Reviews were again mixed. A warning sign were the complaints by some theater managers that audiences were tiring of the Ritz Brothers.

The Ritz Brothers had now fallen under the aegis of Sol Wurtzel. He was known for being able to turn "B" pictures into profitable ones because his standards for the quality of films were said to be low. His unit was known as the Sausage Factory, although he did produce some very watchable entries in the Charlie Chan and Mr. Moto series.

When the Ritzes were placed under his supervision, Harry Ritz famously cracked, "Things have gone from bad to Wurtzel." Wurtzel was later described by author Michael Korda as "a cigar-chewing vulgarian who was reputed to make Harry Cohn [the famously vulgar head of Columbia Pictures] look like a gentleman in comparison."

However, after their next film in 1939, and for a brief time, the Ritz Brothers may well have been the most popular comedy team on the screen. The Marx Brothers, who had achieved dominance in features since their triumph in 1935's *A Night at the Opera*, had seen a decline in script quality and box office returns by 1939. RKO's Wheeler and Woolsey had seen the same decline; Robert Woolsey died in late 1938 at the age of 49. In 1934, they had done *Kentucky Kernels*, about a Hatfield-McCoy–type feud. The Ritzes used that well-worn plot gimmick in *Kentucky Moonshine*.

Following one of their best films, *Way Out West* in 1937, Laurel and Hardy also began a decline. In 1939, Hardy was teamed with Harry Langdon in *Zenobia*, which failed to recreate the L&H magic. (Their eponymous co-star was an elephant.) The beloved duo reteamed a year later but the quality of their films did not improve.

Ole Olsen and Chic Johnson were making sporadic forays into movies but had made only two since 1931, programmers for low-rent Republic. In 1938, they left Hollywood for Broadway and opened in *Hellzapoppin'*, which ran for a phenomenal 1400-plus performances. The Three Stooges continued on their merry maniacal way but they did shorts and only rarely a feature. This left the field to the Ritz Brothers as the most successful of the comedy teams in their most popular feature. They had nowhere to go but down.

THE THREE MUSKETEERS (1939)

In this musical version of the Alexandre Dumas novel, the Ritz Brothers support, and occasionally manage to overshadow, the leading man, the amiable but bland Don Ameche. This is their third pairing and it reverses the billing of their last teaming in *You Can't Have Everything* when the brothers were billed above Ameche. Measured by the amount of screen time each has, the Ritzes are really more the comic relief than the actual leads.

The film's plot deals with that part of the Dumas novel about the theft of a necklace. The Ritzes, who for the first time are not billed as themselves but as the Lackeys, play the inept substitutes for the real Musketeers of the title. It even has some suspense mixed in with the comedy and music. Although *The Three Musketeers* is generally considered to be the best Fox film with the Ritzes in the leads, they were shortly to be cast in what is considered one of their worst.

During the planning of this film, Darryl Zanuck, who had been a big supporter of the Brothers, wanted more of the action centered on them. Then he did an about-face and felt that *too* much of the movie focused on them. The mogul had soured on the trio. In his autocratic opinion, they were becoming too demanding.

THE GORILLA

The Ritzes were unhappy about their follow-up film, the comedy-horror thriller *The Gorilla*. It was based on a failed Broadway melodrama that had already inspired two "B" movies that were quickly forgotten. The Ritzes did not like the script, loudly letting Zanuck know of their displeasure by walking out until their contracts were renegotiated and the script for the old chestnut was rewritten.

A magazine article reported: "*The Gorilla*, which suffered a setback when the Brothers Ritz balked at the script and production set-up, is well underway. The comedians are reported cooperating in every possible manner to offset the lost time, to overcome the poor reception their *Three Musketeers* received, and also to save themselves the money they will be charged for its delay." The statement about the failure of *The Three Musketeers* may be studio propaganda to justify their belief that the Ritz Brothers were no longer worth dealing with, and to ease their ouster.

Zanuck, who did not care to be challenged, had sued them for $150,000 in damages; they had capitulated and the suit was withdrawn. Not being important stars, they were in a weak bargaining position and their bluff was called. On February 4, 1939, a *New York Times* headline reported: "Ban is lifted on the Ritz Brothers."

The article went on to say that the Ritzes "made peace" with the studio and they would report to work the following day. Harry issued a conciliatory statement about Fox being a great place to work and *The Gorilla* was made with predictable results. It is probable that Zanuck had already decided the team had run out their course at Fox.

The Gorilla is a film of the "old dark house" type in which the Ritz Brothers play three Irish private detectives hired to foil the machinations of the arch-criminal called the Gorilla. They spend the brief running time of the film scampering around witlessly while secret panels open and close. As one reviewer noted, it seemed that Patsy Kelly (who plays a perennially frightened maid) got equal screen time. She certainly out-screams everyone else in the cast, and her considerable screen time may have been a deliberate message to the Brothers. Their instincts about the merits of this film, which in every way is mediocre, had been correct. They got some of the worst reviews of their screen career and it seemed their success in *The Three Musketeers* had been pretty quickly forgotten.

Pack Up Your Troubles (1939)

The next film was their last at Twentieth Century–Fox, and it hammered the Zanuck message home. They are not only second-billed to fast-growing child star Jane Withers but are billed below the title. The ads and reviews both reflected the Brothers reduced role; they had been truly put in their place by Zanuck. Interviewed decades later, Withers did not recall the brothers with any fondness whatever. Perhaps they took their frustrations out on her.

The film is a routine World War I comedy-drama. Withers plays a plucky French-American girl searching for her missing father in war-torn France. The Ritzes are broken-down vaudevillians who help her, and along the way do an uninspired number or two. One included getting into a horse costume.

A 1939 article in *Boxoffice* said that Fox was becoming known for punishing their troublesome stars by loaning them out to Republic, then and for years afterwards a low-rent operation. Apparently the Ritz Brothers had been thus threatened in order to bring them back in line—and it had worked, at least temporarily.

Even if they had been given the chance to continue at Fox, they probably had decided that the devil they knew (Zanuck) was *not* preferable to the devil they did not know. They decamped to Universal. Unfortunately, Universal's Abbott and Costello were about to be anointed the new kings of comedy with the big hit *Buck Privates*. The Ritz Brothers would discover they had not improved their prospects.

The Universal Features

It was intended that the trio's first film at Universal would be a screen adaptation of the Richard Rodgers-Lorenz Hart Broadway musical *The Boys from Syracuse* (1938). Starring Eddie Albert and Teddy Hart (younger brother of Lorenz), and based on Shakespeare's *A Comedy of Errors*, it had been a mild success running some 235 performances over eight months. The Ritzes' co-star was to be the professional eccentric Mischa Auer.

The producer of the film was Jules Levey, who had just formed Mayfair Productions as an independent producer at Universal. Levey was a longtime Universal employee, having begun in sales with Universal in 1919. His Mayfair Productions went on to make such films as *Pardon My Sarong* with Abbott and Costello, *Hellzapoppin* with Olsen and Johnson, and Eugene O'Neill's *The Hairy Ape*. One film he was *not* going to make, at least not with the Ritz Brothers, was *The Boys from Syracuse*. Levey announced that they were definitely out of the film, which brought the Screen Actors Guild into the situation in March 1940.

The Guild informed Levey that unless he agreed to have the dispute submitted for arbitration, it would withhold a shop contract from Mayfair. Their investigation discovered that Mayfair had no bargaining contract with the Guild and they sought evidence as to whether Levey was justified in dismissing the Ritzes. Perhaps to save face, the Ritzes contended that they had dropped out of the film over an argument about the size of their roles compared to those of co-stars Allan Jones and Martha Raye.

The film was ultimately made with Joe Penner (whose signature line was "Do you wanna buy a duck?") and Allan Jones; both played their own twins. The boisterous Raye co-starred in this 74-minute film which hardly made a deep impression on the public. It did garner two Oscar nominations, for Best Art Direction and Best Special Effects. Given the plotline, it is hard to see how all three of the Ritz Brothers would have fit in.

Perhaps they were fortunate to have missed it because reviews were generally scathing, at least from well-known modern-day writers. Pauline Kael, the Ritzes' champion, wrote that Universal "should be hanged for what it did to the Broadway show," calling the film "disastrous." Another film historian said it "fell just this side of disaster."

Whether during or after this contretemps, it was reported that the Ritz

Brothers "are planning to produce their own pictures independently, starring themselves in just the types of stories and roles they feel are best suited to their individual and collective talents." This could have been a ploy to speed up negotiations with Universal.

At the time Universal announced the teaming between Mae West and W.C. Fields in *My Little Chickadee*, Harry joked that if spontaneous combustion did not occur with that teaming, he would suggest a film starring both the Ritz Brothers and the Marx Brothers. That may well have been a joke, but it bore the faint scent of wishful thinking, and growing concern about the direction of the Brothers' stumbling film career.

ARGENTINE NIGHTS (1940)

The Ritzes' first Universal film was also the first feature film appearance of the very popular singing trio the Andrews Sisters, LaVerne, Maxene and Patty. The United States was not yet embroiled in the World War but the studios were beginning to produce films set in South America to bolster President Roosevelt's Good Neighbor Policy.

Any good feelings that existed between the Ritz Brothers and the Andrews Sisters before shooting began would soon turn sour. Harry already looks dubious. Al, LaVerne, Harry, Maxene, Jimmy and Patty in *Argentine Nights*, 1940.

Argentine Nights' plot was not much better than those of the Ritzes' last two cinematic misadventures at Fox: To avoid arrest for debts, a group of entertainers flees on a liner to Argentina. They meet stereotypical gauchos, save a rancho and sing some songs, and all ends happily. That plot could have been tailored to *any* country.

The Andrews Sisters were reportedly unhappy about many things. They were inexperienced in front of the camera and believed that Universal did not give them adequate support. Their gaudy costumes were ridiculed; they got no help with their choreography (except possibly from the Ritzes) and did not appreciate the brothers behind-the-scenes clowning, often at their expense.

The Ritz Brothers could not have been happy about their permanent downgrading to "B" film status and were still smarting from the Fox and *Boys from Syracuse* debacles. Ultimately, according to the Sisters, the two trios did not play well together. However, the idea was to highlight South America, and this was among the first films to do that. Luminaries like Orson Welles and Walt Disney were to make highly publicized visits to South America.

One problem at Universal was the studio's extreme frugality. Their shooting schedules for many second features were extremely short and the production staffs were often lacking in depth. Maxene Andrews' frustrated comment "They don't make 'em good, they make 'em by Tuesday" was right on point. The Ritz Brothers undoubtedly felt the same.

During the World War II era, Universal produced a series of peppy "B" musicals that rarely ran over an hour, featuring such young talent as Donald O'Connor, Peggy Ryan and Gloria Jean. *Argentine Nights* was somewhat of a prototype. Often they had song titles: *Six Lessons from Madame La Zonga, I'm Nobody's Sweetheart Now, Ma He's Making Eyes at Me, Ragtime Cowboy Joe*. For war-weary audiences, they were enjoyable and forgettable; Universal's more prestigious musical fare starred Deanna Durbin and Susanna Foster.

Although they were far from being young talent, the Ritzes' remaining films were fit into that cookie cutter pattern. The Andrews Sisters were also cast in a series of such films. At first they had specialties in Abbott and Costello movies which proved to be popular. Then they made several second features in which they were top-billed but were not really the leads.

After signing a new contract, the Ritz Brothers returned for three more films at Universal. *Argentine Nights* had been fairly well received, although one reviewer called it "a nightmare on wheels." Each film was one hour in running time with plots that were mainly a convenience for staging musical numbers. They were released between December 1942 and November 1943. In each, the Ritzes' characters had generic names; they were not called the Ritz Brothers.

Behind the Eight Ball (1942)

In *Behind the Eight Ball*, the Ritzes are dubbed the Jolly Jesters. Among the solid supporting players are Dick Foran, William Demarest and Grace McDonald. It is a murder mystery set against the background of a summer stock production. Because the show is a musical revue, it seems acceptable to cram it full of musical numbers, but it is a far cry from *On the Avenue*, the last picture in which the Ritz Brothers were part of a revue.

Hi'Ya Chum (1943)

This time the Ritz Brothers, billed as the Merry Madcaps, contend not with a murderer but with racketeers. The Brothers run a restaurant that gamblers are eyeing as the site of a crooked casino. The lively cast also includes Jane Frazee and Robert Paige, and plenty of musical numbers. *The New York Times* sniffed that the film suffered from "cheap familiarity," a comment that regrettably was not far from the truth.

Never a Dull Moment (1943)

Their final Universal film, and also their last-ever starring feature, is yet another crime story. Again they portray broken-down vaudevillians, and this time a stolen necklace causes the complications. Now dubbed the Funny Bunnies, the Ritz Brothers are mistaken for three Chicago thugs. They have their strongest Universal leading lady in Frances Langford. This film generally got the best reviews of any of the last three. It was agreed that the writing was a bit stronger, and Langford was then a very popular singer.

There seems no doubt that the Ritzes believed that they had reached the end of their big-screen career. Live appearances were their strength and it was those they would concentrate on for the remainder of their performing lives. For oldest brother Al Ritz, this was his last live feature film appearance. Their cinema career as a trio had lasted less than ten years.

In 1945, a snarky comment in *Boxoffice* read: "There is a possibility that some Magi of Production may yet devise a means through which there can be Andrews Sisters pictures without the Andrews Sisters and Ritz Brothers pictures without the Ritz Brothers." The Ritzes had already decided that on their own.

A modern-day blogger provides some valuable insight into the Ritzes' lack of success as cinema stars in their own right: "Too often the Ritz Brothers were not allowed just to let loose and run away with a picture like the other comedy teams of the time. Even as headliners [in their starring films], they are not really given the chance to shine as characters."

The Final Films

After Al Ritz died in 1965, his surviving brothers Jimmy and Harry were not quite finished with the cinema. In the mid–1970s they appeared together in two more films; then Harry made a solo appearance.

BLAZING STEWARDESSES (1975)

It had been 32 years since all three of the Ritz Brothers had appeared in a feature film. For whatever reason, Jimmy and Harry signed on for what is usually known as a sexploitation film. At least they had substantial cameos and were billed as special guest stars. They actually were replacements for the Three Stooges after Moe Howard fell ill.

Blazing Stewardesses' leading roles were filled by other old-time actors (or, to put it more unkindly, has-beens) such as Yvonne De Carlo and ex–cowboy stars Bob Livingston and Don "Red" Barry. A sequel to the previous year's *Naughty Stewardesses*, the film depicted the further adventures of those lusty ladies.

The two stewardesses find themselves in Palm Springs, and wind up in a brothel. That is the essential plot, which led one reviewer to comment that it is the only film ever made to be *all* padding. The Ritz Brothers are seen in several scenes; they end up as hands on a dude ranch. Jimmy and Harry show every bit of their age, but perhaps to some fans a shadow of what they were is better than none at all.

WON TON TON, THE DOG WHO SAVED HOLLYWOOD (1976)

A misguided attempt to bring back to the screen many old-time stars, this is a failed spoof of Rin Tin Tin, the surly German shepherd that saved Warner Brothers in the 1920s. In fact, one of its working titles was *Won Ton Ton, the Dog Who Saved Warner Brothers*. In the cast are a handful of silent film personalities and a plethora of more recent film actors. Among them are the Ritz Brothers, who reprise their charwomen impersonation from the 1937 Fox film *You Can't Have Everything*.

Like many of the other cast members, their cameo is very brief. Among the reviewers' comments: "unrelentingly crass" and "a smutty film industry in-joke." For Jimmy Ritz (and several other members of the cast), it was the final film appearance.

SILENT MOVIE (1976)

Released shortly after *Won Ton Ton*, this was Harry Ritz's last movie appearance. Mel Brooks was a devoted fan of Harry's and this is undoubtedly meant as a homage. The film itself is a kind of homage to the silent film era as it attempts to recreate the slapstick of that time. Washed-up director Mel Funn (played by Brooks) and two sidekicks try to convince a studio head to let them make a silent movie. Despite the machinations of an evil conglomerate, it is a big hit.

Harry Ritz's screen time could be counted in seconds: He is seen leaving a tailor shop wearing a half-finished suit.

And so the film careers of the Ritz Brothers came to an end.

The Short Subjects

Full descriptions of each short are provided in the entries for each title.

Hotel Anchovy (1934)
Broadway Highlights, #6: High Spots of the Main Stem (1936)
Cinema Circus (1937)
Screen Snapshots, Series 17, #6 (1938)
Hollywood Hobbies (1939)
Meet the Stars, #6: Stars at Play (1941)
Screen Snapshots, Series 22, #5 (1942)
Show-Business at War (1943)
Screen Snapshots, Series 22, #8: *Seeing Hollywood* (1943)
Screen Snapshots, Series 29, #11: *Hollywood's Famous Feet* (1950)
Screen Snapshots, Series 31: *Memories of Famous Hollywood Comedians* (1952)
Screen Snapshots: Hollywood's Invisible Man (1954)
Screen Snapshots: The Great Al Jolson (1955)
Brooklyn Goes to Las Vegas (1956)

Cameo Appearances

Ali Baba Goes to Town (1937)
Take It or Leave It (1944)

The Documentaries (Movie and Television)

The Sound of Laughter (1963)
Hollywood and the Stars: The Funny Men, Part Two (1963)
Hollywood: The Gift of Laughter (1982)
Classic Comedy Teams (1986)
20th Century–Fox: The First 50 Years (1997)
Hidden Hollywood II: More Treasures from the 20th Century–Fox Vault (1999)
Don Ameche: Hollywood's Class Act (1999)

THE FEATURES

Sing, Baby, Sing (1936)

The History

On December 17, 1935, a "First Treatment" titled *Town Hall Tonight*, by Milton Sperling and Jack Yellen, was presented to Darryl Zanuck. (*Town Hall Tonight* was the title of a popular radio show hosted by Fred Allen, whom Zanuck consider casting.) He seemed of two minds, noting "Very very good" and "Too extreme, too hoky [sic]," which seemed to be one of his favorite put-downs. He also expressed another of his favorite maxims: "You must believe [the] premise." This was in line with his frequent admonishment to "legitimize" a story.

His final advice—or command: "Careful on screwy temperament…. Retain comedy and humor, but cut out satire, or farce, or burlesque." It is understandable that he warned against satire because, as the show business maxim went, it was what "closes on Saturday night." Since the story was clearly about John Barrymore, Zanuck also might have been wary about being too explicit about the former idol's increasingly volatile temperament.

On December 30, Zanuck was still lecturing: "Screwy, temperamental people will destroy the sincerity of the picture. It will become a farce like *Twentieth Century* which was a flop." For some time, Zanuck harped on the presumed failure of that now-famous screwball comedy and therein may lie his enmity—if such it was—toward John Barrymore, who starred as the, yes, screwy, temperamental stage director Oscar Jaffe. Zanuck also seemed to encourage the frequent use of alcohol in *Sing, Baby, Sing*. Of course, casting Adolphe Menjou was almost an invitation for one of that actor's often over-the-top comedy performances. Zanuck freely admitted the Barrymore connection: "Stay more to real story of Barrymore—hoke ruins it." At this point, he was considering such talent as Fred Allen, Jack Oakie and Fred MacMurray, plus a "Lupe Velez type" for Rita, a character who would not appear in the final movie.

In the "Scratch Continuity" of February 6, 1936, Zanuck noted that the girl should be at the center of the plot and that Caliban should be the villain. The Barrymore character was originally named Gilbert Caliban in a supposed comparison to Ariel and Caliban in Shakespeare's *The Tempest*. Ariel was presumably to be the Joan Warren character. In *The Tempest*, Caliban is a scorned and detested figure, even bestial, while Ariel is, as the name might suggest, an ethereal being. This idea came from Zanuck, who later apparently decided this conceit would be lost on audiences. At the last minute, he decreed that the name be changed; in the finished film, it was Bruce Farraday.

A "Temporary Script" dated March 31, 1936, bore the final title. Now Brian Donlevy was being thought of as a possible cast member. Zanuck cautioned: "Straight people must all be *very* straight." Presumably he was referring to the non-"screwy" characters, rather than how later generations might interpret that. A week or so later, he was still not happy about some of the dialogue, again using his favorite word "legitimate"—which apparently it was not.

A "Second Temporary Script" issued almost a month later was the first to mention the Ritz Brothers. They actually were to open the movie doing an act at the Club Luigi, later to be changed to the Club 41, described as a swanky modern nightclub. Some time in the next week or so, script changes were made: They were not to be first seen doing their act, but to appear near the club's dressing rooms wearing misfitting bathrobes. The final script ran to 146 pages.

The Film

Directed by Sidney Lanfield. Produced by Darryl F. Zanuck. Written by Milton Sperling, Harry Tugend and Jack Yellen. Music: Richard Whiting, Walter Bullock and Cyril J. Mockridge. Cinematography: J. Peverell Marley. Editor: Barbara McLean. Dates of production: mid–May to early July 1936. Released by Twentieth Century–Fox on August 21, 1936. 90 minutes.

Cast: Alice Faye (Joan Warren), Adolphe Menjou (Bruce Farraday), Gregory Ratoff (Nicholas K. Alexander), Ted Healy (Al Craven), Patsy Kelly (Fitz Craven), Michael Whalen (Ted Blake), The Ritz Brothers (Themselves), Montagu Love (Robert Wilson), Dixie Dunbar (Telephone Operator), Douglas Fowley (Mac), Paul Stanton (Brewster), Tony Martin (Tony Renaldo), Cully Richards (Joe), George Chandler (Intern).

Synopsis: Singer Joan Warren is fired from her job at Club 41, where she has been performing with the Ritz Brothers. She asks theatrical agent Nicky Alexander for help, so he tries to get her a radio job for which she is rejected by Brewster, the network's president. Actor Bruce Farraday hears her perform her final song at the club, then passes out drunk.

Nicky sees this is as a publicity chance for Joan. As the soused Farraday babbles Shakespeare in the hospital, Joan pretends to be Juliet. They try to keep Farraday drunk and tell reporters that he is on his deathbed. The brother of Nicky's secretary pretends to be his doctor.

When Joan is sneaked into the hospital for more publicity, she is photographed with Farraday by Ted Blake, a suspicious reporter. After the actor is released from the hospital, he cannot remember his physician. On the basis of all the publicity, the network president decides to hire Joan after all, but Farraday must also be part of the package.

Robert Wilson, Bruce's manager (and cousin), despises all the publicity and tells Bruce that Joan is a gold digger. He gets Bruce to go to California by train. The network president changes his mind again because of the now negative publicity.

Ted, the once-suspicious reporter, now wants to help Joan, flying her to Kansas City to meet the train. Joan's friends, including the Ritz Brothers, arrange to put on a radio show there. Wilson tries to stop Farraday from joining Joan, but the actor escapes and makes it to the station in time for the broadcast. Farraday publically supports Joan and she finally gets the radio contract.

* * *

In Brazil the film was titled *Novos Ecos da Broadway*; in France, *Chante, Bebe, Chante!*; in Italy, *Radiofolle*, while Scandinavian countries called it by its English title. The song "When Did You Leave Heaven?," written by Richard Whiting and Walter Bullock, and sung by Tony Martin, was nominated for a Best Original Song Oscar at the ninth annual Academy Awards in 1937.

It was widely recognized at the time that this story was a thinly disguised depiction of fading star John Barrymore. His obsessed pursuer and eventual last wife, Brooklyn-born would-be actress Elaine Barrie (née Jacobs), was happily generating much publicity. Whether or not the increasingly addled actor wanted her in his life did not seem to deter her and she did finally land him.

The frequency with which leading characters in films drank to the point of drunkenness was then considered amusing rather than a major problem. It is possible that Zanuck meant this picture to be an unkind dig at Barrymore, but the film-going public did not seem to regard it as such. Publicity touted the film as a "Mad, Merry Musical Delight!"

The seventh-billed Ritz Brothers got a generous amount of screen time in their first feature film, performing at least three numbers at Club 41 and at the radio station. Their debut number was "Dr. Jekyll and Mr. Hyde and Frankenstein." Harry staggers onto the floor of the nightclub where a bunch of chemicals await him; using his full panoply of faces, he gets the mixing directions. With eyes a-whirling, he reads by looking to the side instead of directly at the book and mixes a potent chemical brew.

At first he shrugs, thinking it did not affect him, but then he sinks below the table and emerges with a set of false teeth and contorted face as Mr. Hyde.

(This seems to be a deliberate parody of the transformation of none other than John Barrymore in the 1920 silent film version of *Dr. Jekyll and Mr. Hyde*.) Al Ritz, as his butler, enters to tell him he has a visitor, a Mr. Frankenstein.

"Finkelstein?" inquires Hyde. Corrected, he welcomes brother Jimmy as the Frankenstein Monster, and they dance together. (Jimmy was to again appear as the Monster in the "Horror Boys of Hollywood" number in their next picture *One in a Million*.)

Their next big number is announced via a blurb in *The New Yorker* that the Ritz Brothers are appearing at the Club 41. They emerge costumed in tights vaguely reminiscent of Medieval troubadours to sing "The Music Goes Round and Round." This is performed with a mixture of nonsense syllables and interpolations of other songs such as "When Irish Eyes Are Smiling." Doing a few synchronized dance steps, they go offstage. Harry returns briefly—for no amusing reason whatever—as a bare-chested Tarzan.

The Brothers later do a lively minute-and-a-half dance number, part tap, all synchronized, that displays their true talents as dancers. They may not have been suave Fred Astaires, but they could more than hold their own with most other screen dance teams.

An advertisement for the film touted: "The Ritz Brothers—Nitwits Extraordinary. Three minds without a single thought. You'll wonder how they keep out of the nut house. They panicked the playboys (and girls) in the New York and Hollywood night spots." The ad's dubious description of the brothers was of course referring to their performing personas, but it is an example of how publicity could be over-the-top in those non–politically correct days.

The *LA Times* reviewer compared the Ritz Brothers to the Yacht Club Boys. They were a quartet popular in Vitaphone shorts beginning in 1927, and they made features at about the same time as the Ritzes made their films. They were known for their comic songs and patter, and like the Ritzes they performed in vaudeville and clubs. In features they provided musical interludes unrelated to the plot. The later members were James V. Kern, Charles Sadler, George Kelly and Billy Mann. Kern became a director, including many episodes of *I Love Lucy*. Among their feature films from 1935 to 1938 were *Thanks a Million*, *Artists and Models*, *The Singing Kid*, *Pigskin Parade* and *Cocoanut Grove*.

Reviews

"This picture introduces the Ritz Brothers, song and dance team, widely known when vaudeville was something. Their comedy routines single them out as definitely box office." *Motion Picture Daily*, August 1, 1936.

"This picture introduces a wow comedy trio and they present a show that should be heavy box office in any kind of house." *Film Daily,* August 5, 1936.

"Thanks to the debut of the Ritz Brothers, some clever singing by Alice Faye, and a blithely exaggerated comedy portrayal by Adolphe Menjou, [the film] offers some good entertainment highlights. It might be termed a timely sort of thing, in view of recent transcontinental occurrences in the news involving a certain actor. Of course [it] is just a wild paraphrase…. The Ritz Brothers, mad rivals of the Yacht Club Boys, just about steal the picture." *Los Angeles Times,* August 20, 1936.

"The Ritz Brothers, a vaudeville comedy team, literally steal the show with their boisterous clowning." *Harrison's Reports,* September 12, 1936.

"The Ritz Brothers almost steal this picture." *Motion Picture Herald,* October 3, 1936.

"The Ritz Brothers have several frenzied scenes which will convulse their fans." *Modern Screen,* December 1936.

"While the Ritz Brothers are clever and undeniably versatile, their strident voices and grotesque dances soon become exhausting." *Motion Picture Reviews,* 1936.

"A hit for no other reason than it has three hysterics called the Ritz Brothers who deserve to have their name in lights THAT big." Manager, New Liberty and Ideal Theatres, Fort Worth, Texas.

"The Ritz Brothers perform their often hilarious, often annoying shenanigans, interrupting the story for their routine comic acts." Modern-day commentator.

"The atrocious Ritz Brothers … hogging every going-on-forever second." Modern-day commentator.

One in a Million *(1936)*

The History

The idea for this film, the first for ice skater Sonja Henie, was obviously based on Henie herself (albeit not the movie plot complications). She was a three-time Olympic gold medal winner (1928 to 1936) and a six-time European champion. Darryl Zanuck certainly was high on her possibilities.

There was an initial meeting on July 20, 1936, about what was still informally called the *Sonja Henie Story*. Zanuck thought the proposed story was too thin, needed more plot complications and a big climax. It was agreed that plot points would include the Olympics and Madison Square Garden. Among the possible cast members were humorist Fred Allen and Patsy Kelly.

Five days later, a treatment by Leonard Praskins and Mark Kelly began the story in a little French village near the Swiss border and ended at the Garden. By August 1, there was a second treatment which now began on a Swiss train; Zanuck approved: "Very good—great outline."

By August 3, Zanuck had gotten the idea of putting the Ritz Brothers into the film. He added that the story should develop along the lines of the film *Thanks a Million*, rather than *Sing, Baby, Sing* which he thought had been "too hokey." *Thanks a Million*, released a year earlier, starred Dick Powell, Ann Dvorak and a Zanuck favorite, Fred Allen. Not for the first time did he hark back to the film *Twentieth Century* which he kept insisting had been a flop.

Acknowledging Henie's lack of acting experience (and possible inability to act), he said her dialogue should be as simple as possible, preferably giving her only questions and answers. He floated the idea of Harry Ritz being tested for the role of Tad (ultimately played by Adolphe Menjou), and Al and Jimmy being cast as tap dancers with the band.

Following "Temporary" and "Final" scripts, a revised final script running 146 pages was approved in mid–September 1936. Shooting under the title *One in a Million* soon began. (There had already been a 1934 film with that title, produced by the Poverty Row studio Invincible Pictures.) Famed silent film comedian Raymond Griffith, who according to persistent legend was unable to speak above a whisper, was the nominal producer, although Zanuck usually had his hand in somewhere.

The only child of a wealthy family, Henie knew her way around, and was as hardheaded about business matters as any Hollywood mogul. After her success as an ice skater and subsequent Hollywood interest in her, she asked for $75,000 to appear in a film. There were no takers for that demand, but Fox proposed $60,000. Henie then rented an ice rink and did some shows that attracted enthusiastic audiences. After that demonstration of her drawing power, the studio acceded to her salary demand. On the strength of *One in a Million*'s success, she negotiated a price of $10,000 a night to perform in live shows. On the strength of *that* successful demand, she asked for $100,000 to make another film, plus additional salary if shooting ran over schedule, and so continued to elevate her salary requirements. Other studios offered Fox big money for a loanout.

The Film

Directed by Sidney Lanfield. Produced by Darryl F. Zanuck. Associate Producer: Raymond Griffith. Story and Screenplay: Leonard Praskins and Mark Kelly. Contributing writers (uncredited): Eddie Cherkose, Lester Lee, Samuel Pokrass, Harold Rome. Music (uncredited): David Buttolph and Charles Maxwell. Musical director: Louis Silvers. Cinematography: Edward Cronjager. Editor: Robert Simpson. Sound: Roger Heman and Arthur von Kirbach. Art director: Mark Lee Kirk. Set decorator: Thomas Little. Costume designer: Royer. Dates of production: Late September to late November 1936. Released by Twentieth Century–Fox. 92 minutes.

Cast: Sonja Henie (Greta Muller), Adolphe Menjou (Tad Spencer), Don Ameche (Bob Harris), Ned Sparks (Danny Simpson), Jean Hersholt (Heinrich Muller), The Ritz Brothers (Themselves), Arline Judge (Billie Spencer), Borrah Minevitch and His Harmonica Rascals [including Johnny Puleo] (Adolphe and His Harmonica Ensemble), Dixie Dunbar (Goldie), Leah Ray (Band singer), Montagu Love (Ratoffsky/Sir Frederick Brooks).

Synopsis: Showman Thaddeus "Tad" Spencer, who is short on money, is traveling in the Swiss Alps with his wife, a girl band, the Ritz Brothers comedy trio and a harmonica group. The band singer performs the title song. Tad learns that the Grand Palace Hotel at which they were to perform (and make some money) has burned down. They stay at a modest inn where he sees the innkeeper's daughter Greta ice skating. He envisions her skating in an ice ballet from which he will greatly profit. As a tryout, he arranges for her to skate at a St. Moritz casino; he alone will get paid.

He pawns the band's instruments so Greta can go to skate in Germany. Bob Harris, an American reporter with the *Paris Herald*, arrives to investigate a story involving the burning of the Grand Palace, and its possible connection to a political murder plot against a European statesman. He spots a suspicious-looking character named Ratoffsky (a sly nod to Gregory Ratoff) and tells his photographer to follow him.

Bob also becomes romantically interested in Greta. He learns that her father, Heinrich the innkeeper, actually had won a medal in the 1908 Olympics but lost it because he had innocently accepted money as a gift for teaching. He has now been training Greta for the upcoming Olympics. Bob warns Greta that she too is risking her Olympic eligibility by having performed for Spencer at St. Moritz. Unaware that her skating exhibition had involved any money, she gratefully takes a sleigh ride back home with Bob.

Greta wins an Olympic gold medal for figure skating. Unwilling to lose her medal, she refuses to turn professional to perform in Spencer's show.

Spencer threatens to reveal her paid St. Moritz performance. Her father returns her medal but Bob persuades the secretary of the Olympic Committee that Greta actually was not paid for her performance. Instead, Spencer had used the money for his own expenses.

It turns out that the secretary, Sir Frederick Brooks, used the name Ratoffsky as an alias so he could enjoy a vacation. He restores Greta's Olympic eligibility; now she can keep her medal and also become a professional skater. She becomes the star of the troupe and with them triumphantly performs at New York's Madison Square Garden, where she skates to the title song.

* * *

In the Ritz Brothers' second feature, they continue to be a specialty act playing a version of themselves. Entering the stage on roller skates (to satirize Sonja Henie's ice skates), they sing "The Horror Boys of Hollywood." Harry is costumed as Charles Laughton in his Captain Bligh regalia; Jimmy is Boris Karloff doing the Frankenstein Monster, and Al is Peter Lorre doing…. Peter Lorre.

Although they do not skate, they do a bit of their synchronized dancing. In the climactic big show number, the brothers return as a bull and matador to stage a bullfight; this time they do skate. Harry tries to pull a scam on his too-trusting brothers with a two-headed coin. There is also a scene in which an onlooker in a Nazi uniform can be seen. When the brothers are having an argument with some people in the stands, they quip "We're not in Brooklyn any more"—perhaps a subtle reference to their Jewish roots.

As a result of the Berlin Olympics earlier in 1936, the Nazis were greatly admired by some, and perhaps innocently (or not) by the Nordic Henie herself. She did win a gold medal at that Olympics, and not unsurprisingly had met Adolf Hitler. It was reported that King Haakon VII and Queen Maud of Norway ordered a command performance showing of the film in the royal palace.

Other songs in the picture include "Lovely Lady in White," "The Moonlit Waltz," "We're Back in Circulation Again" and "Who's Afraid of Love?" The popular harmonica troupe of Borah Minnevitch is also crammed into the film to pad out the story. Of course Henie has her own splashy—and icy—specialties.

An advertisement for the film rhapsodized: "Skimming, gliding, whirling, she sets the ice afire and hearts aflame." Henie's notion of acting was to continually smile and be pert and winsome, but she struck a chord with the public and was a top box office draw for several films thereafter. The critics never did consider her to be an actress; instead they lauded her talent for showmanship. The early assessment "Her acting leaves a lot to be desired" did not materially change over time in the critics' community. She did undeniably popularize ice skating in the U.S.

By the following year, Henie was already one of the top ten box office stars. It is interesting that although her character in this film, and that of Don Ameche, have fallen in love, the picture does not end with the usual clinch but with Henie's big skating number. This was possibly at her behest. The Ritz Brothers did well enough with critics and audiences.

When Mel Brooks was writing one his funniest films *Young Frankenstein* (1974), he may have been reminded of one of his favorite comedy teams: the Ritz Brothers. Their rendition of "The Horror Boys of Hollywood" from this 1936 film could well have been one of the inspirations for the hilarious "Puttin' on the Ritz" number performed by Peter Boyle's Monster 38 years later. It is said that a true comedian never forgets a bit, or at least always knows of one he can "borrow."

Reviews

"Lavishly produced, it moves to the tune of pleasing comedy, engaging music, and slight but sufficient romantic content ... and brings into its action the clowning of the Ritz Brothers." *Motion Picture Herald*, December 26, 1936.

"A very entertaining, adroitly mixed cocktail of romance, music, comedy and skating introduces to film audiences Olympic figure skating champion Sonja Henie.... A sweet demeanor, engaging personality, an intriguing Scandinavian accent, and an abundance of poise are among her assets.... She wears the skates a good part of the time, giving various exhibitions that are Pavlova-esque [referring to the famed Russian ballerina] on frozen water." *Variety*, December 31, 1936.

"Plenty of opportunity for Sonia Henie to display her dimpling smile and her dazzling skill and grace on skates, without unduly taxing her ability as an actress.... The Ritz Brothers are amusing." *Motion Picture Reviews*, January 1937.

"[A] new star to the Hollywood horizon. Sonja Henie ... proves that that she has a screen personality.... There is something charming about her, a wholesomeness that is fresh and different and really delightful.... The story is slight and unimportant.... The three Ritz Brothers' goofy antics highlight the picture. Their song 'The Horror Boys of Hollywood' is hilarious comedy as is their bullfight on the ice." Louella Parsons, *Los Angeles Examiner*, January 7, 1937.

"The Ritz Brothers, daffy comedians beyond compare, are in top form. Extraordinarily resourceful in their clowning, they are never tiresome because they never seem to reach the end of their rope." *Picture Play Magazine*, January 1937.

"Splendid box office attraction. The public will pay plenty for pictures like this one." Manager, Strand Theatre, Dryden, Ontario.

"[I] can only add to the good reports already made by other exhibitors." Manager, Avalon Theatre, Clatskanie, Oregon.

"We see the Olympic caliber work of a 1930s era skater, which is far simpler and less dazzling than what we've grown accustomed to. Her 'show stopping' number at the end would be a warm-up for today's super skaters. So as a time capsule thing involving Henie this film is worth watching, but otherwise it's mostly light-headed knockabout nonsense not worth your time." Modern-day commentator.

"[It] would have been so much better without the childish shenanigans of the Ritz Brothers." Modern-day commentator.

"The Ritz Brothers provide some strenuously awful comedy. Harry Ritz mugs so ferociously he looks as if he's herniating himself." Modern-day commentator.

"The Ritz Brothers were such brilliant comics and dancers; it's a major tragedy that they aren't as famous as those other brothers, Chico et al." Modern-day commentator.

"If you fast forward through the Ritz Brothers you'll find it a lot more palatable." Modern-day commentator.

On the Avenue (1937)

The History

On the Avenue began life as *Out Front*. A "Rough First Draft" dated March 5, 1936, was written by William Conselman, with the music and lyrics by Irving Berlin (who had suggested the story). It was presented to Darryl Zanuck, whose initial comments were "Beautiful, charming, clever." But on further reflection, he noted: "Very thin and needs one more twist at finish … needs comedy development (*Enter the Ritz Brothers?*) … needs more cultured tone (*Exit the Ritz Brothers?*)."

The leading man's role had already been penciled in for Dick Powell, who was borrowed from Warner Brothers, as was director Roy Del Ruth. Fox hoped to get MGM star Myrna Loy as the leading lady, and Alice Faye as the second female lead. Faye would soon be that studio's most important musical star. Broadway veteran Helen Westley was to essay the grandmother's role.

A "Revised Rough Draft" followed on March 19. Zanuck became harsher: "Dialogue crude, cheap fresh wisecracks … cheap common Mona [the second female lead] … crude, common throughout." By June 1, the title had been changed to *On the Avenue*. Carole Lombard was now the choice for the female lead, and the character of an aunt had been substituted for that of the grandmother. The role of the secretary Miss Katz was added ("She should be old and ugly").

Another draft, dated June 18, suggested adding such dependable character actors as Walter Catlett, Raymond Walburn, thickly accented Herman Bing and eternally grumpy Charles Lane. On the "Temporary Script" that followed on October 17, Zanuck jotted, "No one should be daffy but the aunt." The "Final Script" of October 28, 1936, changed some character names and finalized the leads. Madeleine Carroll and Cora Witherspoon were now in the cast; the "old and ugly" Miss Katz was to be played by the young and perhaps not so pretty Joan Davis. The Ritzes were, as usual, to play "Themselves," and in spite of Zanuck's dictum they were predictably daffy.

Apparently most of the writing was actually done by Gene Markey, but there was some problem with the Academy of Motion Picture Arts and Sciences' Writer-Producer Code of Practice. It was a violation of the Code to act as both associate producer and a writer on the same film. Fox managed to get around that by claiming that Markey had worked as a writer only before he became the associate producer, and that William Conselman had done the major part of the script. In reality, Conselman did relatively little of it after his initial contribution.

Irving Berlin, already an American icon, was paid $75,000 for the songs, plus ten percent of all gross revenues in excess of $1,125,000. He retained the rights to the songs but agreed not to license them out for at least three years after the film's release, and then only on condition that they not be used in movie production numbers. When Zanuck saw the rushes, he was so happy with Berlin's songs that he assigned the songwriter to work on the film *Alexander's Ragtime Band*.

Because director Roy Del Ruth wanted to take a short vacation before beginning production on his next film, MGM's *Broadway Melody of 1938*, William Seiter was called in to direct some dance numbers. Del Ruth had already rehearsed the numbers so that Seiter did not need much time to complete them.

The Film

Directed by Roy Del Ruth. Fill-in director, William A. Seiter. Executive in charge of production: Darryl F. Zanuck. Associate producer: Gene Markey. Screenplay: Gene Markey and William Conselman. Contributing writers: Eddie Cherkose and Samuel Pokrass. Story: Irving Berlin. Cinematography: Lucien Andriot. Editor: Allen McNeil. Art director: William S. Darling. Set decorator: Thomas Little. Costumes: Gwen Wakeling. Music and lyrics: Irving Berlin. Musical director: Arthur Lange. Sound: Joseph Aiken and Roger Heman.

Dances staged by Seymour Felix. Dates of production: mid-November 1936 to mid–January 1937. New York opening (Radio City Music Hall), February 4, 1937; released by Twentieth Century–Fox on February 12, 1937. 89 minutes.

Cast: Dick Powell (Gary Blake), Madeleine Carroll (Mimi Caraway), Alice Faye (Mona Merrick), The Ritz Brothers (Themselves), George Barbier (Commander Caraway), Alan Mowbray (Frederick Sims), Cora Witherspoon (Aunt Fritz), Walter Catlett (Jake Dibbs), Douglas Fowley (Eddie Eads), Joan Davis (Miss Katz), Stepin Fetchit (Herman), Sig Rumann (Herr Hanfstengel), Billy Gilbert (Joe Papaloupas), E.E. Clive (Cabby).

Uncredited cast members who would become better known included Lynn Bari, June Gale (one of four Gale sisters, she would become Mrs. Oscar Levant) and Marjorie Weaver, the Ritzes' leading lady in *Kentucky Moonshine*. Among those already known for their longtime screen work were Hank Mann, Dewey Robinson and Bess Flowers.

Synopsis: Newspaper columns by Walter Winchell, Ed Sullivan and Mark Hellinger all tout Gary Blake's new Broadway revue *On the Avenue*. One item marvels "Ducats going for $22.00!" at a time when that was ten times the going rate. The very first number in the revue introduces the Ritz Brothers singing, dancing and clowning in "He Ain't Got Rhythm" on a set dominated by a huge telescope. One of the lyrics rhymes "Jupiter" and "stupider."

During the next sketch, "A Quiet Evening with the Richest Girl in the World," Mimi Caraway, her millionaire father and her fiancé seat themselves in the audience. They quickly realize that the sketch is satirizing them: a rich father, a spoiled daughter and a pompous Arctic explorer. The explorer is satirized by the Ritz Brothers, who come out dressed in furs and accompanied by a live seal.

Furious, the Caraways storm out of the theater. Mimi demands that Gary cut the sketch or they will sue, but Gary reminds her that she is a public figure. To accomplish her goal in another way, Mimi decides to play up to Gary by pretending to like him. When they go out for an evening on the town, they fall in love. Gary decides to delete the offensive sketch, but is told by the producers that he does not have the right to do that.

He decides to at least rewrite and soften the sketch, telling Mona to downplay her satire of Mimi. Mona is in love with Gary and is angered by his love for Mimi. She secretly decides to make the sketch even more offensive. Mimi sees it again and thinks Gary has double-crossed her, and she hatches her own plot. She buys the show from the producers unbeknownst to Gary, and plans to have it disrupted to publicly embarrass him.

Mimi arranges to have the show interrupted by noisy claques, and even bribes the Ritz Brothers as part of her plot. She plans to invite important columnists to the show the night this happens. In the middle of Gary's love song, the paid stooges begin to walk out. The Ritz Brothers break into an antic version of "Ochti Tchorniya."

Now it is Mona's turn to be humiliated, and the Ritzes know just how to do it. After she sings "Let's Go Slumming," Harry enters dressed exactly like her and breaks into the same song, making extravagant faces. Dressed in tuxedos, Al and Jimmy join him in some enthusiastic dancing. In his column the following day, Walter Winchell writes that Gary has been made to look like a "sapola."

When Gary discovers that Mimi now owns the show, he tears up his contract. Although Mimi still seems to be in love with Gary, she decides to marry the explorer. On their wedding day, Mona confesses to her that she double-crossed Gary about the insulting revue sketch. Mimi's free-spirited Aunt Fritz talks Mimi into cancelling the wedding and reunites her with Gary. They celebrate their own wedding by going to a diner.

* * *

The Berlin songs in the picture are "The Girl on the Police Gazette," "He Ain't Got Rhythm," "I've Got My Love to Keep Me Warm," "Slumming on Park Avenue," "This Year's Kisses" and "You're Laughing at Me." The latter three became temporarily popular and were featured on the *Hit Parade* radio broadcasts. "I've Got My Love to Keep Me Warm," sung in the movie by Dick Powell and Alice Faye, became an enduring classic.

Zanuck wanted the revue scenes to look as close as possible to the way a real Broadway audience would see them. To create this illusion, they are mostly filmed from the front without many camera angles, unlike the then popular razzle-dazzle of a director like Busby Berkeley. The film was loosely remade as the 1960 musical *Let's Make Love*, with Yves Montand playing the Madeleine Carroll role.

Despite some modern-day critics who think that the Ritzes slow the film down, their numbers are some of its brighter spots. In his commentary on the DVD release of the film, Miles Kreuger, founder and director of the Institute of the American Musical, enthuses, "I love the Ritz Brothers!"

This is certainly one of the more prestigious and popular pictures in which the brothers appeared. It opened at Radio City Music Hall and can still be seen at film festivals. A Ritz number cut from the film features them working for De Luxe Plumbing; it is included on the DVD. It is not up to their usual level so the 1937 audiences did not miss much.

If either Myrna Loy or Carole Lombard had indeed played the part of Mimi, their more feisty screen personas would have been quite different than that of the ladylike Madeleine Carroll. Considering her appearances in prestige films like *The 39 Steps*, *The Prisoner of Zenda* and *Lloyds of London*, this seems a comedown for her; she is colorless and basically miscast.

Dick Powell is his usual pleasant self but his bland performance is overshadowed by livelier supporting players. The energy is supplied by the Ritz Brothers and Cora Witherspoon (who does an imitation of Helen Broderick, the original choice for the role of Aunt Fritz). Most of the supporting players have little to do. Billy Gilbert, borrowed from RKO, is not much seen; Joan Davis is nearly invisible, as are Walter Catlett and Sig Rumann.

Interestingly, the character of Herman played by Stepin Fetchit (née Lincoln Perry) is called "Step" throughout by Powell. That is presumably what the actor was actually called in real life. Only the Ritz Brothers are billed as "Themselves" rather than with character names. It serves to emphasize their casting as a featured act and would be true throughout their time at Fox. They clearly do play fictional characters in *On the Avenue*, particularly when they are in on the plot to disrupt the show. In reality, they are *both* the actual performers and also fictional characters with the same name.

Reviews

"Three cheers for Darryl Zanuck for the first important musical comedy of 1937.... As for those Ritz Brothers they have never been so utterly mad, so funny, or such a comedy asset." Louella Parsons' column, February 11, 1937.

"Motivated by a sound story, the Ritz Brothers are in and out of the film for frequent demonstrations of their clowning.... The show provides plenty to amuse the patrons and a full quota of those angles which aggressive showmen need to sell their offerings." *Motion Picture Herald*, February 13, 1937.

"This offers a satisfactory amount of diversion for those who like this type of musical. The Ritz Brothers are grand if you like them, a little tiresome if you don't.... Scenes from the revue are as gorgeous as those in some of the big stage productions.... The songs have melody and swing, and the plot moves along gaily to its romantic conclusions." *Motion Picture Reviews*, March 1937.

"A mighty swell picture that did not make expenses, but no fault of the picture. The best Dick Powell picture for a long time, good music, good cast." Manager, Owl Theatre, Lebanon, Kansas.

Special Review

In 2012, there was a celebration for the eighty-sixth birthday of Jerry Lewis, a great fan of the Ritz Brothers. There were two Ritz Brothers clips screened from *On the Avenue*: "He Ain't Got Rhythm" and their parody of "Let's

Go Slumming." The March 2012 issue of the magazine *The New Yorker* covered the celebration in its feature "The Clippings File." The writer of the *New Yorker* piece admitted he was not familiar with the work of the Ritzes and had had to research them. About the parody, he wrote,

> What's astonishing about it is its modernity. It looks like a *Saturday Night Live* sketch. In particular Harry Ritz's rubbery expressions foreshadow Will Ferrell.... The Brothers aren't types or emblems, as are the Marx Brothers. Rather their personalities take a back seat to their material, and their teamwork and timing have an acrobatic virtuosity.
>
> Harry Ritz is a performing fury; he gives the impression of punishing himself with comic exertion, with a tense blend of precision and wild expenditure of energy.... The Ritz Brothers have no comic identity without their shtick and so they execute it manically; they're masters of their craft.

Then followed the inevitable comparison: "The Marxes, though brilliantly skilled, are masters of being."

You Can't Have Everything *(1937)*

The History

On December 12, 1936, a "Treatment" by Karl Tunberg of an original story idea by Gregory Ratoff was presented. At that stage, it was titled *Last Year's Kisses*. After reading it, Zanuck said he wanted it to have a "*Libeled Lady* flavor." *Libeled Lady* was an MGM comedy-drama with a high-powered cast: William Powell, Jean Harlow, Myrna Loy and Spencer Tracy.

By January 9, 1937, a "Second Treatment" was ready. Among Zanuck's ambitious ideas for casting were such stars as Warner Baxter, Carole Lombard, Jean Arthur, Claire Trevor, Loretta Young, Claudette Colbert, Fredric March, William Powell and Fred Allen. The latter, a well-known vaudeville and radio humorist, seemed to be a favorite of Zanuck's.

A "Revised Second Treatment" was presented on January 30. Zanuck's most interesting contribution was that Judy Wells' great-grandfather should be Edgar Allan Poe, not Rudyard Kipling. He may or may not have known that Poe had had no offspring, but then he figured that most of the audience probably would not know or care either.

Two months later, the title was changed to *You Can't Have Everything*. By that time, a "Temporary Script" was ready, followed a couple of weeks later on April 7, 1937, by a "Final Script." All of Zanuck's fantasy cast had been replaced by the usual Fox musical leads, Alice Faye and Don Ameche. In the event, the finished film definitely did not have a *Libeled Lady* flavor.

According to a studio press release, Zanuck's original idea was to have only Jimmy Ritz in the film, but it was always all for one and one for all with the Ritz Brothers. They protested such casting and all three appeared in the film. Despite—or because of—this kerfuffle, the brothers were second billed after Alice Faye and before Don Ameche.

The Film

Directed by Norman Taurog. In charge of production: Darryl F. Zanuck. Associate producer: Laurence Schwab. Screenplay: Harry Tugend, Jack Yellen and Karl Tunberg. Original story: Gregory Ratoff. Music (uncredited): Cyril J. Mockridge and Walter Scharf. Cinematography: Lucien Andriot. Editor: Hanson Fritch. Art director: Duncan Cramer. Costume designer: Royer. Sound: Roger Heman Sr. and Arthur von Kirbach. Musical director: David Buttolph. Music and lyrics: Mack Gordon and Harry Revel. Choreographer (uncredited): Harry Losee. Dates of production: April 22 to mid–June 1937. Released by Twentieth Century–Fox on August 3, 1937. 100 minutes.

Cast: Alice Faye (Judy Poe Wells), The Ritz Brothers (Themselves), Don Ameche (George Macrae), Charles Winninger (Sam Gordon), Louise Hovick [Gypsy Rose Lee] (Lulu Riley), Arthur Treacher (Bevins), David Rubinoff [AKA Rubinoff] (Himself), Tony Martin (Bobby Walker), Phyllis Brooks (Evelyn Moore), Wally Vernon (Jerry), Tip Tap and Toe [i.e., Samuel Green, Ted Fraser, Ray Winfield or Wynfield] (Specialty dancers), Louis Prima (Orchestra leader), George Humbert (Romano), Jed Prouty (Mr. Whiteman), Dorothy Christy (Blond woman), Tony Martinelli (Himself).

Among the uncredited supporting cast were two who would become better known as leads in "B" films, Lynn Bari and Robert Lowery. Bari was one of the female leads in the cast of the Ritzes' final Fox film *Pack Up Your Troubles*. Veteran performers included Clara Blandick, Si Jenks, Franklyn Farnum, Mary Gordon, Paul Hurst, Hank Mann and Frank Puglia.

Synopsis: Judy Wells, great-granddaughter of author Edgar Allan Poe, fancies herself a great serious playwright and is in New York to prove it. She has found no success and is living off of basic food that she usually cannot pay for. One night, after hungrily eating copious plates of spaghetti in an Italian restaurant, she is once again financially embarrassed. Another patron offers to pay her bill but she refuses, opting to work off her bill by performing with the restaurant's orchestra and singing the title song.

Her would-be knight in shining armor is the perennially inebriated George Macrae, the producer of less than stellar Broadway musicals. Taken by her voice, he follows her out and offers her a job as a singer while concealing his own identity, calling himself George Blake. Judy scornfully rejects the offer, determined to have her great play on Broadway. She is struggling to write serious plays even though Broadway audiences seem to want frothy confections, not worthwhile plays.

When he staggers back to his apartment, his producer Sam Gordon, girlfriend Lulu Riley and his friends the Ritz Brothers are waiting for him. He persuades Gordon to option her play, although he thinks it has no merit. The next day, as Judy is packing to return home in defeat, she gets the check for the option. Going to Sam's office to discuss plans for her play, she meets George and they agree to go out on a date. At the nightclub, Judy is asked to sing. Sam and Lulu arrive to tell George that the temperamental Evelyn Moore, who was set to start in his musical *Sunny Days*, has quit.

Jimmy, Harry, and Al ogle statuesque Louise Hovick in her very first film. She was soon to become better known as Gypsy Rose Lee. Charles Winninger looks like he's trying to teach her how to do a striptease. *You Can't Have Everything*, 1937.

George happily asks Judy to substitute for Evelyn, but she angrily tells him she does not wish to appear in one of his "stupid musical comedies" and she leaves in a huff. Sam has come to believe that Lulu has been a bad influence on Gordon and asks the Ritzes to find Judy. They gain entrance to Judy's all-girl residence by dressing as charwomen. To clear the field, Sam sends Lulu on vacation and Judy finally does accept the job, believing that her earnings will finance her play. In spite of her disdain for George's taste in musicals, they begin falling in love.

Lulu returns after reading about George and Judy's romance in a gossip column and tells him that he married her while under the usual influence of the booze. Lulu warns Judy to stay away from her "husband" and Judy returns to her hometown to work in a music store selling sheet music. One day she receives music that she realizes is part of an adaptation of her so-called serious play into one of the musicals she so dislikes.

She angrily races back to New York to confront George but when she rushes into the theater, the audience is chanting for the author—namely her. She is now happy and announces to the delight of the crowd that she is working on a new play. George and Lulu arrive, and Harry Ritz notices that the marriage license has fallen out of Lulu's purse. It has never been signed and is therefore invalid. Not only does all end happily between Judy and George, Harry winds up with the seductive but nasty Lulu.

* * *

In Argentina, the film was a strict translation of the English title: *No se Puede Tener Todo*; the Brazilians called it *A Vem o Amore*; in Italy it was dubbed *New York Si Diverte*; in Hungary it was *Tip-Top Folies*, and in Sweden *Halla, Broadway!*

One of the film's odd advertising gimmicks was the distribution of milk bottle tops inscribed with its title. One of the ads, going overboard with its alliteration, promised: "Everything to give the sparkle and splash … the laughter and lilt … the lure and loveliness … the melody and madness." The Ritz Brothers certainly provided some of the laughter and certainly all of the madness, but they were not even mentioned in this ad which featured large photographs of everyone else.

Besides the title song, Alice Faye sings "Danger, Love at Work" and "Please Pardon Us, We're in Love." (Fifteen-year-old Judy Garland recorded "You Can't Have Everything" that same year.) Tony Martin warbles "The Loveliness of You" as part of his role in the stage musical. The other song was "Afraid to Dream."

The Ritz Brothers contribute the specialty number "Long Underwear," which begins with them being dressed in white tie and tails, and ends with them wearing the long underwear of the title. During it, Harry utters some nonsensical pseudo–French words, and at the finale of the number they are all suspended on a clothesline. They also do their usual parody, this time of the title song.

Years later, a Ritz Brothers critic asked director Norman Taurog why he allowed them to carry on in the film; the critic called their antics "extremely tiresome and totally unfunny." Taurog was said to have responded that they were always funny while on the set. "In fact, we were all laughing so much, it was difficult to get a clean take.... In real life they were always clowning around, trying out new routines, just as they do in the movie."

A bonus for movie buffs is the first film appearance of Gypsy Rose Lee under her real name Louise Hovick. It was reported that Fox had received hundreds of letters protesting her appearance. Presumably this was a concerted campaign by some churches because of her naughty but less-there-than-meets-the-eye reputation as a stripper. It also could have been studio publicity.

Bandleader Louis Prima has one of his early cinema roles. African American dancers Tip, Tap and Toe do one of their hot tap dances as part of the stage musical; unjustly, they are little remembered today. Perhaps the Nicholas Brothers overshadowed them—as the Marx Brothers did the Ritzes?

As a sign of their increasingly favored status, the Ritz Brothers had risen steadily in the cast lists since their Fox debut in *Sing, Baby, Sing* when they were seventh-billed. In their next film *One in a Million* they had sixth billing, and *On the Avenue* fourth. *You Can't Have Everything* was to be their last featured role in a Fox musical before earning their first starring role in the programmer *Life Begins in College* the same year.

Another *You Can't Have Everything* ad trumpeted "Hotter 'n' Sweeter than *On the* Avenue," "Faster 'n' Funnier Than *Sing, Baby, Sing*." About the Ritzes it said: "Triple Threats to Gloom.... Give 'em Room.... Give 'em Room!" It was always a good idea to give the Brothers "room."

The Ritzes' number was one of the peppy highlights of a rather mundane musical. Don Ameche, who was not yet 30, is made-up to look older than his actual age with some gray hair and a mustache, presumably to lend him some gravitas in the role of a Broadway producer. While Ameche was made to look older, the Ritz Brothers were getting younger! A *Picture Play* article on this film fudged their ages: Oldest brother Al's age was given as 33; he was about 36 at this time. Jimmy made himself younger by two years, stating his age as 31 when he was 33; Harry shaved a more modest year off, being 30 instead of the article's stated age of 29. The same article reported that while the Brothers had only made $8000 on the stage during the whole of the previous year (a very dubious assertion), they were now making $8000 a week at Fox.

Later in 1937, some of the scenes from *You Can't Have Everything* were reprised on the radio by Don Ameche and the up-and-coming starlet Dorothy "The Sarong" Lamour. During the heyday of radio, this was a very common occurrence; sometimes the entire stories of films were broadcast, often by the stars of the films. Apparently the Ritz Brothers also had been approached to lend their talents to radio; it was reported: "They were still saying no to offers, but more weakly."

Reviews

"Oh, but you can. You have everything right here to make up the maddest and merriest movie of the month. Make it two or three months. You have supremely silly entertainment and you will laugh yourself sick at the Ritz Brothers at their best." *Screenland*, July 1937.

"Fast-moving, high-stepping, rollicking piece of entertainment." *Motion Picture Daily*, July 24, 1937.

"Possesses every ingredient that makes for amusing musical comedy." *Film Daily*, July 27, 1937.

"It is okay as musicals go, with a large dose of the Ritz Brothers. I am afraid Fox is going to wear out their welcome if they use them too much as they seem to be doing.... They are a type of Marx Brothers, but not so clever, and Metro is smart enough to cast them [i.e., the Marxes] in [only] one picture a year." Small-town theater manager.

"We thought this one of the best musicals we have played this season. It seemed to please those who saw it." Manager, Princess Theatre, Lincoln, Nebraska.

"This picture [is] an inferior musical for all its ballyhoo. Did below average business. The Ritz Brothers were not very funny." Manager, Columbia Theatre, Columbus City, Indiana.

"A very fine show that pleased all." Manager, Niles Theatre, Anamosa, Iowa.

"Who else could carry a comedy production about long underwear?" Modern-day commentator.

"There is too much of the Ritz Brothers, and a few of their scenes do go on for too long and bog down the film. Their material is also a mixed bag, sometimes entertaining and sometimes too noisy and tiresome." Modern-day commentator.

"The Ritz Brothers have integrated roles in the plot, ample screen time, and deliver several excellent numbers." Modern-day commentator.

"But the Ritz Brothers? Did people really think they were funny? Jeez, they make the Three Stooges look like George Carlin...."

Fast forward through those three pathetic excuses for entertainment and you probably have a decent movie." Modern-day commentator.

Life Begins in College *(1937)*

The History

The plot of the first starring picture for the Ritz Brothers came about when, in late 1936, Darryl Zanuck wrote that he had "an idea for a new college musical football story." He wanted it written during 1937 because "[o]f course we must have on next year's program a follow-up on *Pigskin Parade*." *Pigskin Parade* was a 1936 Fox programmer which had a routine story, but a solid roster of talent the likes of Jack Haley, Patsy Kelly, Stuart Erwin, Betty Grable, Tony Martin, the Yacht Club Boys (to whom the Ritzes had been compared), and a very young Judy Garland, in her first feature film.

Zanuck had spent much of the silent movie days writing scenarios for Warner Brothers, including some for canine star Rin Tin Tin. Thus, he fancied himself a good writer, although he had been accused of plagiarism at least once. The story he came up with for the *Pigskin Parade* follow-up was unoriginal and treacly, a yarn about saving the job of an old college football coach.

No one at Fox (who wanted to remain employed there) was about to point that out to him, so on December 18, 1936, a treatment by Darrell Ware and Allen Rivkin, with the working title *The Football Story*, was presented to him. On January 6, 1937, another treatment, now bearing the title *Little Black Cloud*, was presented. The title referred to the main character, an "Osage Indian, with a terrific physique, who comes to Lombardy College to learn how the white man studies, lives and loves." His English name was George Black.

On February 1, and with the film idea now retitled *The Pigskin Parade of 1937*, the Osage Indian was changed to a neutral Oklahoma Indian and renamed Little Chief: "He still wants to learn the white man's ways and therefore he is going to a big white man's college." Another treatment emerged in late March 1937. One of Zanuck's underlings wrote to him: "There certainly can be no complaint about the originality in this idea." (Besides being obsequious, this observation probably did not hold up factually.) Because it was a musical, the orchestras of either Paul Whiteman or Fred Waring were suggested; now it was the proposed turn of Shep Fields and His Rippling Rhythm Revue.

On May 8, a revised treatment was offered, written by Karl Tunberg and based on Darrell Ware's *The Little Black Cloud*. Zanuck was not amused:

"Horrible example of ruining a great idea [by which he meant *his* idea]—farce, slapstick, satire, inane nonsense. Almost the same story can be told with human characters ... must be believable like *Pigskin* [*Parade*]. The entire attack is worthless ... must take the same characters and start from scratch.... Have professional backfield or two."

At a conference a few days later, a new cast list was decided upon. With no mention of the Ritz Brothers, it included Jack Haley, Robert Young, Nat Pendleton (who would go on to play George) and Alonzo Stagg, a legendary football coach who was slated to play ... the football coach. (Amos Alonzo Stagg lived to be 102 years of age, dying the same year as Al Ritz.) Seasoned character actors were to include Gene Lockhart, Elisha Cook Jr., and Jed Prouty. The orchestra was now to be Eddie Duchin's.

Zanuck was still unsatisfied: "The treatment submitted, while having a sound premise, contains very little entertainment, as well as presenting casting difficulties." On May 22, a "Temporary Treatment" suggested: "This is a story of how three brothers [enter the Ritzes!], working their way through college, suddenly find themselves with a tremendous income to spend." Zanuck's reaction: "Good, can be improved ... dialogue punch up ... football opening." A new leading man was floated, Joel McCrea.

In the middle of June, a "Temporary Script" elicited this comment: "The Ritz Brothers, particularly, are working in well." The "Revised Temporary Script" of June 28, 1937, was (finally!) titled *Life Begins in College*, with original scenario by Karl Tunberg and Don Ettlinger. Zanuck now said: "The lines of the Ritz Brothers have been split up too much. Give the sock lines to Harry and the secondary lines to the other two ... as Harry is actually the only one that can deliver a line."

From this point on, the title would alternate between *Life Begins* **in** *College* to *Life Begins* **at** *College*. A "Final Script" appeared on July 5, 1937, and a "Revised Final Script" three days later. This film had taken so long to gestate that a title of *Pigskin Parade of 1938* was being considered.

Although Zanuck seemed to really like his "original" idea, there had been many earlier movie football stories besides *Pigskin Parade*. The Marx Brothers made *Horse Feathers* in 1932, the same year that Wheeler and Woolsey did *Hold 'em Jail*. Others in the talkie era included *College Coach, Rose Bowl, Huddle, Hold 'em Yale* and *College Rhythm*. Even the Three Stooges got into the act with *Three Little Pigskins*, featuring a very early screen appearance by Lucille Ball. In the silent era, Harold Lloyd's *The Freshman* had been very popular, and there was *Brown of Harvard* (made twice), *The Quarterback* and *West Point*. Legendary player Red Grange even made a football-themed serial, titled after his nickname: *The Galloping Ghost*.

The Film

Directed by William A. Seiter. Produced by Harold Wilson. Executive producer: Darryl F. Zanuck. Screenplay: Karl Tunberg and Don Ettlinger. Based on a series of magazine stories by Darrell Ware. Additional material (uncredited): Ray Golden, Sid Kuller and Samuel Pokrass. Cinematography: Robert H. Planck. Editor: Louis R. Loeffler. Art director: Hans Peters. Costume designer: Royer. Musical director: Louis Silvers. Dates of production: July 12 to early September 1937. Released by Twentieth Century–Fox on October 1, 1937. Approx. 85 minutes.

Cast: The Ritz Brothers (Themselves), Joan Davis (Inez), Tony Martin (Band Leader), Gloria Stuart (Janet O'Hara), Fred Stone (Coach Tim O'Hara), Nat Pendleton (George Black/Little Black Cloud), Dick Baldwin (Bob Hayner), Joan Marsh (Cuddles), Jed Prouty (Oliver Stearns Sr.), Maurice Cass (Dean Moss), Ed Thorgerson (Radio Announcer), Marjorie Weaver (Miss Murphy), Robert Lowery (Sling), Lon Chaney Jr. (Gilks), J.C. Nugent (T. Edwin Cabot), Fred Kohler Jr. (Bret), Elisha Cook Jr. (Ollie Stearns), Charles C. Wilson (Coach Burke), Frank Sully (Acting Captain), Norman Willis (Referee).

Synopsis: Lombardy College was founded in 1847 "to give the Indian Nations of North America access to higher education." Little Black Cloud, whose English name is George Black, enrolls after crashing his motorcycle and is hazed by football player Bob Hayner and his fraternity brothers. They dress him in a nightgown, blindfold him and send him into a women's physical science class while giving a war whoop.

Student Janet O'Hara is drenched with a bucket of water meant for George. She is naturally angry at Bob. Humiliated at his treatment, George decides to leave Lombardy. But first he takes his torn trousers to the Klassy Kampus Kleaners, which has been unsuccessfully run for seven years by the Ritz Brothers. They have also been Lombardy students for seven years.

The Ritzes see that he is carrying a large amount of money, and is actually very wealthy from owning oil wells. Determined to save old football coach Tim O'Hara's job, they convince George to stay in school and play football. O'Hara (Janet's father) has been asked to retire because of his age, and the arrogant Bob Hayner was on the committee that ordered it.

Although Bob, who is in love with Janet, now tries to save O'Hara's job, the dean announces his retirement anyway. Another student, Inez, madly pursues George. The Ritzes ask George to use his money to pay the coach's salary, but he replies that he wants people to like him for himself, not his money. The brothers offer to help spend his money for him, using some for themselves and giving

Perhaps Al, Harry and Jimmy are celebrating being in their first starring film. Or maybe they're just enjoying their seven years—and counting—as very mature college students. *Life Begins in College,* **1937.**

$50,000 to reinstate O'Hara. Another condition is that they be allowed to play on the football team. They even establish their own fraternity, with George as the only other member.

Bob and George are now sworn enemies because Bob made an insulting remark about his Indian heritage. O'Hara makes George the star of the team and they score victories, no thanks to the awful playing of the bumbling Ritzes.

To get rid of Inez, George tells her she must get a tattoo of a snake if she wants to marry him. Janet, who had begun believing Bob was sorry about his treatment of George, now turns on him again because she see him with Cuddles, an old girlfriend.

Thinking she can make Bob the team star again, Cuddles schemes to reveal that George cannot play for the team because he played football for an oil company team in Oklahoma and therefore has lost his amateur status. George admits it, but says he did not keep any of the money. He is still deemed ineligible to play. The coach is prepared to dismiss Bob from the team as well for his role in George's ouster, but relents when it becomes apparent that Bob was not to blame.

With George ineligible to play, Bob becomes the star again, but during the big game he suffers a broken collarbone with the other team ahead by five points. The Ritzes get onto the field to try to help, but commit errors that make things worse. At the last second, Harry catches his own pass and scores the winning touchdown. Bob and Janet are reunited, and Inez shows George that she has gotten the tattoo. He kisses her so passionately that, frightened, she tries to rub the tattoo off.

* * *

In the U.K. the film was called *The Joy Parade*.

Obviously, this was *not* originally intended to be the Ritz Brothers' first starring film. They were not even considered for the cast until later in the planning process. It is not known with certainty what caused Zanuck to decide that they would star. Perhaps their specialties in the preceding four features earned them that opportunity. Or possibly continuing frustration with the script led him to the decision to juice it up. Some version of the latter scenario seems the most probable.

The character of George Black was, in the opinion of many, reminiscent of the great Native American athlete Jim Thorpe, and it would have been thought of as such by audiences of the 1930s. Like George Black in the film, he had lost his amateur standing. Thorpe was deprived of the gold medals he had won in the 1912 Olympics because he had played minor league baseball during a couple of previous summers. This was also a plot device in Sonja Henie's first film *One in a Million*.

In the early silent movie days, Native Americans were often portrayed sympathetically as valiant warriors. By 1937, audiences were used to seeing them on the screen either as bloodthirsty villains to be shot down, or as comic figures who spoke in monosyllables and grunts. Reviews of that time would have rarely or never mentioned such stereotyping. (See Louella Parsons review below.)

There were an unusually high number of songs packed into the running time, which was eventually edited down by almost 15 minutes. Reviews written at the time the film opened listed the original running time as 94 minutes; within a short time, it became 80 minutes. This suggests that it was originally envisioned as a minor "A" film, like *Pigskin Parade*. The cuts may have been accomplished by the elimination of some songs, perhaps some trimming in the football sequences. It would then be closer to bottom-of-the-bill length when it went into wide release. Small town and rural filmgoers did not necessarily clamor to see college musicals.

In her later years, Gloria Stuart had some nice things to say about working with the Ritz Brothers. This was leading man Dick Baldwin's first film, but his career did not prosper. He made a few more by 1938, then disappeared from the screen before returning briefly in 1944. Among this cast of experienced and often antic actors he seemed very bland indeed. Marjorie Weaver was to be the Ritzes' leading lady in *Kentucky Moonshine*.

Tony Martin, given no character name beyond Band Leader, continued his slow rise toward leading man status; second-billed Joan Davis was on her way to becoming one of the more raucously successful comediennes of the late 1930s and 1940s. Martin, Davis and Stuart (possibly dubbed) all sing. Songs include "Big Chief Swing It," "The Rhumba Goes Collegiate," "Our Team Is on the Warpath," "Fair Lombardy," "Why Talk About Love?" and "Sweet Varsity Sue."

The Ritz Brothers perform their usual specialty numbers, none of which showcased them very effectively, except perhaps their rumba exhibition in which Harry dresses in drag. Another included their being pulled in on a float by coeds and, dressed as Indian braves, singing and dancing a so-called Indian number with a mix of disparate lyrics. The final one was at the football game where they enter behind the large school band (whose members all wear Indian chief headdresses). This time the Ritzes are in colonial garb and do a number loosely based on *Yankee Doodle Dandy*.

Fox put on a big blitz to advertise the film. When the Ritzes were invited to put their hands and feet into the Chinese Theatre cement, there was a tie-in with the film. An edition of the newsreel *Fox Movietone News*, narrated by journalist Lowell Thomas, opens with Thomas intoning, "Life may begin at college...." The Ritzes enter the Grauman Chinese Theatre forecourt in raccoon coats and football helmets which they quickly discard to reveal one-piece bathing suits. They salaam in front of the cement square where they will place their hands and feet, as Thomas quips: "Another of their goofy jokes, pretending that they know how to write." They proceed to put their names, handprints and footprints in the cement; Harry's is done in bare feet. They kiss the bemused Sid Grauman while Thomas relates how Grauman not too long before had turned the brothers down as entertainers in that very theater. The same scene appears in the *Screen Snapshots: Hollywood's Famous Feet* short subject of 1950.

Suggested catchphrases for ads and posters, all using immodest capital letters and exclamation points, included: "The Three-Ritz Circus Is Coming to Town!" "We're Putting on the Ritzes and They're Putting on a Riot!" "Wotta Life! Wotta Riot! Wotta Laffa-Palooza!" "They Go Collegiate! You Go Nuts!" "The Mad Merrimaniacs of *You Can't Have Everything* Wilder and Wackier Than Ever!" and "The World's Newest Fun Favorites in Their First Starring Laugh Sensation!"

There were newspaper contests, one of which was to submit the game scores of the six teams Lombardy plays against during the picture. Football tie-ins were encouraged: "Invite members of visiting teams to attend your theater as guests," "Arrange with local radio stations for announcements before, during and after games," "Arrange with college bandleader to play songs from the picture during intermission" and the especially inventive "Use captive balloon to announce [the showings]. Moor it near stadium."

Reviews

"[The film] doesn't make a lot of sense but it's a whale of a lot of fun.... [The Ritz Brothers] are without a doubt the hardest working cohort of entertainers the picture business ever has had. They battle so hard to make the audience laugh that they succeed, and once in a while they pull a gag so screamingly funny that even the gloomiest onlooker might bust a gallus laughing." *Daily Variety*, September 25, 1937.

"[The film] is disappointing. It demonstrates pretty thoroughly that the Brothers Ritz, excellent as they are as incidental performers, cannot carry a whole picture, and there is vastly too much of them in this one.... The chief defect is the lack of a basic comedy idea." *Hollywood Reporter*, September 25, 1937.

"The Ritz Brothers provide a lot of laughs with their nonsensical entertainment. Although their routines lack the bang-up physical antics that characterized their previous work, and which helped to get those socko results, they still clown, dance, sing and chatter in a manner that makes the piece very enjoyable." *Film Daily*, September 27, 1937.

"Anyone who enjoys their clowning will probably enjoy the picture. Others will be bored." *Motion Picture Reviews*, October 1937.

"Clearly the thing to do with the Ritz Brothers is not to try to explain them. In no time at all they have shot up from vaudeville stage and nightclub floor to a screen eminence acknowledged here by stellar billing. They are given expanded opportunity to display their deliberately demoniac talents.... The brotherly comics, it may be pertinent to remark, are stars of the picture only obliquely and by sheer weight of preponderant emphasis." *Motion Picture Herald*, October 2, 1937.

"Has enough laughs to please their adherents." *Independent Exhibitors Film Bulletin*, October 1937.

"A fast-stepping well-told college football yarn of amusing improbabilities, offers ace laugh entertainment for any audience." *Motion Picture Daily*, November 6, 1937.

"[The Ritz Brothers] give it the works.... They contribute some revamped versions of their familiar routines, but they wring out the laughs." *Philadelphia Ledger*, October 8, 1937.

"Those mad, mad Ritz Brothers are up to all their old zany tricks, and some brand new ones, in their first starring picture.... Apparently the movie fans just can't get enough of these genially insane comedians.... Fundamentally the picture is built completely around the Ritzes, and they more than prove their ability to carry a production on their own.... Nat Pendleton's Indian makeup is very effective and he grunts his way to one of his best and funniest performances." Louella Parsons, October 14, 1937.

"Too Ritzy! These birds are OK in support, but when you have to look at them most of the time it sure does get tiresome. And they are so silly." *Motion Picture Herald*, December 25, 1937.

"Grand production in any spot. Will stand extended run. Pleased all and will please you." Manager, Strand Theatre, Old Town, Maine.

"[T]he American Indian [character] rings the changes of just about every possible stereotype ('me-um,' 'how,' etc.) that the most gutter-minded person could imagine. It's not quite at the level of *Birth of a Nation* but it comes close. I know this was a different and less sensitive time.... It is an indicator of how far we have come in the eighty years since it was filmed." Modern-day commentator.

"This just isn't a good movie. The Ritz Brothers' comedy is limited, best in their dance numbers and very weak in the dialogue passages. They can't carry a feature-length film on their own.... The script is obvious and lame-brained.... And then there's the blatant racism.... Eighty minutes of tedium and embarrassing racism." Modern-day commentator.

The Goldwyn Follies *(1938)*

The History

Samuel Goldwyn (*née* Shmuel Gelbficz) was, like most Hollywood moguls of his time, a self-educated man, but driven and shrewd for all that. It is understandable that he wanted to be taken seriously as a producer in any genre he might undertake; possibly to be a film impresario at the level of Broadway's Flo Ziegfeld. He had already produced the successful movie musicals *Whoopee*, *The Kid from Spain* and *Roman Scandals*, all starring *Ziegfeld Follies* alumnus Eddie Cantor.

The word *Follies*, with its aura of enduring success, no doubt appealed to him and thus may have born the idea for *The Goldwyn Follies*. He would gather diverse talents from all areas of show business, including "cultured" performers from opera and the ballet, and meld them into a harmonious whole. It would be a blending of his interest in prestige projects: the production of films drawn from classic novels, with more glitzy material suitable for lovers of his comely Goldwyn Girls and gaudy Technicolor musicals. It was reported that Goldwyn wanted to make a whole series of three-hour, $2,000,000 films that would, as he said, "put an end to the double feature."

Apparently playwright Lillian Hellman, whose controversial play *The Children's Hour* had been (sorta) filmed by Goldwyn, was one choice for the writer, as was Dorothy Parker. Ben Hecht seemed like an odd choice too, but he did go on to write the film. His idea may have been to make a film that had a producer resembling Samuel Goldwyn trying to make a film like *The Goldwyn Follies*. It was perhaps a kind of mischievous satire that the imperious Goldwyn might not have realized. The scene where Kenny Baker sings a fine Gershwin love song to a grilling hamburger would certainly indicate that.

The idea of using George Gershwin's 1928 ballet score for *An American in Paris* for Zorina's great ballet set piece was supposedly rejected by Goldwyn on the grounds that the "miners in Harrisburg wouldn't understand it." Instead, songwriter Vernon Duke provided his score which, to some, seemed inferior.

It was speculated that Vera Zorina's character was based on the real-life Russian actress Anna Sten, unsuccessfully pushed by Goldwyn for stardom a few years earlier. A well-regarded biography of Goldwyn suggests that his interest in Zorina (as she was usually billed) was more than professional. The producer also had dreams of snagging French director Rene Clair, but settled for workmanlike George Marshall. Perhaps having to "settle" was not in the best interest of the film.

The Film

Directed by George Marshall and (uncredited) H.C. Potter. Produced by Samuel Goldwyn. Associate producer: George Haight. Story and screenplay: Ben Hecht. Specialties and songs: Sid Kuller and Ray Golden. Additional comedy: Sam Perrin and Arthur Phillips. Cinematography: Gregg Toland. Editor: Sherman Todd. Set decorator: Julia Haight. Costume designer: Omar Kiam. Makeup: Max Factor. Color designer: Richard Day. Sound: Frank Maher. Ballet music: Vernon Duke. Music: George Gershwin. Lyrics: Ira Gershwin. Musical director: Alfred Newman. Ballet conceived and staged by George Balanchine. Released in the United States from January 28 (Miami, Florida) to February 20, 1938 (New York). [Extant version] 115–117 minutes; [Copyright version] 122 minutes.

Cast: Adolphe Menjou (Oliver Merlin), The Ritz Brothers (Themselves), Vera Zorina (Olga Samova), Kenny Baker (Danny Brewster), Andrea Leeds (Hazel Dawes), Edgar Bergen (Himself/Charlie McCarthy), Helen Jepson (Leona Jerome), Phil Baker (Michael Day), Bobby Clark (A. Basil Crane), Ella Logan (Glory Wood), Jerome Cowan (Director in the film), Charles Kullmann (Alfredo in the opera), American Ballet of the Metropolitan Opera (Ballet dancers), Nydia Westman (Ada), Frank Shields (Assistant director in the film).

Among the uncredited cast were the very young Alan Ladd as the first singer to audition; Barry Norton, leading man in silent films; Alfred Newman, the actual musical director, playing the same role in the film, and Buddy Roosevelt, a "B" cowboy actor.

Synopsis: Two young small-town women watch a movie scene being filmed with diva Olga Samova. One of the women, Hazel Dawes, comments on how unrealistic the scene is. She is overheard by the film's producer Oliver Merlin, who asks her to accompany him back to Hollywood. She will be his advisor on making his films "real" and he dubs her "Miss Humanity." He forbids her to talk to any actors and to stay away from the set so she will remain unspoiled. When Merlin tries to get into his studio, the gate is blocked by the animal training act of the Ritz Brothers, who want to break into films. They are thrown off the lot.

Miss Humanity is installed in an apartment with a young chaperone. She gives Merlin advice such as remaking *Romeo and Juliet* with a happy ending in which they both live. Every bit of advice she gives him is greeted with his reaction of "Amazing!" and he adopts everything she says. She also tells him how a "good girl" is supposed to behave. The Ritz Brothers have gotten into a film and they perform the "Here, Pussy, Pussy" number which is basically that word repeated endlessly while they prance around, followed by a multitude of real cats.

Bored with her seclusion, Hazel goes to an eatery where the cook Danny Brewster is flipping hamburgers to the accompaniment of George and Ira

Gershwin's "Love Walked In." He and Hazel begin a romance. Edgar Bergen and Charlie McCarthy periodically appear in the film, the dummy being much the livelier one of that duo. He is even wooed by Samova to appear with her in a film. (In their interactions, it is often difficult to tell which is the more wooden.)

Also popping in and out is the character of Michael Day, usually wearing his accordion like a bulky jacket. He is a bit actor who is either never given a role, or if he is, the character is always being changed at the last minute. He and Charlie McCarthy continually insult one another, à la the then-current McCarthy–W.C. Fields "feud" on Edgar Bergen's radio show. Opera star Helen Jepson in her only film role occasionally bursts forth with arias from *La Traviata*.

Oliver Merlin is making a film starring Samova, the plot of which is never revealed except that it seems like some sort of revue. The Ritz Brothers reappear in Cossack outfits and run in and out of Samova's room kissing her passionately. It is unclear whether this is part of the movie being made or "for real." In a very brief number as gondoliers-mermaids, the Ritzes sink beneath the waves of the canal on the Venice set, this after scatting "The Serenade to a Fish."

Danny has also been signed for the film after appearing on a radio show singing the second Gershwin love ballad "Our Love Is Here to Stay." In her set piece ballet number, Zorina rises from a fountain (shades of the Ritzes disappearing into the canal) and dances in an Art Moderne setting. Hazel sneaks onto the set to watch Danny perform and he spots her. Misunderstanding the situation, he breaks off their romance.

Merlin realizes he is in love with Miss Humanity and prepares to propose to her at a party. When he learns that she and Danny are an item, he threatens to fire Danny from the film. Love finally conquers all: Hazel and Danny are reunited and he is signed to a five-year contract.

* * *

In the countries in which the film was released, it mostly retained something similar to the English title. In France it was called *Hollywood en Folle*; in Italy, *Follie di Hollywood*, and in Spain *Asi Nace una Fantasia*.

Perhaps because of its pretensions (and sometime pretentiousness?), *The Goldwyn Follies* has become a cult film, and not necessarily in a good way. One of the more modest ads for the film read: "Samuel Goldwyn Presents the Greatest Array of Stars from the Screen, Stage, Radio, Opera, and Ballet." Another trumpeted: "Hollywood's Greatest Show—Samuel Goldwyn's Most Important Production Will Gloriously Reflect Its Brilliance at the Box-Offices of the World." Perhaps not even *Gone with the Wind* or any other epic production could have lived up to such puffery.

No effort was spared to publicize the film. It was reported that distributor

United Artists sent 17 "exploitation men" into the field to handle the major openings. At the film's grand opening, there was a tie-in with a Charlie McCarthy doll. A ventriloquist holding one of the dolls perched on a platform in front of the theater and did an act. It was said that the "real" Charlie McCarthy was so affected by the response to his acting that he had to be carried out of the theater after the preview.

A Chicago theater featured "street ballyhoo." A five-room model apartment called the Miss Humanity Home, based on that of Andrea Leeds' character in the film, was created in New York City by "more than twenty home-making industries." In one city a parade was organized with the mayor at its head and a police escort. The topper may have been the revelation that carrier pigeons were used to deliver the acceptances of "notables" to the world premiere at the State Theatre in Miami, Florida.

Earlier in the week, the birds had been delivered to these notables with the instruction to place their acceptances into metal containers on the birds' left legs. They were then taken up to the various roofs and were allowed to fly off. It was claimed that upon the opening of the film, it was continually sold out, and that thousands of people had to be turned away.

These over-the-top efforts have been an inevitable invitation for derision over the years, possibly because there *are* no really great stars in it. A reputed budget of $2 million bought the thinnest of plots as a thread to support specialty acts. With such lines as Danny's "Me and the hamburgers will be waiting for you with a song on my lips," this film does almost seem like a parody. Yet the line is seemingly delivered with total sincerity after Danny has sung "Love Walked In" to one of the hamburgers.

There are a legion of such cringe-making lines in the film including the supposedly sophisticated Oliver Merlin crying out: "I can't buy common sense, I cannot buy humanity!" If all this is looked upon as a deliberately written satire by Ben Hecht, then some of the reappraisal which has taken place may be worth thinking about. Some modern-day reviewers have called it self-referential.

On paper this film did have the "A" team working on it. Samuel Goldwyn had produced and would go on to produce a string of prestigious films dating back to silent film days. Hecht was famous for his realistic writing. Gregg Toland would become renowned for his cinematography on *Citizen Kane*. It presents the last film music of George Gershwin, who died during production. Ira Gershwin had worked as his younger brother's lyricist with great success. The picture earned Oscar nominations for Best Score and for Art Direction.

It is obvious that the second-billed Ritz Brothers were somehow induced to imitate the Marx Brothers in the scene when they each make love to Samova. It is a direct rip-off of scenes from the Marxes' *Horse Feathers* and *A Day at the Races*. Their major number, "Here, Pussy, Pussy," could well have been interpreted in a different way than the filmmakers intended. It was later alleged in an article in the magazine *The Animals' Friend* that cruel methods had been used to keep the 200 cats on the set for this number.

If modern-day critics of the Ritzes have only seen this one film of theirs, it is likely that many regard them with less than admiration. On the other hand, some have praised their zany contribution to it. It was the first time all three of the brothers were seen together in a Technicolor feature, although one or two of them would be seen in their "true colors" in the future.

Adolphe Menjou, who often played theatrical producers of one kind or another, seems a bit tamped down in the film. Whether he was aware of the kind of lines he is given is unknown but he always seemed comfortable hamming it up, as evidenced by his madly frenetic Russian charity show producer in *Gold Diggers of 1935* and other films of that era.

Andrea Leeds goes through the entire movie rather blandly with a wan smile on her face. After a series of uncredited roles, she finally achieved status with an Academy Award nomination for Best Supporting Actress in the previous year's *Stage Door*. The role of Miss Humanity, and her strong resemblance to Olivia de Havilland, did not help to further her career and after a few more films she left Hollywood.

German-born Vera Zorina (*née* Eva Brigitta Hartwig), one of the many wives of ballet master George Balanchine, was primarily a ballet dancer who did a few films and a handful of Broadway shows, some very successful. This was her first American film. As a relatively untrained actress, she came across onscreen (perhaps deliberately) as humorless, icy and stone-faced.

When asked in later years if she liked doing *The Goldwyn Follies,* Zorina replied,

> Yes, because Balanchine worked on the dance numbers, the water ballet, which, as far as I'm concerned is the only good thing about the film. The rest of it, the Ritz Brothers and Edgar Bergen and Charlie McCarthy, oh, I didn't know what they were talking about with their jokes. The Ritz Brothers made a joke in that film, something like "Do you know Zorina?" and another one replied, "Yeah, I have it for breakfast every morning." A joke on Farina, right? Ha, ha, ha.
>
> Everyone laughed but me. I didn't get it. It's just a terrible joke. Working with the Ritz Brothers, they were just not for me. My whole interest in that film was working with Balanchine.

Although the "joke" she recalled is not in the film, no doubt the Ritzes were capable of teasing her. In the same interview, she said that Goldwyn, with whom she had a seven-year contract, kept loaning her out for films she did not much like either.

Of the nominal leads, Kenny Baker (who some dubbed a less talented Dick Powell) was basically a one-note actor. He performed the two Gershwin love songs with his usual pleasant tenor voice but neither was sung to the nominal female romantic lead Andrea Leeds. One was sung to a hamburger, the other over the radio. That same year, he did *At the Circus* with the Marx Brothers.

Bobby Clark, late of the comedy team of Clark and McCullough, went on to significant Broadway fame, as did Ella Logan. They were both pretty much wasted in nominal roles. Helen Jepson had a distinguished operatic career to return to, as did Charles Kullmann. The "actor" who may have come out as the wittiest in this was a wooden dummy, by way of his self-effacing (at least on the screen) creator Edgar Bergen. Although there were some respectable and even glowing reviews at the time of its release, the film was a flop and Goldwyn lost much of his investment.

In *The 50 Worst Movies of All Time*, author Harry Medved sums up *The Goldwyn Follies* with "[C]ertainly more than a folly, it is a travesty." He also characterizes the ballet sequences as "intended to add a touch of culture, but instead add a touch of indigestion." The dancers look like they are "having their innards squeezed out by tutus that are much too tight." The Ritz Brothers are "a knockabout comedy team with a dubious track record." This opinion of the film probably has been one of the reasons for its poor reputation in recent decades, but perhaps in light of current reevaluation, that has proven to be overly facile.

Reviews

"A hefty eyeful.... A lavish production in which certain individual performers and ensembles erase the memory of some dull moments." *Variety*, December 31, 1937.

"Sets a new standard for sheer screen beauty and sumptuous production.... In its assembly of talent and established names of great pulling power, the picture has something for all tastes. The comedy runs the gamut from sly satire to the broadest slapstick.... The most gorgeous and effective use of Technicolor to date.... The Ritz Brothers incorporate their characteristic zany antics and manage to make them jibe with the more restrained elements of humor by other members of the troupe." *Daily Variety*, January 26, 1938.

"An incredible blending of entertainment elements that is superbly effective and stunningly beautiful. Technicolor has never been used with such consummate skill and taste and, combined with the magnificent artistry of a lavish production, it weaves a magic spell of loveliness…. The Ritz Brothers, with good material, are unfailingly uproarious." *Hollywood Reporter*, January 26, 1938.

"The [film] disappoints, a draggy overlong musical." *Independent Exhibitors Film Bulletin*, February 26, 1938.

"The most beautiful and tasteful of musical shows is one of the mildest. It misses being the knockout it could have been, even with Technicolor to glorify it and an almost limitless roster of talent. 'Pleasing' is the word for this two-hour lavish outlay. 'Sensational' is the word I had hoped to use." *Picture Play Magazine*, April 1938.

"Comments divided. Had seven walkouts on Sunday and a few the other nights. However, it is a very fine production." Manager, Mason Theatre, Mason, Michigan.

"My opinion, very good, but I didn't make any money in it." Manager, Grand Theatre, Lemmon, South Dakota.

"It's a wonderful picture that everybody was enthused over." Manager, Rialto Theatre, Saguache, Colorado.

"This below average musical was producer Samuel Goldwyn's failed attempt to recreate the kind of revue that made showman Florenz Ziegfeld famous…. Unless you love ventriloquist Edgar Bergen, or more improbably the Ritz Brothers and their antics, you're unlikely to enjoy much of this movie." *Classic Film Guide*.

Re-release Reviews

Despite some of the negative reaction that this film has earned over the years, the tincture of time—namely seven decades—can make a difference. With the release of a carefully produced DVD in 2009, there were some different perspectives on the film.

"A particularly memorable skirmish in Hollywood's continuing battle between high art and low…. A fascinating mash-up whose ill-assorted elements are a major part of its odd appeal…. The water-nymph sequence … is immediately recognizable as the inspiration for the 'Dance of the Hours' in Walt Disney's *Fantasia*. Where [it] does succeed, it's not as high art but as elevated craft…." *New York Times*, May 1, 2009.

"Not half as bad as we've been led to believe all these years…. I found *The Goldwyn Follies* wonderfully entertaining, along with possibly the best use of Technicolor in a Hollywood film, startlingly naturalistic and visually stunning…. Although the storyline has a tendency to totter and weave, there's always something to catch one's eye, not to mention one's funny bone.... No one could come up with a story that would combine [all the stars], not to mention, God help us, the Ritz Brothers.... While certainly not the *Citizen Kane* of musicals [it] is consistently entertaining and continually fascinating, both from a historical standpoint, as well as for the crazy-quilt high and low musical culture." *Films in Review*, May 18, 2009.

"It is the antics of the infamous Ritz Brothers that steal the show.... [T]he rest of the cast seems to be sleepwalking through the picture by comparison. The underrated by posterity Ritz Brothers were a talented trio who were capable of far more than is revealed in this picture, as anyone who ever saw them dance could attest to. They could leave you breathless at their agility and finesse, while at the same time have you rolling in the aisles laughing.... They do deserve special mention here, as they get ignored by others too often." Modern-day commentator.

Another reevaluation seems to have come about from modern-day viewers about the Ritzes' "Here Pussy, Pussy" number. Contemporary comments include: "Their song about the pussy cat can make a modern audience cringe"; "All I can hear in my head is 'Here Pussy Pussy' and I have nightmares of that; not to mention those guys were scary as all Hell"; "Their pussy cat song is truly a jaw-dropper"; "That song about the pussy cat has to be one of the worst ever," and a rare contrary opinion: "Not many people understand or appreciate the Ritz Brothers today. I think they were super-talented nightclub-trained comedians with a finely honed edge to their bits, especially the pussy cat number."

Kentucky Moonshine *(1938)*

The History

The earliest extant treatment of the film that was to become *Kentucky Moonshine* came in the form of a "Skeleton Outline" dated September 25, 1937. The writers were M.M. Musselman and Jack Lait Jr. Others who contributed along the way included Art Arthur, Curtis Kenyon and James Gruen. Originally it was a story about a traveling circus run by the Ritz Brothers and the discovery of a fountain of youth (actually an illegal still). Potential cast members included Jean Hersholt, singers Leah Ray and Tony Martin, Joan Davis, Slim Summerville and Jane Darwell. It was to be the Ritz Brothers' second starring film.

An October 20, 1937, story outline entitled *Moonshine Over Kentucky* changed the entire storyline. Zanuck was not enamored of the new proposal. There was "twice too much story" and he wanted several characters dropped. He also wanted Jack Haley in the film and toyed with the idea of Sonja Henie. His notes include the word "dame" several times, as in "No marriage, [she's] just a dame." Titles like *Honolulu Goes Hillbilly* and *Kentucky Goes Hawaii* were considered.

In discussing the new draft, Zanuck repeated a concept that was a practically a mantra with him: He often stated that stories needed to be "legitimized." This story needed to be logical for this reason: "We are dealing with clowns like the Ritz Brothers and Joan Davis [who was not cast in the film] who will go completely haywire. The underlying plot must be completely sound to overcome their wildness." He did not offer an idea of how to make a story about three New York entertainers who disguise themselves as hillbillies "logical."

Zanuck's reaction to a "Revised Treatment" dated November 5, 1937, was that it was several reels too long. He again repeated his theory about legitimizing the story, and ordered the removal of such unsavory actions as tobacco-spitting, taking off shoes, etc. He ordered that it be funny but not goofy, and that Harry Ritz be given "the best breaks in lines and business all the way through." Also: "Take out all references to Bill Robinson [a dancer] and Peters Sisters [an African-American singing trio]—we don't intend to use any colored talent in this story."

He also expressed concern that the "hillbilly craze was old news." He was probably referring to the spate of such films that came out in the late 1930s, like *Down in "Arkansaw," The Arkansas Traveler, Mountain Music* and *Swing Your Lady*. (The "craze" was far from over; the 1940s saw many such comedies being made, including those of Judy Canova, the Weaver Family, Bob Burns and Lum and Abner.)

Now being considered for the cast were tough guy Warren Hymer and Marjorie Weaver, who had played bit parts in earlier films in which the Ritzes appeared. Zanuck flirted with the idea of Mickey Rooney for the role of Reef, because Rooney had a "tough" image. (The entirely contrasting John Carradine ultimately played the role.) At this point, the movie was slated to have both hillbilly and Hawaiian specialty acts.

A "Temporary Script, Parts One and Two" followed on December 4 with the new title *Kentucky Moonshine*. December 16, 1937, saw the emergence of a "Revised Temporary Incomplete Script, Parts One and Two." Zanuck's notes included: "Open with sock song" and "Dull—what about boys" [i.e., the Ritzes]. He instructed that everyone be laid off without pay until *Moonstruck* was rewritten. (*Moonstruck* was also a title which was being considered.) He suggested Snozzle [sic] Durante and Bert Lahr as possible cast members.

At this point, Zanuck had the brainstorm of making the Ritzes real hillbillies instead of Broadway zanies posing as such. He thought the actual hillbillies in the story would get the laughs and wanted the brothers to be "the cream of the comedy." This changed the whole thrust of the film. As real mountain people, they would naturally be "slow-moving, lazy, shiftless," according to Zanuck, who obviously had absorbed some of the prejudices of his time.

He suggested calling them Hank Poke (Harry), Reef Poke (Jimmy) and Alf Poke (Al), which would be the first time the Ritzes had not played themselves. And they would each play an instrument: cigar box banjo, jug and bellows, and that would lead to their being discovered as "great rural talent" and being taken to New York. This totally unoriginal idea was not adopted.

As 1937 came to an end, Zanuck was still expressing some displeasure. He thought the script was on the wrong track because it was a Ritz Brothers vehicle but they had little to do: "They are heading nowhere, they have no objective." A new storyline was devised, and both Musselman and Lait were taken off the picture. Zanuck ordered that all or most of the key lines were to be given to Harry Ritz. "He should be the one who does most of the hillbilly dialogue…. He will of course keep missing cues so that Jimmy and Al can pick on him and bawl him out on the side."

A "Final Script" dated January 11, 1938, was presented to Zanuck. Other suggested cast members now were Lon Chaney Jr. and Alfalfa of the *Our Gang* series. A "Revised Final Script" was dated January 18, 1938; a January 24 "Shooting Final Script" resulted in the start of production.

Another Zanuck suggestion: "12 girls from *Rebecca*; 3 kids from *Sally, Irene and Mary*." The latter was a Fox film starring Alice Faye, Joan Davis and Marjorie Weaver which was released a couple of months later. The three kids referred to were probably the young singing sisters, Betty, Doris and Gwen Brian, who did appear in *Kentucky Moonshine*. The reference to *Rebecca* is presumably to *Rebecca of Sunnybrook Farm*, a Shirley Temple vehicle released in early 1938.

It is not surprising that the combination of Kentucky and hillbillies appealed to Zanuck as a story idea. Presumably because horse racing and mountain feuds make for good drama or comedy, the state of Kentucky has engendered literally hundreds of films. As far back as 1905, the one-reeler *A Kentucky Feud* hit the nickelodeon screens. There followed so many others that titles were re-used. *My Old Kentucky Home* was almost bound to be one—and it was.

One of humorist Will Rogers' last films was *In Old Kentucky* (1935); that title had also been used on a 1927 silent film. There were *Kentucky Foes, Kentucky Days, Kentucky Girl, Kentucky Pride, A Song of Kentucky, A Kentucky Cinderella, Hills of Kentucky, A Feud in the Kentucky Hills* (with Mary Pickford),

Kentucky Kernels (with Wheeler and Woolsey) and on and on. In 1938, the year *Kentucky Moonshine* was released, there was a movie simply called *Kentucky*. For that Technicolor film, Walter Brennan won an Oscar for Best Supporting Actor.

The producer Kenneth Macgowan's budget showed that the Ritz Brothers received $60,000 for their work; long-time character actor Slim Summerville was the second highest paid at $2000 a week. Several of the other supporting players made higher weekly salaries than the leading man Tony Martin, who was paid $450 a week, and newcomer Marjorie Weaver, who was penciled in for $300 a week.

The film ran into some legal problems. Three writers sued Fox, claiming that the plot was a steal from *Nitwit's Holiday*, a script that they had previously submitted. A director claimed that he had sent *Kentucky Moonshine* director David Butler the script of a two-reeler with a similar storyline that had starred comic El Brendel. Apparently one lawsuit demanded damages of a million dollars but was settled for the bargain price of only $300.

The Film

Directed by David Butler. Story: Jack Lait Jr. and M.M. Musselman. Screenplay: M.M. Musselman and Art Arthur. Contract writers (uncredited): James Gruen and Curtis Kenyon. Additional dialogue [and comedy songs]: Ray Golden and Sid Kuller. Associate producer: Kenneth Macgowan. Producer: Darryl F. Zanuck. Music (uncredited): Murray Cutter, Cyril J. Mockridge and Gene Rose. Cinematography: Robert H. Planck. Editor: Irene Morra. Art directors: Lewis H. Creber and Bernard Herzbrun. Set decorator: Thomas Little. Costume designer: Royer. Dates of production: January 26, 1938, to April 7, 1938. Released by Twentieth Century–Fox on May 20, 1938. 87 minutes.

Cast: The Ritz Brothers (Themselves), Tony Martin (Jerry Wade), Marjorie Weaver (Caroline), Slim Summerville (Hank Hatfield), John Carradine (Reef Hatfield), Wally Vernon (Gus Bryce), Berton Churchill (J.B.), Eddie Collins ("Spats" Swanson), Cecil Cunningham (Landlady), Paul Stanton (Mortimer Hilton), Mary Treen (Sugar Hatfield), Francis Ford (Grandpa Hatfield), The Brian Sisters [Betty, Doris, Gwen] (Singing Trio), Clarence Wilson (Attorney), Frank McGlynn Jr. (Clem Hatfield), Jan Duggan (Nurse), Si Jenks (Buckboard Driver), Irving Bacon (Hotel Clerk), Olin Howlin (Tom Slack), John Hiestand, Carroll Nye, Tom Hanlon (Radio Announcers).

An uncredited cast member who would become better known was Robert Lowery; he went on to be a leading man in many 1940s "B" pictures. Among those who were already known for their frequent screen work were Claud

Allister, who played in several *Bulldog Drummond* films; Harold Goodwin, a leading man in silent films; Milton Kibbee, who had almost 400 screen appearances to his credit (he was the younger brother of character actor Guy Kibbee); Jack Norton, eternally typecast as a friendly drunk, and the unforgettably named Joe Twerp (*née* Escott Boyes).

Synopsis: In New York, Jerry Wade's swing music radio show for Sunshine Soap is falling in the ratings. Announcer Gus Bryce suggests a hillbilly theme because, after all, they are the people who are most in need of soap. Jerry offers to find some real ones; he thinks that previous hillbilly programs have failed because people discovered they were phonies.

When Jerry calls off the auditions for new talent, Caroline, a singer who is actually from Kentucky, is disappointed. She returns to her boardinghouse to talk to her friends the Ritz Brothers, unemployed performers. They have been faking injuries from an automobile accident to collect insurance, but give up when they find the driver who hit them is both uninsured and on relief.

They all decide to head down to Kentucky and pose as real hillbillies; Caroline will pose as the Ritzes' sister. She gets the money for the trip from her suitor Spats by telling him her aunt needs new teeth. Once in Kentucky, the Ritzes are mistaken for the Slack brothers who have been involved in a long-running feud with the Hatfields. Some shooting ensues.

The Ritz Brothers and Caroline perform for Jerry and are hired to do a radio show from a local barn. They sing "Reuben Reuben I've Been Swinging," after which they spot the Hatfields in the audience and pretend to have hiccups so they can make their escape. Jerry fills in by warbling "Moonshine Over Kentucky," aided by the Brian Sisters, the eldest of whom bears a close resemblance to Judy Canova. Caroline warbles "Harvest in the Hills."

When the brothers see that the Hatfields have fallen asleep, they resume performing. The Hatfields wake up and begin shooting. The show does not get transmitted to New York because of technical problems. Jerry brings them all to New York, still unaware of the trick they are playing on him. Caroline refuses to go but then she and Jerry play a game that results in a kiss. Caroline, who is falling in love with Jerry, decides to end the charade.

Once they are back in New York, Spats threatens them with exposure, demanding $300. The Ritzes give him the money but he decides to squeal anyway. A fight results in two of the brothers being knocked out; Harry knocks Spats out. When Gus the announcer discovers they are fakes, they tie him up and leave him in a bathtub.

Caroline tells the brothers that she will not appear on the show because she refuses to hurt Jerry, but does not want to spoil their chances for success. She decides to go to Chicago but Jerry finds her at Grand Central Station while

Broadway "hillbillies" Al, Harry and Jimmy are hoping to finish the radio broadcast before they are relieved of their false beards—and possibly their lives—by the Hatfield clan. *Kentucky Moonshine*, 1938.

the Ritzes do the show as their real selves. They wow the audience by imitating various radio stars and with a Snow White parody. They end with a parody of the Brian Sisters while wearing gingham dresses and aprons, and then perform one of their patented synchronized dance routines. All ends happily when Caroline agrees to marry Jerry.

***

The story is a mélange of elements that never fully jell and little is ultimately made of the Kentucky feud that the Ritzes stumble into. It is one of numerous films of the era that deal with radio shows and unhappy sponsors, not to mention stereotyped hillbillies. Whatever zip it has is supplied by the Ritz Brothers, especially by their typically animated performances.

Although Marjorie Weaver has a genuine regional accent (she was from Tennessee), the romantic leads are bland and most of the supporting players are severely underused. This includes Slim Summerville, who by this time was anything but slim. Berton Churchill does his patented harrumphing, and Eddie Collins performs his usual tongue-clicking routine.

The Brian Sisters, who are given little to do, appeared in nine features and shorts from 1935 to 1940. Amazingly, they still have fans today. One of them blogged that he was not happy—a full 60 or more years later—that the youngsters had been "set up" by the Ritzes' parody.

One influential person who did like the film was Pauline Kael, long before she became an influential critic. She said: "I had trouble dating because I often disagreed about the quality of a movie. One boy was so upset at my laughing at *Kentucky Moonshine* that we never went to a movie again." She continued to laugh with the Ritz Brothers when others forgot or denigrated them.

The film was released in many European countries between June 1938 and June 1941. On the latter date it began playing in Portugal, a neutral country during World War II. There it was known as *Os Tres Vagabundos*. It was known as *Les Pirates du Micro* (France), *Vagabondi al Chiaro di Luna* (Italy), *Tre Tokiga Tenorer* [Three Crazy Tenors] (Sweden) and *Det Glade Vanvid* (Denmark).

One advertisement with caricatures of the Ritzes as hillbillies, and a photo of Tony Martin and Marjorie Weaver in a romantic clinch, blared: "It's Fun o'Clock, Mountain Time!" It continued: "Ain't been so much to laugh at since Gran'maw shot the galluses off'n that revenoor. Public maniacs 1, 2, and 3 [i.e., the Ritz Brothers] gone hillbilly ... and making *Life Begins in College* look like a false start!" Aside from the appeal of the ad to juvenile stereotypes, it was probably a poor idea to knock the stars' last starring picture. And how did the Ritzes like being characterized as "public maniacs"?

In Norwalk, Connecticut, a movie house staged this publicity stunt: Three young men impersonating the Ritz Brothers drove around in an old car with a banner bearing the movie's title. It "broke down" at several intersections so that passersby could see the advertisement on the banner.

Reviews

"Using the Ritz Brothers as ammunition, Darryl F. Zanuck has scored another box office bulls eye.... As stimulating from the standpoint of sheer entertainment as is the fiery liquid from which it derives its name.... The stellar trio at its best.... Definitely establishes the artistically screwy Ritz Brothers as the tops in cinematic mirth-provokers. Picture will bring uproarious laughter from the customers." *Daily Variety*, April 30, 1938.

"Those zippy zanies, the Ritz Brothers, have loosed a mirthquake ... that will shake the sides of the nation. They ride to new glory on a roaring gale of laughter.... This is all merry madness.... Never were the Ritzes better.... Could turn a funeral into a fiesta." *Hollywood Reporter*, April 30, 1938.

"Packed with laughs.... It's a field day for the Ritz Brothers who sing, dance and clown to make this a rollicking laugh fest. Their imitations and skits are most enjoyable.... This is the best thing the boys have been in and proves that with fair support, they can carry a picture. ..Swell comedy entertainment for the masses." *Film Daily*, May 3, 1938.

"What a nosedive it took at the box office. I still contend that the Ritz Brothers have not enough on the ball for two or three pictures a year.... There is no originality in what they do. They do the same thing in each picture; the only change being in the dialogue. When you have seen them once you have seen it all. [The] lowest weekend gross in three years." Manager, Columbia Theatre, Columbus City, Indiana.

"Crude comedy but some folks seemed to enjoy it. However I didn't take in film rental [i.e., the theater did not recoup the film's rental cost]." Manager, Star Theatre, Lupton, Colorado.

Perhaps the success of the Ritz Brothers' films in both big cities and in small towns and rural communities depended on what other film was shown, e.g., "Played on a double bill with a Gene Autry western and it did top business." Manager, Myrtle Theatre, Detroit, Michigan.

"Gives the Brothers Ritz an opportunity to carry a film with star billing. Unfortunately they don't rise to the occasion. Their stuff at times can be funny and it's amusing here. But it's not the stuff [of which] classic comedy is made." Modern-day commentator.

"As usual not enough Ritz Brothers in this, but they get some good moments, the best—perhaps one of their finest sequences captured on film—is their performance at the end. Worth the wait. Phenomenal dancing. Just hilarious and entirely Ritz-ian." Modern-day commentator.

Straight, Place and Show *(1938)*

The History

This film was based on the unproduced play *Saratoga Chips*, written by a seemingly odd team: author and beloved New York "character" Damon Runyon and songwriter Irving Caesar. It was originally titled *Blue Plate Special* and was based on a Runyon short story called "That Ever Loving Wife of Mine" published in the September 1931 issue of the magazine *Hearst's International-Cosmopolitan*.

Fox supposedly paid the authors $50,000 for the rights to the play, said to be the highest price paid to date by a Hollywood studio for an unproduced play. (Film rights to the novel *Gone with the Wind* had previously fetched the same price.) It was originally intended be the basis of a musical comedy picture starring Eddie Cantor and Ethel Merman, who had already been teamed in 1936's *Strike Me Pink*. The possibility of contributions by George Gershwin was discussed. Harold Lloyd was rumored to be interested in the project. Merman did appear in the Ritz Brothers version.

A "Screen Treatment" dated November 21, 1936, was written by Leonard Praskins. Darryl Zanuck expressed his dislike for it in no uncertain terms: "Insane hoke" ("hoke" and "hokey" being among his favorite insults). "This is Sennett hoke," and just to make his meaning clear: "Awful." He did not completely shoot down the idea, saying it had the basis of a strong story but that the treatment was "the wrong foot completely."

On December 12, a "Second Treatment" was discussed, along with actors Eddie Cantor, Gregory Ratoff and Mischa Auer. At that point, Zanuck brought up what seemed to be a favorite setting, Kentucky. (See the entry for *Kentucky Moonshine*.) A couple of weeks later, a "Revised Second Treatment" emerged. Zanuck reminding everyone about "legitimacy," another of his favorite concepts.

In discussing a "Third Revised Treatment" presented to him on the final day of 1936, he was still thinking about Cantor and a "Glenda Farrell type." The idea then seemed to expire. It was revived more than a year later, in February 1938, with a treatment entitled *Straight, Place and Show* by writers M.M. Musselman and Jack Lait Jr. Now the Ritz Brothers were slated to star, but Zanuck called the writers' treatment "too involved, complicated, a jumble."

A few days later, Zanuck commanded that all the Ritz Brothers have equal roles. He though the idea was still "too rambling and vague." A week and a half later, Zanuck called the "Revised Treatment" by Musselman and Allen Rivkin "confused and muddled." He said that it must add "sympathy."

A "First Revised Continuity" (April 7, 1938) was better in Zanuck's opinion, but needed to "develop characters more." Zanuck thought it was the best vehicle the Ritz Brothers ever had, but there was still "too much hokum." He now backed off from his earlier command that all the Ritzes be equally treated. He said that Harry should always have the gag line topper and the other brothers the feeder lines. He also instructed that the character played by diva Ethel Merman not be portrayed as a "bitch." (Apparently he and Merman were social friends.)

He said about her character in this film: "She can still be the clever, smart and sophisticated girl that she starts out to be with a great sense of humor, etc., and she should end up that way. We must avoid the feeling … that she is trying to thwart the situation." Actually, during the course of the film, she does try to do just that, but she redeems herself in the end.

Two weeks later, a "Temporary Script" emerged, and very shortly thereafter came a "Revised Temporary Script" now written by Lew Brown. It turned out that Zanuck had had two sets of scripts written simultaneously and he liked different parts of each one. The task was then to meld them together. Zanuck warned that the final version of the script was to be delivered to the Ritz Brothers the day they arrived in Hollywood: "So no arguments!"

Whether the last command was a sign of Zanuck's impatience or the brothers' demand, a "Final Script" and a "Revised Final Script" were ready by mid–May 1938. After 33 days of production, the film was $33,000 over its projected budget of $717,000. It wound up costing three-quarters of a million dollars. The chief reason given was the replacement of male lead Robert Allen with the better-known (and similarly named) Richard Arlen.

The Film

Directed by David Butler. Associate producer: David Hempstead. Executive in charge of production: Darryl F. Zanuck. Based on a play by Damon Runyon and Irving Caesar. Screenplay: M.M. Musselman and Allen Rivkin. Additional dialogue: Lew Brown. Contributor to screenplay (uncredited): Jack Lait Jr. Cinematography: Ernest Palmer. Editor: Irene Morris. Art directors: Lewis Creber and Bernard Herzbrun. Set decorator: Thomas Little. Costume designer: Gwen Wakeling. Sound: Alfred Bruzlin and Roger Heman. Music: Louis Silvers. Dances: Nick Castle. Dates of production: May 25 to July 1938. Released by Twentieth Century–Fox on September 30, 1938. 68 minutes.

Cast: The Ritz Brothers (Themselves), Richard Arlen (Denny Paine), Ethel Merman (Linda Tyler), Phyllis Brooks (Barbara "Babs" Drake), George Barbier (Mr. Drake), Sidney Blackmer ("Lucky" Braddock), Will Stanton (Truck driver), Ivan Lebedeff (Ivan Borokov), Gregory Gaye (Vladimir Borokov), Rafael Storm (Boris Borokov), Stanley Fields (Slippery Sol), Tiny Roebuck (Terrible Turk), Ben Welden (Promoter), Edward Gargan (Detective Globe), Pat McKee (Referee).

Among the uncredited cast are several old reliables with many hundreds, if not thousands, of screen appearances between them. They include Willie Best (AKA Sleep'n'Eat), Grace Hayle (forever cast as a variation of "Stout Woman"), George Chandler, Harry Hayden and Fred Kelsey. Two were on their way up to some measure of stardom: Lon Chaney Jr. and Robert Lowery.

Synopsis: The opening credits are animated and show the three Ritz Brothers riding on a single horse. (No doubt this was done to point out a comparison to the popular play and film *Three Men on a Horse*.) Society horsewoman Barbara "Babs" Drake arrives very late to a swanky party held in honor of her engagement to Denny Paine, "a noted gentleman rider." Her lateness was due to her riding in a van with her beloved horse Playboy. Denny complains that her whole life is devoted to the horse and they argue. The Ritz Brothers are in quite another sphere: They run a pony ride in a rundown city lot.

The Ritzes act on an overheard tip from professional gambler "Lucky" Braddock, preparing to put a small bet down on the horse he touts. Instead they accidentally bet on Playboy, who brings them a big payday of more than $3000. They buy a luxury car and even a ranch, hoping that Playboy will continue to bring them luck. Denny tells Barbara that it is either the horse or him. He makes a deal with her that he will take Playboy if the horse does not win again within three months. When that actually happens, she is furious, even though she has made the deal.

Playboy escapes from a van and goes to look at the Ritzes' ponies. Denny given them the horse. They discover it is a natural jumper. Barbara calls off her planned wedding and convinces the Ritzes to turn the horse into a steeplechaser. She gets 25 percent ownership from them and plans to pay Playboy's entrance fee. She asks her friend Linda for a loan, and tells her she can pursue the now-jilted Denny for herself. Linda turns on her former friend, informing Barbara's father about her plans, and he cuts off her allowance.

Now the Brothers have to raise some money for the entrance fee; they do it by Harry wrestling the Terrible Turk for $1000. Harry calls himself Running Deer, claiming he is the country's wrestling champion west of the Mississippi. His brothers, dressed as Indian braves, help him win by turning out the lights and hitting Turk over the head with a hammer. Now they have the money. Denny regrets what he did to Barbara and offers to ride Playboy. Barbara fears that he is only riding to make Playboy lose, but the now-chastened Linda assures her that he is doing it for love of Barbara.

The Ritzes overhear three Russian jockeys, the Borokov brothers, plotting to make Playboy lose. They lock the Borokovs up, steal their uniforms and ride three horses in the race. Al and Jimmy fall off their horses but Harry stays in the lead despite doing everything to let Denny win. He keeps making his horse do jumps while Denny and Playboy win. Denny and Barbara are happily back together; the Ritz Brothers shakily recuperate in an ambulance.

* * *

In the United States the film was advertised as *Damon Runyon's Straight, Place and Show*. In the U.K. it was called *They're Off*; in Sweden *Tre Glada Jockeyer* (*Three Happy Jockeys*), and in Portugal *Tres Malucos a Cavalo* (*Three Crazy People on a Horse*).

Some of the outdoor scenes were shot at the Santa Anita Racetrack and the Los Angeles Arboretum, both located in the little suburban town of Arcadia, east of Pasadena. An advertisement: "A new high in nonsensicality for the rollicking Ritzes in this mad scramble of horseplay and horse-laughs."

It can be speculated that Fox revived the idea of a racing film starring the Ritz Brothers because the Marx Brothers had made a hit in the MGM musical racing story *A Day at the Races* in 1937. That film undoubtedly had a lavish MGM budget. It also had the luxury of a six-month shooting schedule, as opposed to little more than one month for this film. The Marx Brothers film ran just under two hours, almost an hour longer than *Straight, Place and Show*.

A plethora of plot and music is crammed into the film. The Ritzes perform the "Russian Cowboys" number in front of a group of laughing children. It ends with Al holding all the cowbells and being shaken up by his brothers for a cacophonous finale.

Ethel Merman's character perhaps is not completely a "bitch," as Zanuck had directed (and as she was often portrayed in real life and on the stage), but neither did a role like this help her less than stellar film career. Billed third in the credits, she sings two songs, "Why Not String Along with Me?" and "With You on My Mind." In later life, she claimed to have despised this film. Indeed the seven features she had appeared in prior to this film had mostly been "A" productions with leading stars, including the hits *Anything Goes, Alexander's Ragtime Band* and *Happy Landing*. Even if the films were big, though, Merman never was a big star in movies. It was said that her oversized personality was more suited to reaching the back of a Broadway balcony than being contained within the confines of an intimate movie screen.

Following this, she made no films in the 15 years from 1938 to 1953, except for a small cameo together with many other stars in 1943's *Stage Door Canteen*. Eventually Merman did play one of the screen's greatest "bitch" parts: a mother-in-law from Hell. She literally hollered and screamed her way through the entirety of the very lengthy comedy *It's a Mad Mad Mad Mad World* in 1963. Had Harry Ritz been in that picture, he surely would have delivered his patented refrain of "Don't holler, please don't holler!"

Richard Arlen had become a major leading man in the late silent and early talkie days in the important films *Wings, Beggars of Life* and *The Virginian*, but by 1938 he had been reduced to some leading roles in "B" pictures and in later years supporting parts in westerns. He did enjoy a lengthy career lasting into the television era.

Reviews

"The odds are not in favor of this Ritz Brothers comedy…. The boys don't have the weight to carry it, while the stilted romantics, plus the disappointing story fail to take up the slack." *Boxoffice*, September 24, 1938.

"This is the Ritz Brothers at their merriest, and the result is a very heavy total of laughs. They employ many new antics and capers and enjoy a field day.... There is never a dull moment.... The material is refreshing." *Film Daily*, September 29, 1938.

"A noisy affair crammed with the antics of the Ritz Brothers who sing, shout, gesticulate, roll in the mud, and keep up a perpetual jamboree. Their fans will find them excruciatingly funny and others will laugh sometimes in spite of themselves." *Motion Picture Reviews*, October 1938.

"A fair comedy. The Ritz Brothers are not at their best here, owing to the weakness of the material given to them.... The serious end of the story is slightly tiresome and unbelievable." *Harrison's Reports*, October 10, 1938.

"Too much of the same pattern. My patrons are getting sick of them." Manager, Garlock Theatre, Custer, South Dakota.

"Nothing to get excited about but it was OK. Double featured it." Manager, Rialto Theatre, Paynesville, Minnesota.

"If the Ritz Brothers are funny then I have had a mistaken conception all my life of what constituted comedy." Manager, Empress Theater, Waurika, Oklahoma.

"Part of this is O.K. entertainment, but a lot of it is overly silly, and the net result rates the show below average." Manager, Westby Theatre, Westby, Wisconsin.

"That's it, I give up on the Ritz Brothers.... [The] pace is appropriately zippy..., but there's no getting around the fact that the central premise pulls up lame, and worse: The Ritz Brothers aren't all that funny ... at least not here.... It looks like [the film] was cut to ribbons ... with obvious, sometimes incomprehensible holes in its choppy construction." Modern-day commentator.

The Three Musketeers *(1939)*

The History

Residing in the rather scant Twentieth Century–Fox production files for this film is the lengthy script of the 1935 RKO version of *The Three Musketeers* starring Walter Abel and Paul Lukas. It is not entirely clear why it was decided to make this 1939 version. Like most of its predecessors, the 1935 movie was a straight dramatic retelling. One assumption could be that it seemed like a natural story for a trio, and Fox was looking for the next Ritz Brothers film. (See Appendix Three: Versions of *The Three Musketeers*.)

A May 3, 1938, treatment had Zanuck's note: "Great idea but not yet Ritz, too much dialogue without them"; "Get twice as much Ritz into it; should have comedy premise." The lead characters were described as an "Allen Jones type" for D'Artagnan and a "Kitty Carlisle type" for Lady Constance. Zanuck insisted: "It must be the Ritz Brothers' story—we must tell the story from their viewpoint."

On May 19, a revised treatment written by Sam Hellman appeared, followed three days later by the "First Draft Continuity." It was not until August 29 that a "Temporary Script" was issued, now with the working title *One for All*. It was extremely unusual for a gap like that to occur between a continuity and a not-even-final script. Things had definitely changed in those three-plus months, going from not enough Ritz Brothers to a surfeit of them.

In a conference with Zanuck two days later, the writers were told: "Too much Ritz Brothers in it…. They should come on now and then and do a sock piece of entertainment. Take out a lot of their stuff. Harry should get the best lines [i.e., of the Ritzes' material, not of the entire film]." In September 1938, both the "Revised Temporary Script" and "Final Script" were ready.

It might be speculated that Zanuck's change of heart was due to the Ritz Brothers' firm objections to their proposed next film *The Gorilla*. However, the initial *Gorilla* treatment was not issued until November 1938, two months later. The Ritzes of course may have heard about the planning of it, or it they might have made demands about other things. They had definitely begun flexing their muscles, perhaps mistakenly believing they had more power than they did.

It does seem apparent from the May 1938 discussion that *The Three Musketeers* was originally meant to be a fully Ritz Brothers starring film. Why the autocratic Zanuck went sour on them will remain speculation. It was thus at the height of the Brothers' rise that their decline, at least in the movies, was put into motion.

The Film

Directed by Allan Dwan. Executive in charge of production: Darryl F. Zanuck. Associate producer: Raymond Griffith. Based on the novel by Alexandre Dumas. Screenplay: M.M. Musselman, William A. Drake and Sam Hellman. Special material: Sid Kuller and Ray Golden. Music (uncredited): Charles Maxwell, Cyril J. Mockridge and Ernst Toch. Cinematography: J. Peverell Marley. Editor: Jack Dennis. Art directors: David S. Hall and Bernard Herzbrun. Set decorator: Thomas Little. Costume designer: Royer. Sound: Roger Heman and

George Leverett. Production began in early October,1938. Released by Twentieth Century–Fox on February 17, 1939. 73 minutes.

Cast: Don Ameche (D'Artagnan), The Ritz Brothers (The Three Lackeys), Binnie Barnes (Milady De Winter), Gloria Stuart (Queen Anne), Pauline Moore (Lady Constance), Joseph Schildkraut (King Louis XIII), John Carradine (Naveau), Lionel Atwill (De Rochefort), Miles Mander (Cardinal Richelieu), Douglass Dumbrille (Athos), John King (Aramis), Russell Hicks (Porthos), Gregory Gaye (Vitray), Lester Matthews (Duke of Buckingham), Egon Brecher (Landlord), Moroni Olsen (Bailiff), Georges Renavent (Captain Fageon), Montague Shaw (Ship Captain), Jean Perry, Fredrik Vogeding (Guards).

The uncredited cast members include Gino Corrado, who had over 400 screen credits going back to the mid–1910s, and June Storey, cowboy star Gene Autry's leading lady in several of his popular singing westerns.

Synopsis: The opening title reads: "Once upon a time (to be exact, 314 years ago), a young Gascon with a stout heart and a song on his lips set forth to Paris to enlist in the service of his king." This is the newly minted musketeer D'Artagnan, who rides toward Paris singing all the way. He is awaited at the Tavern Coq d'Or by the Three Musketeers: Athos, Porthos and Aramis. D'Artagnan has insulted them all for trivial reasons (one's hat, one's walk, one's mustache) and he demands a duel with each. In the meantime, they encounter the three lackeys who work at the inn and demand tankards of wine.

The three lackeys sing "Chicken Soup" as they prepare a huge vat of the stuff, throwing in all kinds of goodies. The Musketeers insist they join them in drinking to every King Louis starting with the first. By Louis XIII, the present king, all the Musketeers are dead drunk. The lackeys try on their uniforms, unaware of the edict that condemns to death anyone falsely wearing the uniform of a musketeer.

When Cardinal Richelieu's guards enter the inn, the lackeys and the newly arrived D'Artagnan drive them off, he with his sword and lackey Harry Ritz with a bellows filled with hot chicken soup. D'Artagnan discovers a secret relationship between the queen of France and the English Duke of Buckingham. The oily and devious cardinal, always looking to stir discord, also learns about it and plots to get the emerald brooch that the queen has given to the duke. The valiant D'Artagnan begins a romance with Lady Constance, the queen's lady-in-waiting.

The cardinal's scheming ally Milady De Winter is enlisted to get the brooch back from Buckingham in London, which she does. D'Artagnan enlists the lackeys, still in musketeer's uniforms, to accompany him to Calais to waylay Lady De Winter when she returns. Despite the lackeys' comically inept "assistance," De Winter has D'Artagnan captured and driven in a coach toward Paris.

The lackeys take the coach over, leave De Winter behind, and with D'Artagnan drive to a chateau where Lady Constance is held prisoner. Posing as minstrels, the four gain access to the chateau and entertain until Lady De Winter arrives. Once again there is swordplay. The lackeys, D'Artagnan and Constance escape in the cardinal's coach to Paris, to return the brooch to the queen.

At the king's palace, the cardinal asks to see the brooch, which the queen still does not have. Posing as a beggar, Harry distracts the palace guards while the other four enter the palace and return the brooch just in time. The three lackeys become real musketeers at last.

* * *

In later years, the film was also shown under its former title *One for All*, presumably to differentiate it from all the other versions of *The Three Musketeers*. In the U.K. it was also known as *The Singing Musketeer*. In nearly all of the other countries in which it played, the title was translated exactly. According to publicity, *The Three Musketeers* was awarded the Grand Prize that year at the Hungarian National Film Festival in Budapest.

For Don Ameche, who gets top billing, this was the third and final time he appeared with the Ritz Brothers. The opening credits read: "Don Ameche and the Ritz Brothers in A Musical Comedy Version of Alexandre Dumas' *The Three Musketeers*." This reverses the billing of *You Can't Have Everything* and Ameche deserves it, although a modern-day critic called him a golden-voiced but less than athletic leading man. In an advertisement for the film which boasted: "The Happiest Entertainment Idea Since the Movies Began to Move!" Ameche's smiling image was at least five times greater than the Ritzes, who were depicted in a small cartoon to one side.

Ameche went on to become a dependable leading man in both musicals and dramas. Because of his title role in the 1939 biopic *The Story of Alexander Graham Bell*, radio comedians joked for many years thereafter that Ameche invented the telephone. For a brief time, his surname was actually used as an alternate name for the telephone itself, as in "Answer the Ameche!"

At about the same time as the Ritz Brothers were making *Argentine Nights* in 1940, Ameche made *Down Argentine Way*. The difference was that it was a lushly produced "A" Technicolor musical, while the brothers were to be stuck in "B" films from then on. Ameche did copy the brothers in one way: In 1940, he staged a walkout from Fox to protest a loan-out. The studio claimed he had cost them $170,000 but his star was on the rise so the protest seems to have worked. The Ritzes' threatened walk-out did not.

A modern-day critic opined that *The Three Musketeers* had a "four-song score and a one-joke script." That is actually meant to be a compliment for director Allan Dwan, who, he said, had created "a terrific entertainment." In addition to the "Chicken Soup" number, the tunes are "Viola," "Song of the Musketeers" and the love ballad "My Lady." As part of their deception when posing as minstrels, the Ritzes perform one of their synchronized dance numbers with cymbals attached to various parts of their bodies.

The Ritzes are truly comic relief in this film, not the stars, and they are absent from significant chunks of it even though still billed above the title. This is considered by many to be their best film, aided by notable production values and a solid supporting cast. It is a step up for them since they became the stars of their own films with *Life Begins in College*. It could be described as a minor "A" effort, but not really "their" film.

As has often been pointed out, the film does somewhat adhere to that part of Dumas' novel *The Three Musketeers* relating to the theft of the emerald brooch. Its theatrics provide some light thrills and suspense so it is watchable even without the Ritz Brothers' antics.

Not all critics of the time agreed that it had much relation to the original novel. One said, "Many admirers … will groan aloud at the liberties Darryl Zanuck has taken with their favorite adventure tale … as the basis for a broad and often burlesqued musical comedy. Mr. Zanuck would be howled out of Hollywood by the thousands who have carried that sword [i.e., that of D'Artagnan] in imagination.… It plunges into the intense antics which are the Ritz Brothers' stock in comedy.… Once the Three Musketeers strode gallantly through danger; now they romp wildly through slapstick comedy."

Reviews

"The idea of having the three Ritz Brothers play this has turned out quite as badly as one might have anticipated." *New York Herald Tribune*, February 18, 1939.

"That isn't a buzzing in your ears you've been hearing; it's Dumas *fils* spinning in his grave…. We're not outraged by it, only terribly, terribly hurt that the burlesque was not carried far enough, far enough at least to escape the clutches of the Ritzes themselves…. Maybe they are funny but they leave me as cold as a marinated herring and twice as limp. They ogle, posture, milk a gag until it curdles, try to steal scenes that aren't worth taking, and generally behave as though they were being paid to act at so much the square mug. It must be worth a fellow actor's life to stand on the set when it's their cue." *New York Times*, February 18, 1939.

"Okay as hokum. [It] combines the personable qualities of Don Ameche with the inanities and laugh guarantees of the Ritz

Brothers and comes up with a picture that will give general satisfaction.... The whole measures up as satisfactory while leaving a feeling of irritation as one wonders why it shouldn't have been better." *Box Office Digest*, February 18, 1939.

"Merry travesty of the classic.... [The] Ritz Brothers clown comedy rather less crude than usual." *The Educational Screen*, March 1939.

"Those who like the Ritz Brothers brand of humor will rock in their seats. Armchair adventurers who like their gallantry straight should think twice before besieging the box office." *Movies ... and the People Who Make Them*, 1939.

"A nutty comedy that is a flop in any language. Leave this in the can and play the cheapest western you can find, for it will please more." Manager, Tivoli Theatre, Knoxville, Tennessee.

"Patrons complained about casting the Ritz Brothers with Don Ameche, declaring they liked him but just couldn't stand the silly Ritz Brothers. This hurt our business, even on bargain night. The picture is pretty good and the Ritz Brothers are not in long enough to hurt, but these picture patrons are plenty picture-wise." Manager, Princess Theatre, Lincoln, Kansas.

"I only saw about a third of this one, but that is a third more than most people saw." Manager, Owl Theatre, Lebanon, Kansas.

"One reel of this is enough ... a weak silly plot and the Ritz Brothers kept them away." Manager, Temple and Vernon Theatre, Viroqua, Wisconsin.

"Shades of Dumas; what they did to his immortal story is plenty. A burlesque on it and it classes as screwball at its very screwiest." Manager, Columbia Theatre, Columbus City, Indiana.

"We consider the Ritz Brothers no adornment to the show. Their slapstick stuff seemed out of place or overdone. Without that, it would be one of the best costume shows." Manager, Cornish Theatre, Cornish, Maine.

"Would have been a pretty good Ritz Brothers vehicle if the ending had any punch. As it is, it turns out to be sort of a fizzle." Manager, Bethel Theatre, Bethel, Vermont.

"The Ritz Brothers are all but forgotten but they were consummate clowns.... This marks their finest hour on screen.... The songs are forgettable but the comic set pieces hold up well, anticipating Bob Hope.... Royally entertaining, this treasure will delight Dumas fans and old school comedy buffs eager to be puttin' on the Ritzes." Modern-day commentator.

> "The Ritz Brothers are an acquired taste—like arsenic! Try as I might, every film I have seen these guys in, I have thoroughly despised them." Modern-day commentator.

> "It makes one wonder why the Ritz Brothers are all but forgotten by the general public." Modern-day commentator.

Special Award for Brevity

> "No draw; no money; no like." Manager, Rialto Theatre, Paynesville, Minnesota.

The Gorilla (1939)

The History

The idea of apes as dangerous killers of human beings, as veritable fiends, stretches at least as far back as Edgar Allan Poe's short story "The Murders in the Rue Morgue." It reached its apogee with the 1933 classic *King Kong*. Beginning in the silent era, many films have picked up on this theme; some of them were shoddy horror flicks. Among the latter are *Gorilla at Large* (its "horrors" were in 3-D) and *The Ape Man*. More recent films like *Ape* and *Congo* have carried the baton.

The idea of such menaces has expanded to include killer orangutans, chimps, monkeys (e.g., *Monkey Shines* and *Link*) and even malevolent baboons in *In the Shadow of Kilimanjaro*. There is even a subgenre of films about apes being turned into men and vice versa (e.g., *Island of Lost Souls*, *Bela Lugosi Meets a Brooklyn Gorilla*). The *Planet of the Apes* canon put its own stamp on this fantasy. The genre may have reached its low point with the cheapie 1969 Mexican film *Night of the Bloody Apes*.

The Ritz Brothers reached their own low point 30 years earlier with *The Gorilla*. The brilliant pioneering detective Auguste Dupin of "The Murders in the Rue Morgue" is replaced by three bumbling zanies in a badly done film which immediately followed their biggest hit to date.

The comedy-mystery-thriller was a popular stage genre going back to the days of broad-gesture Victorian melodrama. The genre reached its zenith on Broadway with the phenomenally successful 1920 production *The Bat*, about a murderous thief and a frightened household. This production ran two years and almost 900 performances. It starred "the four E's," Effie Ellsler and Edward Ellis, both later respected character actors in the movies.

The *Bat*'s popularity undoubtedly led to the production of more comedy-horror films in the silent cinema. Among the better-known were *The Cat and the Canary* (1927), *The Last Warning* (1928), *The Monster* (1925) with Lon Chaney, and the long-sought Chaney film *London After Midnight* (1927). D.W. Griffith was among the first to join the parade with his film *One Exciting Night* (1922) starring Henry Hull. That year also saw *The Ghost Breaker* with Wallace Reid. Even Harold Lloyd parodied the genre in his *Haunted Spooks* and *Dr. Jack*.

On the Broadway stage, there was the hapless *The Gorilla* (subtitled on the play's typescript: "A Chilling, Thrilling, Killing Mystery"). Doubtless hoping to emulate *The Bat*'s success, it opened and closed rapidly in May 1925 after only 15 performances. Up to that time, the playwright Ralph Spence (1890–1949) had only written for such glamorous musical revues as *The Ziegfeld Follies* and *Earl Carroll's Vanities*.

The publicity for the very short-lived production promised: "Now out-bats *The Bat*—Outcats *The Cat and the Canary*—Outwarns *The Last Warning*. You'll laugh, roar, howl and scream." The use of made-up words might be novel, but the only roaring, screaming and howling probably came from playgoers demanding their money back!

This play was not the last Broadway show to try to match *The Bat*'s popularity. The melodrama *Sh, the Octopus* (with another mysterious villain and frightened people, this time in a lighthouse) opened and closed rapidly in 1928. It too was made into a movie, with more dramatic title punctuation, 1937's *Sh! The Octopus* with Allen Jenkins and Frank McHugh.

Given this background, Hollywood in its wisdom decided to make a silent film version of *The Gorilla*. This they did in 1927 with respected director Alfred Santell, popular comic actor Charles Murray as detective Garrity, and Fred Kelsey (later to be typecast as policemen and detectives) as Mulligan. As in the play, there were only two detectives investigating the criminal known as the Gorilla. In retrospect, the most interesting thing about this version is one of the early appearances of durable leading man Walter Pidgeon.

Because that version sank with little trace, Hollywood decided to remake it in the early talkie days. The 1930 version, directed by the very competent Bryan Foy (one of the famous Seven Little Foys), starred comics Joe Frisco and Harry Gribbon. Pidgeon reprised his 1927 role. (He went on to sing in screen operettas before finding his permanent niche as a solid—and stolid—leading man.)

This adaptation also failed to light up the box office, but Hollywood decided to try it yet *again*, perhaps thinking the third time was a charm. Enter the Ritz Brothers. On November 16, 1938, a "Screen Treatment" by Jack Yellen and Rian James "from an original play by Ralph Spence" appeared. That phrase alone should have given someone pause but it apparently did not.

Again, Zanuck opined that it should have "the flavor of legitimacy." By this he presumably meant disguising the fact that the story was so incredible that no one could take it seriously. He also liked the idea of "the boys [i.e., the Ritzes] being clunked over the head with a metal vase." He believed that the comedy should come from their reactions of fright, making it clear that they are the "shyster type of detective." The fact that such men are involved in preventing a murder would lead to "a lot of natural comedy."

November 24 brought an "Incomplete First Draft Continuity" by Rian James. Zanuck's comments included: "Could we have more of a plot?" (a seemingly reasonable *demand*; coming from Zanuck it really was not a question); "Put girl in room alone with butler for menace." The butler was to be played by Bela Lugosi, and menace is certainly what Lugosi was cast for. (Reginald Owen and Peter Lorre also had been considered for the part.) Zanuck also noted: "More Mulligan and Garrity." This was an order to enlarge the roles of Al and Jimmy Ritz. Harry was set to play Harrigan.

On December 10, 1938, James came in with a "First Draft Continuity—First Draft Intact." Not even a month had passed since the 18-page "Screen Treatment." Zanuck was apparently interested in getting this project up and running quickly after the success of *The Three Musketeers*. On Christmas Eve, another script, labeled "Second Script, Incomplete," was ready. This time co-writer Sid Silvers was added; he was to stay with the project until production. A "Temporary Script" came on January 9, 1939. More cast members were suggested including perennial villains George Zucco and Lionel Atwill.

Zanuck felt the story should be told "honestly, *with the exception of the comedy* [italics mine]." Director Dwan was not too happy with the script. Zanuck now backtracked on his instruction to give Al and Jimmy Ritz more emphasis. He instructed that their lines be shortened to give them more comedy business instead of dialogue. He wanted the entire movie considerably shortened. This was perhaps an insight into the lowered value he now placed on the production—and the Ritzes. The "Final Script" appeared on January 17, 1939, and a five-week shoot was authorized.

The proposed budget for the Makeup Department included more than $3000 for the costuming of the gorilla, played by Art Miles. Makeup and hairdressing expenses for the whole rest of the cast came to less than half that. Director Dwan's suggested changes were approved by Zanuck. A too-long absence of the Patsy Kelly character was addressed. It was decided that a "hair-standing on end" gag for Harry Ritz could only be used once. The name of the detective agency was changed to "Acme" instead of "Keyhole." On January 25, 1939, there was a "Revised Final Script" and production began.

The Film

Directed by Allan Dwan. Associate producer: Harry Joe Brown. Screenplay: Rian James and Sid Silvers. Based on the play by Ralph Spence. Music (uncredited): David Buttolph, Alfred Newman and David Raksin. Cinematography: Edward Cronjager. Editor: Allen McNeil. Art directors: Lewis Creber and Richard Day. Set decorator: Thomas Little. Costume designer: Gwen Wakeling. Makeup (uncredited): Perc Westmore. Executive in charge of production: Darryl F. Zanuck. Production began in early February 1939. Released by Fox on May 26, 1939. 66 minutes.

Cast: Jimmy Ritz (Garrity), Harry Ritz (Harrigan), Al Ritz (Mulligan), Anita Louise (Norma Denby), Patsy Kelly (Kitty), Lionel Atwill (Walter Stevens), Bela Lugosi (Peters), Joseph Calleia (The Stranger), Edward Norris (Jack Marsden), Wally Vernon (Seaman), Paul Harvey (A.P. Conway), Art Miles (The Gorilla).

Synopsis: In Walter Stevens' mansion on the proverbial dark and stormy night, the maid Kitty is reading *Romeo and Juliet* when a hairy hand reaches in through the window and hands her a note. She is terrified. The note is from a master criminal, the Gorilla, who has already killed several people, and it is a death warning to Stevens. Instead of calling the police, Stevens hires bumbling private detectives Harrigan, Garrity and Mulligan of the Acme Agency to safeguard him. They arrive in an open car in the pouring rain with one umbrella to cover them.

Stevens' niece Norma arrives with her fiancée Jack. The stolid butler Peters skulks around, looking appropriately menacing. He tells the young couple that they cannot leave because their car will not start; Norma says he gives her the creeps. Jack keeps reassuring her that he does not believe anything bad will happen.

The incompetent Harrigan keeps getting into trouble: running into doors, getting locked outside in the downpour, tripping on stairs, and having an ironing board fall on his head. The detectives verbally spar with the maid, who delivers zinger after zinger at their expense while they sputter in return. She wants nothing more than to leave the house, but Stevens prevails upon her to stay.

A mysterious face is seen at the window. After the lights flicker out, a note wrapped around a rock is thrown through the window with the ominous words "At midnight." A real gorilla is unleashed by an unknown person. Near midnight, the radio turns on and warns Stevens that he only has two minutes to live. At the stroke of 12, the lights go out and he disappears. A gorilla's arm reaches out of a closet. A few moments later, the door opens and an unconscious seaman falls out. The gorilla is not there.

Hapless detectives Mulligan and Harrigan (Jimmy and Harry Ritz) look apprehensive as they face menacing butler Bela Lugosi in *The Gorilla*, 1939.

The detectives reenact the disappearance and one by one they disappear as well. A smirking stranger enters through the French doors. He rescues Harrigan from a closet, but when questioned he handcuffs the hapless detective and exits through a secret panel. Garrity and Mulligan are found tied up. Another man arrives at the house, telling everyone that Stevens owes him $250,000 and he wants to collect. He claims Stevens has been cheating his clients.

As they search the cellar, the detectives encounter the real gorilla, but Harrigan thinks it is actually the arch-criminal in a gorilla suit. While the animal runs amok, Norma is menaced by the real criminal. Harrigan and Kitty are chased around by the gorilla, while the mysterious stranger re-emerges from one secret panel and exits through another. He is obviously searching for something.

The seaman says that he is the gorilla's trainer. He was told to bring the beast to the house that night but does not know who hired him. He is searching for his gorilla, which he says is dangerous. The radio comes on again to announce that Walter Stevens is dead and his body is in the garage. While the others race to the garage, Harrigan guards Norma, only to be knocked out. Kitty is found locked in the gorilla's cage. The animal grabs Norma and dangles her from the roof. At the seaman's command, it drops her safely. The mysterious stranger is seen trying to open the safe; he is chased through a secret panel by the animal.

The seaman finds his gorilla and takes him away. The stranger emerges and tells the others that he is a Securities and Exchange Commission investigator and has been investigating Stevens. They find the supposedly dead Stevens tied up; the investigator claims that Stevens is actually the Gorilla. He accuses Stevens of wanting to murder his niece to get sole possession of any inheritance and then blame her death on the arch-criminal.

As the stranger prepares to leave the house, Harrigan shakes his hand, revealing a hairy arm underneath. The stranger pulls a gun and admits he is the Gorilla. He has been searching for the $250,000 Stevens had supposedly embezzled. The butler comes up behind him and makes him drop the gun. All finally ends happily.

* * *

In Spanish-speaking countries, the film was called *El Gorila*; in Denmark, *Gorillaen*; in France it was *Le Gorille*, and in Brazil *Segure Este Gorila*. The Swedish title took a different tack: *Tre Tokiga Detekiver* (*Three Demented Detectives*). The film opened at the Roxy Theatre in New York and was not sent abroad until September 1939. Because the war began on the first day of that month, it was distributed to countries not yet embroiled in the conflict.

The blame for this misfire can be spread around, starting with Darryl Zanuck. Allan Dwan, a celebrated director in the silent days, seems to have settled for directing potboilers. The romantic leads deliver their lines seemingly by rote as if they did not believe a word of what they were saying. Bela Lugosi underacts to the point of somnolence.

In contrast, the ever-frenetic Patsy Kelly reprises her well-worn persona as a screamer, and the mugging Ritzes run around perpetually frightened. Harry Ritz keeps ordering "Mark that down, Garrity" and "Make a note of that, Garrity" as if that is somehow funny and bears constant repetition.

The Brothers' usual energetic performances are reduced to such overused shtick as their hair standing on end from terror. This is the kind of stereotyping that the movies ordinarily used to assign to Black performers like Willie Best and Mantan Moreland. If the Ritzes had cried out "Feets, get moving," it would have completed the dismal effect. The plot has continuity problems which often lead to confusion, certainly the fault of the screenwriters, the editing and possibly the original play.

By 1939, the conventions of the mysterious masked killer, a gloomy mansion, secret panels and shrieking servants were already overdone. The revelation that the self-proclaimed investigator is actually the killer is a direct steal from

The Bat, and also happens to be the plot device of Agatha Christie's eternally playing *The Mousetrap*.

It is apparent from Zanuck's comments during pre-production that his ideas about comedy remained on a rather juvenile level. He may have felt that because of the Ritz Brothers' comic personas, such material was their forte. They obviously disagreed about that, probably feeling that he did not understand their appeal. A walkout seemed to them to be their best option.

They also had to contend with rowdy Patsy Kelly, who competed for the title of the most raucous female second banana of the 1930s and '40s with such other broad comediennes as Joan Davis and Martha Raye. She was a scene-stealer but not in the subtle way of some other actresses; she simply barged into a scene and yelled her way through it. This was bound to detract from the Ritzes, especially in a film that ran only a bit more than an hour. It has to be wondered whether her prominence was a deliberate effort on Fox's part to deliver a message to the brothers. Her wisecracking brought forth an occasional laugh, while they mostly reacted to events and had little to add to a lifeless story. The *New York Times* review got it right when it stated that this comedy-thriller was neither funny nor thrilling.

Reviews

"Tailored to the wants and needs of the Ritz Brothers, the new resuscitation of *The Gorilla* pretty much 'goes to town' as entertainment. Outside of those who may hold an innate aversion to the antics of the comics, it should be a first rate hit, and even those who hold such antipathy should make due allowances in this case. The Ritzes contribute liberally to the fun.... They're right in their element for lunatic goings-on." *Los Angeles Times*, May 18, 1939.

"This version of the old play will afford no solace to champions of screen uplift. It is unblushingly slapstick, packed with Ritz monkeyshines.... In its class it is a fairly acceptable job.... The Ritzes are pitching like gibbering demons for the major portion of the film." *Hollywood Reporter*, May 18, 1939.

"Thoroughly dotted with laugh moments and equipped with an artistically strong supporting cast, offering should reach beyond bounds of stellar trio's fixed following and satisfy general audiences, especially juves [i.e., juveniles].... Work of Ritzes will win them added boosters." *Variety*, May 18, 1939.

The portions of the *Hollywood Reporter* and *Variety* reviews dedicated to Patsy Kelly may give some clue as to one of the reasons that the Ritz Brothers were unhappy with this film: "Patsy Kelly as the hysterical housemaid doing her best—and very well—to match the Ritz antics." "Patsy Kelly, whose role carries her through major portions of footage … giving her prominence equal to that held by the top-liners."

> "[It] has not, we regretfully report, enhanced the standing of the comic muse, nor has it contributed much to the enjoyment of patrons…. Even the [Ritzes] antic buffoonery is not equal to the task. The real comedian of the show is the gorilla…. It's all supposed to be either very funny or shockingly thrilling…. We couldn't see it either way." *New York Times*, May 28, 1939.

> "Just when I had made a resolution never to run another Ritz Brothers picture they come along with this one…. Plenty of comedy and suspense. It's so good I'd like to see it again and Patsy Kelly deserves a few words of praise." Manager, Star Theatre, Lupton, Colorado.

> "You say you've never heard of the Ritz Brothers? You should count yourself among the fortunate ones. [A]nother of those 30s–40s slapstick comedy teams which I detest so much…. Nor are the Ritz Brothers the sole source of painfully unfunny comedy in this film [referring to Patsy Kelly]…. Even ten minutes of the Ritz Brothers is a long, grueling slog. At full feature length this movie would be simply unendurable." Modern-day commentator.

Pack Up Your Troubles (*1939*)

The History

A tepid title for what was to be a tepid movie, *Pack Up Your Troubles* had already been used for a 1932 Laurel and Hardy World War I comedy-drama. Working titles for this 1939 film included *Tin Hats* and *Roughnecks*. The latter was the title announced in the Twentieth Century–Fox *Studio Special* issue of August 1938. It might be assumed that neither of the working titles was used because they would have put the focus on the Ritz Brothers rather than the Jane Withers character. Hers was going to be the name above the title.

On May 1, 1939, when it was still to be titled *Roughnecks*, an outline by Lou Breslow and Owen Francis was presented, with the Ritz Brothers' characters called the Schultz Brothers. This was followed ten days later by an 87-page "First Draft Continuity" that suggested the Brothers' comedy would be presented in thick German accents. June 1 saw a "Revised First Draft Continuity" of 131 pages. Only one week later, a "Final Script" was ready; in it, the Ritz characters show business act was the Silly Schultzes.

Advertisements all emphasized the photos of Jane Withers and the typography of her name was larger than that of the Ritz Brothers, who were featured below the title. Many ads used the same tagline: "Jane's the bravest little ma'amselle in all France." If the Ritzes were mentioned, it was with such taglines as: "Three new friends" and "With the Ritzes helping her to keep things merry." These were among the unsubtle indications that emphasized their inferior status in the film.

One publicity idea for exhibitors was to mention that the Ritz Brothers "were added to her latest picture." It was suggested that Withers' authorized merchandise be displayed in prominent places, including the dolls in her image, leather fabrics, children's hats, books, paper dolls, writing paper, raincoats and children's swim suits. This may have been about the last year in which such Withers merchandise could be used. Not only was she a teenager now but she was becoming quite tall and proto-womanly, as was noted by some reviewers.

The Film

Directed by H. Bruce Humberstone and Otto Brewer. Produced by Sol Wurtzel. Original screenplay: Lou Breslow and Owen Francis. Music (uncredited): Samuel Kaylin. Cinematography: Lucien Andriot. Editor: Nick De Maggio. Art directors: Richard Day and Albert Hogsett. Set decorator: Thomas Little. Costume designer: Helen A. Myron. Sound: William H. Anderson and Bernard Fredericks. Released by Twentieth Century–Fox on October 20, 1939. Approx. 75 minutes.

Cast: Jane Withers (Colette), The Ritz Brothers (Themselves AKA The Silly Schultzes), Lynn Bari (Yvonne), Joseph Schildkraut (Hugo), Stanley Fields (Sgt. "Angel Face" Walker), Fritz Leiber (Pierre), Lionel Royce (General), Georges Renavent (Colonel Giraud), Adrienne D'Ambricourt (Mme. Marchand), Leon Ames (Adjutant), William [Wilhelm] von Brincken (Mueller), Edward Gargan (Sentry), Robert Emmett Keane (Kane), Henry Victor (Colonel).

Among the uncredited cast members were such old reliables as Irving Bacon, Billy Bevan, William Benedict, Clyde Cook, Harold Goodwin (a co-star with Sydney Chaplin in the hit World War I silent comedy *The Better 'Ole*) and Mary Foy, one of the two girls in the famous Seven Little Foys family.

Synopsis: In 1917, the Ritz Brothers are washed-up in vaudeville and locked out of their rooming house. Dubbing themselves the Silly Schultzes, their act consists of comedy and songs done in thick German accents. Soon they are put in uniforms and are actually on their way to fight real Germans. They expect to join the "cushy" cavalry but when they arrive in France, their charges turn out to be a company of stubborn mules. The brothers already have experience with that breed, having adopted a baby mule named Margie.

In a small French village, they befriend young Colette, who gives them some milk for Margie. Believing that her father is dead, Colette has been singing at Madame Marchand's inn. There she meets her father's old friend Pierre, who is actually a French intelligence officer. Her friend Yvonne also entertains there; she is actually a spy for the Germans.

Yvonne tries to keep Pierre occupied while her fellow spies search his room, but he returns and is fatally injured in a fight. Just before he dies, he tells Colette that her father is alive and spying on the Germans. Colette wants to pass this intelligence on to Colonel Giraud and has the Ritzes smuggle her past a sentry. But Giraud is at the front and unreachable.

Determined to get to the front, Colette hides in a troop transport that is heading there. The Ritz Brothers' nemesis Sergeant Walker, whom they call "Angel Face," has been giving them a hard time. When he falls for Yvonne, not realizing she is a spy, the brothers write to General Pershing complaining about the sergeant's inappropriate behavior. They also tell the general that he, Pershing, is not running the Army very well, and add, "If you want to know more, give us a buzz."

To entertain their fellow troopers, the Ritzes revive their old German act; they are actually mistaken for the enemy by French soldiers while wearing their German uniforms. Pursued, they disguise themselves in a horse costume and escape by hot air balloon. Over No Man's Land, the balloon's basket is shot away little by little while they hold on for dear life. The Germans believe that the Ritzes, now posing as real Germans, are part of a battalion that has been missing in action.

The brothers unexpectedly meet Collette and her father in the headquarters of the German High Command. Yvonne has also come there to report her findings to the Germans and she recognizes Colette. The German general grows suspicious of Colette's father and gives him false information to set a trap. Her father falls into it by passing the phony information along to Colette. The general orders him to be executed but he is rescued by the Ritzes. They not only help Colette and her father to escape, but they bring the German general back to the French lines with them.

Due to a misunderstanding, the Ritz Brothers are sent to a prisoner of war camp as German soldiers. Fortunately, the intelligence that Colette's father has obtained is given to the French. The brothers are finally rescued by Collette and her father and recognized as heroes. To top off their triumph, they discover that the letter they wrote to General Pershing about Sergeant "Angel Face" has resulted in his demotion.

* * *

The precocious Jane Withers not only sings "Who'll Buy My Flowers," but also imitates George M. Cohan singing "I'm a Yankee Doodle Dandy" and Eva Tanguay doing her defiant signature song "I Don't Care." The fact that her character Colette seems to be a lot more American than French is explained by her having had an American mother. Withers' genuine Southwestern twang was put to more convincing use in her later and best adult role in *Giant* (1956).

She had been in films since the early 1930s and remained active through most of the 1940s. Although *Giant* was the acme of her later cinema career, she became really famous (and no doubt wealthy) via her long-running television commercials playing the hearty Josephine the Plumber for Comet Cleanser. For movie buffs, she is no doubt best remembered for being the nasty spoiled little girl who was mean to sweet Shirley Temple in *Bright Eyes*.

The only major number the Ritzes get to do opens the film as a sample of the German act they have been performing in vaudeville. This paring-down of their song-and-dance numbers to almost nothing was no doubt Zanuck's idea. When you were on your way out, he helped by figuratively kicking you down the studio steps.

This movie was called *We're in the Army Now* in the U.K., which may be the reason the British felt free to title their own 1940 film *Pack Up Your Troubles*. To add to any slight confusion, a 1937 British film had been titled *You're in the Army Now*, as was a 1941 American film. The Ritz-Withers film was shown in neutral Portugal in 1940 but it was not released in most European countries until after Europe's liberation in 1945.

As the *New York Times* review indicates, this movie was not only a comedown for Al, Jimmy and Harry Ritz, but no doubt for distinguished actors Joseph Schildkraut and Fritz Leiber. Schildkraut, who was the scion of a distinguished theatrical family including his father Rudolph, was a Broadway star and had been in numerous silent and sound films. His last great role came as Otto Frank, father of Anne, on the stage and in the film version of *The Diary of Anne Frank*. He also appeared with the Ritzes in *The Three Musketeers*.

Leiber was a Shakespearean actor who made scores of films, including the legendary lost 1917 Theda Bara film *Cleopatra*, from the 1910s to the time of his death in 1949. Hulking German-born character actors Wilhelm (here called William) von Brincken and Henry Victor were to have busy careers playing nasty or comic Nazis in a string of World War II films. They both passed away at the end of the War.

The film was premiered at the Palace Theatre in New York so perhaps the Ritz Brothers and Jane Withers' names still had some cachet. Or more likely it was just that Twentieth Century–Fox had that much clout.

Reviews

"Although the prospect of Jane Withers, the First World War and the Ritz Brothers all in a single picture seems calculated to shake the nerves of a sensitive cinemagoer, the combination at least serves to remind us that Miss Withers is growing even if the art of the Ritzes is not. In favor of [the film] is that it packs off the boys in something other than a [starring] vehicle, for a welcome change. Though technically in reduced circumstances so far as billing and plot position are concerned, there are moments when they seem almost funny again." *New York Times*, October 27, 1939.

"The former screen tomboy has grown up to be a very nice and personable young lady. Jane Withers and the Ritz Brothers (who in the opinion of many have yet to grow up) are the alternating centers of attraction of this picture.... The Ritz Brothers play themselves with customary ebullience. The gags they contribute from being nursemaids to a parcel of donkeys are peppy.... Somehow the sight of little Miss Withers dodging enemy shellfire doesn't seem to belong to the same world inhabited by the carefree three." *The Movies ... and the People Who Make Them: A Continuing Survey...*, 1939.

"Jane Withers has what it takes. She deserves better backing up than the Ritz Brothers can give her." Manager, AM Theatre, Blaine, Washington.

"Just a fair program show that failed to draw. Jane not so popular and the Ritz Brothers too darn silly." Manager, Bocanta Theatre, Scottsboro, Alabama.

"Don't let the adverse critics fool you.... The best I have had from the Ritz Brothers. Had [a] good draw." Manager, Wells Theatre, Kingsland, Georgia.

"The Ritz Brothers are terrible and should never be cast in another picture. As for Jane, if they keep giving her this kind of material she'll be a has-been in no time. Barely made expenses on this one, and it didn't seem to please the few who did venture in." Manager, Palace Theatre, Exira, Iowa.

"[The film] seems less like a Twentieth Century–Fox film than one from Universal ... but it is better than its reputation. By the way, demeaning the Ritz Brothers is a demonstration of poor judgment." Modern-day commentator.

"[This] is one of their worst films.... The Ritzes are basically supporting players here.... The comedic material for the Ritzes is close to non-existent." Modern-day commentator.

Argentine Nights (1940)

The History

See the section on Universal in the chapter "An Overview" for the events leading up to this film's production.

Argentine Nights was the picture that the Ritz Brothers agreed to do—or were contractually forced to do—in lieu of the aborted effort to cast them in *The Boys from Syracuse*. Their late casting delayed the start of this film for a month or so. Its production was in line with the resuscitation of the Good Neighbor Policy following the outbreak of World War II in Europe.

Because of their recording success and well-attended live appearances, the Andrews Sisters were certain to come to the attention of Hollywood, always on the lookout for new faces. The supposed immediate impetus to offer them a contract was the result of an agreement between Jack Kapp, head of Decca Records, and Nate Blumberg, president of Universal.

Universal was already known for its cheaply made "B" films which generally had very short running times. The studio's motto at that time could be summed up in the phrase "Don't get it right, just get it writ" or, as one of the Andrews Sisters reportedly observed, "They don't make 'em good, they make 'em by Tuesday." The studio was soon to launch a series of musicals which, after America's entry into the war, were balm for home front audiences. *Argentine Nights* was among the first, although at 72 minutes it was longer than many of its successors.

The Ritz Brothers had already sunk to the "B" film level at Fox, but were to continue to be top-billed at Universal. Nineteen forty was also the year that Bud Abbott and Lou Costello made their first film, Universal's *One Night in the Tropics*. With its silly plot about love insurance, it was no great hit, and Abbott and Costello were only supporting players. In their next film, the military comedy *Buck Privates*, they were starred and made a roaring success. The fate of the Ritz Brothers as Universal's leading comedy team was sealed. From then on, their feature film career would be in decline.

Enter the Andrews Sisters. A photograph shows them in big hats looking very happy at the signing ceremony for the film with the Ritzes, Harry mugging as usual. A magazine article memorializing this event was titled "A Trio of Cinderellas." It began: "For eight long years the Andrews Sisters sang for their suppers, but seldom made enough for breakfast and dinner too." The implication: All that would change with the launch of their cinema career.

The article continued: "They are amazed that Hollywood, reputedly so hardboiled, is so nice." Among the *other* polite fibs in the article were the ages of the Sisters. LaVerne chopped a cool five years off her age, claiming to be 24 (she was about 29 by then). To make that birth date plausible, Maxene and Patty each trimmed their ages by a more modest two years. The Ritz Brothers too were sometimes less than punctilious about their own ages (*see You Can't Have Everything*).

Another magazine improbably reported: "New songs, familiar harmony, and their own particular brand of clowning caused the studio to expand the parts of the Andrews Sisters after their first day on the set." That was most unlikely, but if true could have signaled the studio's hedging their bets about the Ritz Brothers.

The Film

Directed by Albert Rogell. Associate producer: Ken Goldsmith. Original story: J. Robert Bren and Gladys Atwater. Screenplay: Arthur T. Horman, Ray Golden, Sid Kuller and Edmund Joseph. Contributors to the dialogue and screenplay (uncredited): Paul Gerard Smith and Olive Cooper. Music: Saul Chaplin and (uncredited) Hal Borne, Hugh Prince, Don Raye, Vic Schoen and Frank Skinner. Lyrics: Sammy Cahn. Cinematography: Elwood Bredell. Editor: Frank Gross. Art director: Jack Otterson. Set decorator: Russell A. Gausman. Costume designer: Vera West. Sound: Bernard B. Brown. Musical director: Charles Previn. Dates of production: June 20 to July 17, 1940. Released by Universal on September 6, 1940. 72 minutes.

Cast: The Ritz Brothers, The Andrews Sisters (Themselves), Constance Moore (Bonnie Brooks), George Reeves (Eduardo Estaban), Peggy Moran (Peggy), Anne Nagel (Linda), Kathryn Adams (Carol), Ferike Boros (Mama Viejos), Paul Porcasi (Papa Viejos).

Among the uncredited cast were such familiar veterans as Heinie Conklin (one of the silent era's Keystone Cops), Vinton Hayworth, Russell Hopton, Fred Malatesta, Matt McHugh (another silent film comic), Frank Puglia, Dewey Robinson and Dave Willock. Relative newcomer Craig Stevens would later become a "B" film leading man and TV star.

Synopsis: The Ritz Brothers are the directors of Colossal Ideas, Inc., but because their ideas are *too* colossal and impractical they are on the brink of bankruptcy. An entire hall is filled with their creditors hoping the brothers won't declare bankruptcy. The Ritzes hire Bonnie Brooks, leader of an all-girl band,

and the Andrews Sisters to perform for their creditors in hopes of getting further investments.

This idea is a failure and the Ritzes are forced to flee to avoid jail. They stow away with the band on a ship bound for Buenos Aires where they have a booking at a resort. When they are discovered, they are made to swab the decks. The Andrews Sisters hijack the boat's orchestra and Bonnie's band plays instead. Bonnie becomes infatuated with the dashing Eduardo Estaban, but as soon as the ship docks, he is arrested.

It is actually a stunt to welcome him home as the captain of a victorious polo team, but Bonnie thinks he is a real criminal. Dressed as a gaucho, Eduardo leads a victory parade. In the meantime, the Ritzes, the Andrews Sisters and the band discover the resort is really a small rural hacienda. The brothers decide to turn it into a dude ranch. The owner, Papa Viejos, tells them a story about a bandit named El Tigre, who Bonnie thinks must be Eduardo.

When she sees Eduardo and his friends dressed as gauchos, she thinks there must be a reward, and she and the girls in the band capture them. The confusion eventually gets cleared up. The polo team has a big party at the hacienda;

Al, Harry and Jimmy have fled to Argentina to avoid their creditors but may have gone from the frying pan into the fire, in *Argentine Nights* (1940), their first film for Universal.

Eduardo reveals he is not only *not* an outlaw but a wealthy man. Bonnie, the Ritzes, the Andrews Sisters and the owners of the renovated hacienda happily look forward to the future.

* * *

With the war now raging in Europe, the overseas market for this film was limited, but it did make it to neutral Sweden and Portugal. In the countries in which it played, the titles were almost all literal translations of the English title, but in France, which got it several years after the end of the war, it was called *L'Auberge des Loufoques*. The film was re-released in the U.S. in 1948. It was claimed that the president of Argentina had been so upset by the way his country was portrayed that he had the film banned. This smacks of Universal publicity insofar as it created a bit of a buzz around the film and helped the box office.

Argentine Nights premiered at the Fordham Theater in the Bronx, New York. The advertisements ranged from mild to over-the-top, but that was not unusual for that time when audiences were presumably thought to be less sophisticated. Most of the ads emphasized the Latin American connection, as in: "Swing and Sway the South American Way, with Gangsters and Gauchos, Songsters and Senoritas" and "Gay Gauchos! Sultry Senoritas!"

For some reason, there were ads that connected a film that had the very word "Argentine" in its title to Brazil: "Rolling Down to Rio with Romance and Laughter"; "Swing and Sway with Brazilian Nuts and Sultry Senoritas"; "Roll Down to Rio.... Nights of Romance and Daze of Daffiness." This could have been a result of the popularity of the tempestuous Brazilian discovery Carmen Miranda.

As would be expected, the Andrews Sisters get the lion's share of the songs. They perform "Hit the Road," "The New Lick," "Oh, He Loves Me" and "Rhumboogie," which, as the title indicates, is a combination of the rhumba and boogie-woogie. It is their first number onscreen and is belted out as only the Sisters could. It would become one of their hits.

The Ritz Brothers do "The Spirit of 77-B," both as a "tribute" to the Bankruptcy Act and a travesty on the "Spirit of '76," something they had already done in *Life Begins in College*. They also do a specialty number to "Brooklynonga," another combination word for the style of jitterbugging in Brooklyn (the borough of their upbringing) and the conga. The brothers explained it this way: "You wriggle your shoulders, shuffle your feet, and then swing out your arms like a gaucho throwing a rope." In the film, they do this dance while gauchos crack whips around their ankles. Pretty leading lady Constance Moore warbles the romantic "Once Upon a Dream" and "The Hall of the Mountain Queen." Leading man George Reeves sings (or possibly is dubbed) doing "Amigo, We Go Riding Tonight."

Among the Ritz Brothers' shtick are the purloining and eating of huge sandwiches, and using their version of sign language to communicate with an Argentinean bus driver. They also impersonate their female co-stars (this time it is the turn of the Andrews Sisters), donning blonde wigs, garish costumes and silk stockings. There is a lot to parody. In the "Rhumboogie" number, the Sisters are dressed in incredibly loud patterned and ruffled "Latin" outfits which, were the film shot in blazing Technicolor, would have caused mass migraine auras in the audience.

In the "Oh, He Loves Me" number, the Sisters are given equally bizarre outfits and fitted with blonde wigs. Their synchronized dancing style was at least influenced by that of the Ritzes, and reputedly may have been taught to the Andrews *by* the Ritzes. Maxene later credited Patty with creating their choreography. At any rate, there was no credited choreographer—probably because Universal did not want the added expense.

By all accounts, the Sisters were sensitive about their appearances, particularly LaVerne. Her strong dark features, inherited from her Greek father, did not translate well to a big movie screen. It is said that she wanted to change from her usual right-hand position in the trio to the left because she thought her profile looked better from that angle. Patty resembled her strongly, although the bleaching of her dark hair helped to soften her features.

Pleasant-faced Maxene was always considered the "pretty one." *The Harvard Lampoon* dubbed their debut "the most frightening of the year." Whether that mischievous edict was directly intended to refer to their looks and/or their acting abilities, their appearances were frequently commented on throughout their career. Later in their filmmaking days, they were made to look more glamorous.

The Andrews Sisters were generally unhappy about what they perceived as Universal's cutting corners on them; being new to the picture business, they did not have much clout. They felt they were not given enough care makeup- and wardrobe-wise. Patty complained that they looked like the Ritz Brothers in drag. In the future they would claim that the film had been shot in a quick ten days, although production notes put it closer to one month.

The Ritz Brothers were not easy to work with, given their penchant for practical jokes and teasing. A later biography quoted the Sisters as complaining that the Ritzes were overbearing and rude. A *Hollywood Magazine* article reported:

> The Ritz Brothers wasted no time. The minute the Sisters timidly entered the sound stage each Ritz grabbed himself an Andrews, clasped her in a half-nelson, and showered her with a burlesque conception of torrid Latin kisses. It wasn't any use to fight; there was no place to run. The Ritzes were making so much noise it would have been useless to scream. They were just getting ready to fight.

If the Ritzes had been unhappy with their last two films at Fox, their luck would not change much at Universal. They would make three more mediocre films as a trio, and then return to their vastly more successful career in clubs and on theater stages. The first line of *Daily Variety*'s *Argentine Nights* review mentions that Universal gave them "Better material and better *executive guidance* [italics are the author's]." This may reveal the industry's understanding of how the Ritz Brothers had been treated by Darryl Zanuck in their final year at Fox. The part about getting better material is highly debatable.

On the other hand, the Andrews Sisters' cinema appeal would begin to change with their very next Universal film. In 1941, they were hooked up with Abbott and Costello in *Buck Privates*. The Sisters were spotted throughout the film singing some of their most memorable songs, particularly "Boogie Woogie Bugle Boy" and "I'll Be with You in Apple Blossom Time," two of the virtual anthems of World War II. They again appeared with Abbott and Costello in *In the Navy* and *Hold That Ghost* before getting a "B" series of their own, beginning with *What's Cookin'?* (1942) and ending with *Her Lucky Night* three years later.

They always received top billing, playing Themselves as the Ritz Brothers usually did. In these later pictures, comedienne Patty was given a chance to stand out; the other two were usually only given a few token lines, and they were nearly always dressed identically. Despite their billing, the actual leads were those actors playing the romantic couples. Like the Ritz Brothers, the Sisters were only too happy when their Universal contract ended. They continued to make radio and theater appearances and turn out hit records, which was always their greatest claim to fame.

Constance Moore was a pleasant leading lady in several minor films. George Reeves received the bulk of his fame playing television's *Superman*. He would always have the cachet of appearing as one of the red-haired Tarleton Twins in *Gone with the Wind*. He died a mysterious death and conspiracy theories abound to this day.

Reviews

"Given better material and better executive guidance than they have had in some time, the Ritz Brothers open up and deliver a line of top clowning which raises their stock considerably and starts them off on a new phase of their career. At the same time the Andrews Sisters, radio warbling names, show talent which promises important future placements. Between the two aggregations of comics, working harmoniously, Universal's romantic travesty with music comes through as sock entertainment, alive with music, dance, funny antics and amusing routines." *Daily Variety*, August 30, 1940.

"It's a gay romp for the Brothers Ritz all the way, and they easily cop what honors accrue.... The Andrews girls ... have legions of followers who may find themselves a bit disappointed in their queens since this, their first appearance in pictures, by no means proves their photographic worth.... Since the story was obviously written around the Ritz boys, the action seems to stop when they're not around. The story itself means nothing. In this type of picture it rarely does." *Hollywood Reporter*, August 30, 1940.

"I saw the picture and I don't believe it myself, but then sense is the last thing you would expect of a picture starring the slaphappy Ritz Brothers and the swing-happy Andrews Sisters.... One of the daffiest endings ever filmed. You will, however, get plenty of gags, some of them side-splitters, some just mildly amusing, and some pretty flat.... The Ritz Brothers have some of the funniest material they've had in a long time and make the most of it, even if you don't go for their brand of comedy.... Wisely no attempt has been made to glamorize the [Andrews Sisters], they are played strictly for comedy." Harriet O. Parsons [daughter of Louella Parsons], *Los Angeles Examiner*, August 30, 1940.

"There isn't much plot ... its makers having resorted to the time-proven formula for musical comedy.... None too lavish in production, [the] direction is undistinguished; consequently the film barely rises above mediocrity." *Boxoffice*, September 7, 1940.

"An entertaining musical comedy with never a dull moment." *National Board of Review Magazine*, October 1940.

"Instead of real South American romance you have the Ritz Brothers and the Andrews Sisters gently poking fun at conventional Latin legends. There isn't much story and what there is is lost in monkey business.... If you go for the Ritz Brothers you'll like them fine here." *Photoplay*, November 1940.

"Although it has been said more times than Universal cares to remember, the Ritz Brothers cannot carry a picture by themselves. Their latest nightmare on wheels has plenty of good gag situations, or at least enough to make the customers think they are having a good time.... The Andrews Sisters play a loony obbligato to the Ritz lead." *The Exhibitor*, November 1940.

"Loud, crude, senseless farce-riot of hectic action, crazy slapstick, maudlin dialogue, and much radio 'acting'.... Insane adventures.... Incessant laughs for Ritz addicts." *The Educational Screen*, December 1940.

"Little by way of plot or authentic atmosphere. A lot of monkey business on ocean liners and such." *Photoplay*, December 1940.

"If you don't like the Ritz Brothers then avoid this Universal 'B' movie. It is not, I hasten to say, a complete waste of time…. It is a pleasant enough time waster to make you stay through to the end, although it won't make fans for any of the talent involved." Modern-day commentator.

"The musical itself is very corny and dated, but every time the Andrews Sisters get to sing it comes alive…. Whether or not the audience takes to the Ritz Brothers will be based on their tolerance to their antics…. Here they score only a few laughs." Modern-day commentator.

"The Ritz Brothers are not everyone's cup of tea. Imagine making a career of portraying lousy comedians, which they were…. Lots of mugging, making faces, rolling eyes, synchronized silly dance steps…. They run true to form in this breezy musical that will help pass the time on a rainy day." Modern-day commentator.

Behind the Eight Ball (1942)

Directed by Edward F. Cline. Produced by Howard Benedict. Original story: Stanley Roberts. Screenplay: Stanley Roberts and Mel Ronson. Cinematography: George Robinson. Editor: Maurice Wright. Art director: Jack Otterson. Set decorator: Russell A. Gausman. Costumes: Vera West. Sound: Bernard B. Brown. Music: Ted Cain, Gene de Paul and Sonny Dunham. Words and music: Don Raye. Choreography: Eddie Prinz. Dates of production: June 17 to early July 1942. Released by Universal on December 4, 1942. 59 minutes.

Cast: The Ritz Brothers (Al Jester, Jimmy Jester, Harry Jester, known as the Jolly Jesters), Carol Bruce (Joan Barry), Dick Foran (Bill Edwards), Grace McDonald (Babs), Johnny Downs (Johnny), William Demarest (McKenzie), Richard Davies (Clay Martin), Russell Hicks (Harry Kemp), Vinton Hayworth (Bobby Leonard), Sonny Dunham and His Orchestra.

Synopsis: The notoriety caused by the murder of guest star Jack Daily on the opening night of the musical revue *Fun for All* draws a big crowd on the second night. Thus the Green Barn Playhouse is packed when Daily's replacement Wally Raymond is also shot dead. Police Chief McKenzie decides to arrange a third performance thinking he can trap the killer. Producer Joan Barry and her boyfriend Bill Edwards protest that no act would be foolish enough to go on.

Theatrical agent Harry Kemp agrees but sends them anyway to the Club Royale to scout acts. The Jolly Jesters—once a vaudeville trio, now washroom attendants—barge uninvited onto the stage and perform their specialty act "Charles Atlas (Did It for Me)." Harry, dressed in a leopard skin leotard, has nails pounded into him by Al and Jimmy to prove how strong he is. They end the act with Harry supposedly lifting Al and Jimmy up into the air by his own might and main. Actually suspended on wires, they go flying off into the wings.

The hapless trio is tossed out of the club and Kemp persuades them to perform at the Green Barn Playhouse. Once there, they learn of the two murders and try to flee; the chief forces them to stay. Joan tells them they can go if they like, but the show may be headed to Broadway so this is their big chance.

They decide to take that chance but overhear a plot to drive everyone off the farm on which the theater is located by means of an explosion. The explosion takes place and the brothers report what they overheard to Bill.

In the middle of the show, the chief stops the performance to announce that Bill himself is the actual killer. He has found incriminating chemicals in Bill's laboratory and declares the murders are now solved. Backstage, Bill and the Jesters later discover a secret passage which leads to a short wave radio set. The killers are Nazi spies who want the theater for their nefarious activities.

The Jesters perform an imitation of bandleader Ted Lewis, borrowing the clarinet played by band member Clay Martin. It turns out that Clay is a Nazi agent and has a hidden gun in the instrument; this is how he committed the two murders. The gun is primed to shoot when the clarinet player hits a high C. Fearing being accidentally shot himself as the clarinet is being played, he confesses. Harry continues playing and the clarinet shoots a bullet into the ceiling. After the spies are rounded up, the show goes on, and it is a success.

*　*　*

Behind the Eight Ball marked the return to the screen of the Ritz Brothers more than two years after their first Universal film, 1940's *Argentine Nights*. Its working title was *Off the Beaten Track*. In Mexico the film was titled *Siempre en Apuros*; it did not reach our southern neighbor for over a year and a half. It took more than two years to get to neutral Portugal where it was called *Os Tres Mosquiteiros de Risota*. Ads carried such taglines as "The Laugh Boys Are Here Again—Crazier Than Ever!" and "A Riot of Fun with the Maddest Zanies of Stage or Screen!"

The major reason to have a plot that involved putting on a musical show was the amount of music that could be crammed into it. This was a plot device also used at Fox so the Ritz Brothers could do their specialties. In one of their numbers, they hark back to their vaudeville act of ten or twelve years earlier in which they wore togas.

Several songs are shoehorned into the short running time; the Brothers perform four. Besides their "Atlas" number, they sing "Keep 'Em Laughing," "The Bravest of the Brave" and "When My Baby Smiles at Me," a classic song long associated with Ted Lewis.

One they do not perform was to become a minor classic of the World

The Jolly Jesters (Al, Jimmy and Harry), washed-up vaudevillians, are still blissfully unaware they have been set up as bait to trap a mysterious killer in *Behind the Eight Ball* (1942).

War II era, "Mr. Five by Five." The other numbers are "Don't You Think We Ought to Dance?," "Riverboat Jamboree," "Golden Wedding Day" and "Wasn't It Wonderful?"

The brothers' dialogue does not rise above the level of low comedy groaners, but that was now their lot in bottom-of-the-bill fare. An example:

"There's the patter of tiny feet at my house."
"Your sister have a baby?"
"No, she married a midget."

And a play on words on the title of the popular Broadway play *Three Men on a Horse*:

"I'm glad we got out of there before they called it *Three Men in a Hearse*."

Because it was now wartime, such films were probably satisfying enough to home front audiences, particularly when they played with a major "A" film. This fits right in with the extensive Universal slate of musical quickies and might explain the fairly positive contemporaneous reviews.

Reviews

"Zany as ever, the Ritz Brothers are on the loose again.... Entertaining with their usual violence, the Ritzes knock themselves out in their efforts to be amusing and, where they are popular, will give this lesser musical considerable bounce.... Unfortunately, this basic idea doesn't come out as funny as it might have." *Hollywood Reporter*, December 3, 1942.

"The Ritz Brothers lend their buffoonery to the daffy doings.... [The director] lets the fun run free, minimizing story elements to show off the musical acts and tunes. The Ritz Brothers are appropriately themselves and swing the fun along with several routines sure for top laughs." *Daily Variety*, December 3, 1942.

"The Ritz Brothers are in the fore throughout, after they enter the proceedings, indulging their liking for rough house comedy and song.... [They] carry the film." *Motion Picture Daily*, December 8, 1942.

"Although the story is a hodgepodge of nonsense, this comedy with music is more than satisfactory comic fare.... The hilarious routines and slapstick clowning of the Ritz Brothers are mainly responsible for the film's entertainment value." *Harrison's Reports*, December 12, 1942.

"Here's a programmer that will sell if the Ritz Brothers are an attraction in your neighborhood. Zany as ever." *Showmen's Trade Review*, December 12, 1942.

"Seemed to give the kids a lot of laughs but the adults acted differently. Had no draw." Manager, Koronis Theatre, Paynesville, Minnesota.

"Will fit neatly into the duallers [i.e., double features]." Small town theater manager.

"A murder mystery with plenty of slapstick comedy by the Ritz Brothers.... Your patrons won't guess who the murderer is until the final reel." Manager, State Theatre, Rivesville, West Virginia.

"You have to like the Ritz Brothers act to enjoy this one, for there is not much else here. Thankfully I do, so it was wild enough for me." Modern-day commentator.

"Not terrible if you can stand the twee musical numbers, pop-eyed schmaltz, and antique vaudeville routines from the Ritz Trio." Modern-day commentator.

"Finally the Ritz Boys put to good use. Actual characters rather than just a backdrop for a boring love story." Modern-day commentator.

Hi'Ya Chum (1943)

Directed by Harold Young. Produced by Howard Benedict. Story and screenplay: Edmund L. Hartmann. Cinematography: Charles Van Enger. Editor: Maurice Wright. Art directors: Ralph M. DeLacy and Jack Otterson. Set Decorator: Russell A. Gausman. Costume designer: Vera West. Sound: Bernard B. Brown and Jess Moulin. Music: Ted Cain, Hans J. Salter and Frank Skinner. Songs composed by Eddie Cherkose, Gene de Paul, Jacques Press and Don Raye. Choreography: Edward Prinz. Dates of production: August 24 to mid–September 1942. New York premiere, February 25, 1943. Wide release by Universal on March 15, 1943. 60 minutes.

Cast: The Ritz Brothers (The Merry Madcaps), Jane Frazee (Sunny Lee), Robert Paige (Tommy Craig), June Clyde (Madge Tracy), Paul Hurst (Archie Billings), Edmund MacDonald (Terry Barton), Lou Lubin (Eddie Gibbs), Andrew Tombes (Jerry Macintosh), Ray Walker (Jackson).

Synopsis: When their show *Fancies of 1943* closes in the Midwest, the brother act the Merry Madcaps and the singing act of Sunny Lee and Madge Tracy head for sunny California. They fail to make it when their car breaks down in the wartime boom town of Mercury, formerly known as Rustler's Gulch. At the Brewster Club restaurant, the Madcaps complain so much about the food that the only cook in town quits.

This does not please the war workers at the Brewster Chemical Works, who force the Madcaps to assume the cooking chores. They are so bad at it that the workers almost resort to violence until Sunny and Madge take over. They make a hit with their cooking and are asked to stay on and run the restaurant. They agree and the reluctant Madcaps become the dishwashers. Sunny and Tommy, one of the chemical workers, begin to fall in love. The Madcaps are anxious to leave town and, dressed as cowboys, they attempt in vain to get their car from the garage owner. Posing as a cowboy, Harry Ritz runs for sheriff.

Gambler Terry Barton wants to turn the restaurant into a casino, but Sunny refuses to sell because she does not approve of his plans. Madge has Sunny buy out her interest and she becomes the manager of Barton's new casino. It is far out of town so he still wants the restaurant because of its location. He lures the Madcaps into a crooked crap game. The idea is not for them to lose, but to win enough money to leave town so that Sunny will not have her friends around her.

After they collect their winnings, the brothers turn the tables on Barton by giving the money to Sunny so she can turn the restaurant into a nightclub. Barton warns them he will get revenge. Sunny brings in Hollywood showgirls for the opening, which Barton plans to disrupt by hiring some hoodlums to break

The Merry Madcaps (Jimmy, Harry and Al) hope to sneak out of the little town of Mercury disguised as cowboys in *Hi'Ya Chum* (1943), the trio's penultimate feature.

the club up. Madge regrets her split with Sunny. Upset that Barton is cheating at the casino, she warns Tommy about the plot.

The nightclub is a success, one number being a ballet parody by the Merry Madcaps. As the hoods try to disrupt the show laughing gas is used to subdue them. This does not make Barton forget his threat against the Merry Madcap. They find themselves at the bottom of a river with balls and chains around their necks.

* * *

The working title of this film was *Passing the Buck*. In the United Kingdom, it was called *Everything Happens to Us*. One poster for the film promised: "Bevies of Beauties! Bonanzas of Joy! A Host of Hostess Honeys Show a Boom-Town How to Boom! Hey! Hey! It's a Mirthful Mess of Music, Maids and Madcap Miners!"

Others had these taglines: "They're the Nuggets as They Strike It Rich in a Laugh Bonanza!"; "More Laughs Than You Can Shake a Pick At!"; "Merry Maids from Broadway.... Mania Miners of the West.... See Them Dig It"; "Take a Pick and Swing It! Grab a Gal and Dig It!" One ad called the Ritz Brothers "Three Zoot Zanies," zoot suits being much in the news then. They were described as "Crazier Than Ever" and the "Maddest Zanies of Stage or Screen."

Among the campaigns to publicize the film was a suggestion that corn stalks be placed around stills of the Ritz Brothers in theater lobbies and that actual corn be scattered around. Candy corn was to be distributed with the packaging legend "If you like corn you'll get a bellyful of laughs at the corny Ritz Brothers." Because of the restaurant in the plot, a contest called "1943 Good Eats" was suggested, with the best wartime menus winning a prize.

Yet another suggested marketing campaign was that theaters hang imitation hams in the lobby with a sign calling the hams the Ritz Brothers. It was also suggested that Ritz Brothers imitators march up and down in the street with advertising for the film on their backs. They were cautioned to fill their trays with plastic food in case they decided to do a funny stumbling routine.

Songs were "He's My Guy," sung by Robert Paige and Jane Frazee, and "Two on a Bike" and "I'm Hitting a High Spot," sung by Frazee and June Clyde. "You've Gotta Have Personality," "The Doo Dat" and "Cactus Pete for Sheriff" were performed by the Ritzes.

In their three Universal films after *Argentine Nights,* the Ritz Brothers are not cast as themselves, but (unlike almost every other comedy team) neither are they given character names that distinguish one from the other. This feeds into the commonly expressed criticism that they are basically the same person in their films.

Their designations as the Jolly Jesters, the Merry Madcaps and the Funny Bunnies continued to strengthen the perception of indistinguishable personalities. They had but one feature left at Universal, and they were no doubt happy about that. It was increasingly obvious that the studio very much favored the still very popular Bud Abbott and Lou Costello.

June Clyde entered films in 1929 and was now at the tail end of her cinema career. Robert Paige and Jane Frazee were the leads in many a "B" film, particularly in the period just before and during World War II. Both were competent performers but lacked the charisma which might have made their careers more important. Darkly glowering Edmund MacDonald made villains a specialty; the actor met an early death in 1951.

Reviews

"An enjoyable program comedy with music. What there is in the way of a story is nonsensical, but it should more than satisfy the followers of the Ritz Brothers' routines, most of which are of the slapstick variety. A fast-moving film designed for laughs and it gets them." *Harrison's Reports,* February 13, 1943.

"A program offering that is beamed at the Ritz Brothers fans, for in it they go to town with their own brand of antics. In those houses that have made money on pictures featuring the Ritz Trio this newest edition looks like a very satisfactory moneymaker. The facial contortions, dancing and singing all but crowd out the story." *Showmen's Trade Review*, February 13, 1943.

"The nature of the Ritz Boys' affability, and of the picture as a consequence, is that of a show-off youngster trying hard to draw attention to himself. Their, and this Universal picture's, cheap familiarity is exactly the kind which, in this quarter, breeds a mild contempt." *New York Times*, February 26, 1943.

"A very good one day picture. Followers of the Ritz Brothers told me they liked it." Manager, Lincoln Theatre, Columbus, Ohio.

"I love the Ritz Brothers, but this film is horrible…. The film never resolves, it just stops. I guess Universal could not put any care into this vehicle. They were much too busy with Abbott and Costello." Modern-day commentator.

"Probably the film that killed the career of the Ritz Brothers as a screen team…. Poor script, poor comedic material, poor production value…. The entire film feels like a thrown-together quickie." Modern-day commentator.

Never a Dull Moment *(1943)*

Directed by Edward Lilley. Produced by Howard Benedict. Screenplay: Mel Ronson and Stanley Roberts. Cinematography: Charles Van Enger. Editor: Paul Landres. Art directors: John B. Goodman and Martin Obzina. Set decorators: Russell A. Gausman and Ted Offenbecker. Costumes: Vera West. Music: Hans J. Salter, Charles Previn, Paul Sawtell, Frank Skinner and Ted Cain. Sound: Bernard B. Brown and Edwin Wetzel. Songs composed by Joseph Reed Alden, Eddie Cherkose, Walter Donaldson, Raymond B. Egan, Ange Lorenzo, Jacques Press, David Rose, Richard Whiting and George Whiting. Dates of production: February 22 to mid–March 1943. Released by Universal on November 19, 1943. 60 minutes.

Cast: The Ritz Brothers (Al, Jimmy, Harry, known as The Funny Bunnies), Frances Langford (Julie Russell), Mary Beth Hughes (Flo Parker), Franklin Pangborn (Sylvester), Stuart Boyd Crawford (Dick Manning), George Zucco (Tony Rocco), Elizabeth Risdon (Mrs. Schuyler Manning III), Jack La Rue (Joey), Sammy Stein (Romeo), Barbara Brown (Mrs. Lizzie Van Drake), Douglas Wood (Commodore Barclay), The Rogers Dancers (Dorothy Rogers, George Rogers, Don Kramer), Igor Dega, Grace Poggi (Exhibition dancers).

Also seen in the movie, uncredited: the familiar faces of George Chandler, Milton Kibbee, Ruby Dandridge (mother of Dorothy, playing her usual maid role), Bess Flowers (known as the Queen of the Extras) and Spec O'Donnell (the heavily freckled child actor).

Synopsis: Dick Manning brings his socialite mother to the Club Algiers to meet his fiancée, singer Julie Russell. Club owner Tony Rocco plans to steal Mrs. Manning's $500,000 diamond necklace. Julie innocently persuades Mrs. Manning to hold the engagement party at the club; Tony believes that will be his chance to pinch the necklace. He does not want to use his own men so he calls a Chicago theatrical agency which is actually a front for hiring thugs.

The Funny Bunnies, a broken-down vaudeville act, happen to be in the office and take the call. When Rocco asks for three "smart" men (by which he means crooks), they think he wants them to perform at the club. They arrive at the engagement party to entertain; Rocco thinks they are his hired thugs using their act as a cover.

While Harry is dancing with Flo Parker, a pickpocket confederate of Rocco's, she takes the necklace from Mrs. Manning and puts it into Harry's pocket. He discovers it and returns it to Mrs. Manning. Flo steals it again. When Harry's brothers filch some food from the club, they are chased out, unaware that they still have the necklace. They do not learn that until they read the newspaper the next morning. The Bunnies are now fugitives from the law.

The Bunnies manage to pick the worst possible place to hide out, a police station. Because Julie suggested that the engagement party be held at the club, she is now under suspicion. To prove her innocence, the Bunnies turn the necklace over to the police and manage to convince them they are also guiltless. Agreeing to help snare Rocco, they return to the club. Rocco is tricked into confessing; the police arrest him and his gang.

The Funny Bunnies decide to try to revive their none-too-successful career by going back to Chicago. When someone calls the Club Algiers looking to hire two gangsters, Harry answers the phone as he did at the theatrical agency. He explains to his brothers that it is for the benefit of the theater audience in case they missed the beginning of the movie.

* * *

An advertisement for the film declared "The Hit of the Soldier-Boys Overseas.... Latest Smash Comedy Hit from the Universal Studios.... Famous Vaudeville Acts.... Romance and Action!" Another promised: "You'll Never Have a Dull Moment When You See the Ritz Brothers Teamed with Frances Langford in the Latest Smash Comedy Hit from Universal." Whatever success the film had was due in part to the honey-voiced Langford's wartime popularity. She went on many overseas tours with Bob Hope to entertain countless thousands of G.I.s.

The film made references to the current wartime shortages and rationing of food. In one scene, Harry is seen cutting a three-inch–thick New York cut steak. He turns directly to the camera and says: "Don't get excited, folks, it's only a prop." This was not the only time this kind of a scene was inserted in a movie.

The film's songs were "My Blue Heaven," "Sleepy Time Gal," "Hello," "Yakimboomba" and "Once You Find Your Guy." Langford performed two, as did the Ritzes.

Other films with the title *Never a Dull Moment* included a 1950 romantic comedy starring Irene Dunne and Fred MacMurray, and a 1968 family comedy with Dick Van Dyke, Edward G. Robinson and Dorothy Provine. It was also the title of a Canadian short subject in 1979, a Canadian television movie of 1997 and a documentary in 2014. Numerous episodes of TV shows have also borne that title.

In the case of the Ritz Brothers film, there could hardly be a dull moment in a music-loaded picture that runs for barely an hour. This was the final feature film in which all three Ritz Brothers appeared live. From then on, they concentrated mainly on their successful club career. Jimmy and Harry did two film cameos together, and then Harry did one as a solo. There was also television, on which they appeared infrequently.

This was the next to last film for leading man Stuart Crawford, billed here as Stuart Boyd Crawford. He appeared in only eight films, the final one in 1944. He was so little-known that the film's posters had his name in small type below that of Franklin Pangborn. Suave and usually villainous George Zucco worked steadily until illness ended his career in 1951.

Reviews

"A good comedy with songs and a pinch of romance." *Showmen's Trade Review*, October 29, 1943.

"Although the plot is as old as the hills, the Ritz Brothers bring it up to date with some very funny comedy material covering present-day shortages.... The weight of the film is carried by the Ritz Brothers' antics with the accent on hokum, but as usual the speed at which they work keeps the show rolling at a lively clip. You get a good solid slice of fun and entertainment with emphasis on juvenile appeal." *Showmen's Trade Review*, October 30, 1943.

"Lives up fully to its title. It's never any less than extremely funny, at times it's positively hilarious. The Ritz Brothers turn in their finest screen work in a long time.... A fast-moving musical that hits the bulls-eye. For the first time in moons, the comic triumvirate have been supplied with material that's genuinely funny." *Film Daily*, November 5, 1943.

"The Ritz Brothers fail to get what are apparently their best lines and antics across in this one due to re-soled gags for the main part." *Motion Picture Herald*, November 6, 1943.

"Good program fare. Wherever the Ritz Brothers are popular, this should please. It develops into a slapstick farce with hilarious situations. [It] depends for entertainment on the antics of the Ritz Brothers." *Harrison's Reports*, November 6, 1943.

"The Ritz Brothers fail to get their best comedy lines and antics across.... A weak script." *Motion Picture Daily*, November 8, 1943.

"This picture didn't do as well as I thought it would. After looking at Abbott and Costello, the Ritz Brothers aren't as funny." Manager, Florida Theatre, Daytona Beach, Florida.

"This is just what the title implies. I played it to a pleased audience." Manager, Empress Theatre, Lloydminster, Saskatchewan.

"There wasn't too much plot to this picture and it didn't draw well or go over too strong." Manager, Winema Theatre, Scotia, California.

"There is never a dull moment is right. These fellows are crazy and my patrons like them that way." Manager, State Theatre, Rivesville, West Virginia.

"The Ritz Brothers may be an acquired taste, but if you have acquired that taste you'll probably find them fairly funny. They have lots of crazy routines, throwaway lines, and two deliberately nonsensical musical numbers." Modern-day commentator.

Blazing Stewardesses (1975)

The History

The working titles of the film were *Wild Stewardesses* and *The Jet Set*. It had also been called *Texas Layover*, *The Great Truck Robbery* and *Up Like a Shot*. It is a tamer sequel to the previous year's *The Naughty Stewardesses*. In an interview almost four decades after this movie was made, the writer-producer Samuel Sherman stated that it was meant as a "takeoff" on the 1942 Abbott and Costello film *Ride 'Em Cowboy*. That picture itself was a takeoff on the singing westerns which were popular in those days.

The Three Stooges, to consist of Moe Howard, Emil Sitka and Joe De Rita, were originally slated to appear in the movie. Moe, the only original member of the Stooges, was already ill and passed away in May 1975. Earlier in the year,

Jimmy and Harry Ritz had been cast in their place. Former star Rita Hayworth was supposedly offered the lead role but it was the fading Yvonne De Carlo who was finally cast. Although budget constraints were given as the official reason Hayworth was not cast, she was already displaying signs of Alzheimer's and could not remember lines.

Apparently former western actor Rod Cameron was sought for the male lead but Don "Red" Barry, another old "B" western star, was in the final cast. Yet another ex–oater star, Robert (Bob) Livingston, was also in the film. He reprised his role as Ben Brewster from *The Naughty Stewardesses*. For good measure, he was also in the similarly titillating *Girls for Rent*.

The potential appeal of this film limited it to a very selective release schedule. It may have been seen primarily as a drive-in theater attraction. Originally announced to open in wide saturation in North and South Carolina, it had its "premiere" in San Diego, California. Other venues in which it played included such widely diverse places as Aberdeen, South Dakota, Richmond, Virginia, and Cleveland, Ohio. It did not make it to Los Angeles until March 1977, two years after its production in Southern California, primarily in the high desert community of Palmdale and in the low desert resort town of Palm Springs. An end credit stated that it been filmed at the White Sun Guest Ranch in Palm Springs.

The Film

Directed by Al Adamson. Produced by Samuel M. Sherman, Irwin Pizor and Dan Q. Kennis. Screenplay: Samuel M. Sherman and John R. D'Amato. Story: Samuel M. Sherman. Songs composed by Barry Keenan, George Moslener, Gene Nash and Lee Zahler. Music: Roy Kohn and Gene Nash. Cinematography: Louis Horvath. Editor: John Winfield. Costumes: Georgette [Regina Carrol]. Music: Herman Stein. Visual effects (title animation): Bob Le Bar. Makeup: Melanie Levitt. Sound: Robert Dietz. Dates of production: March 1 to about May 1975. Produced by Producers Commercial Productions; distributed by Independent-International Pictures and released on August 14, 1975. Approx. 80 minutes.

Cast: Yvonne De Carlo (Honey Morgan), Robert (Bob) Livingston (Ben Brewster), Donald "Red" Barry (Mike Trask), Geoffrey Land (Bob Travers), Connie Hoffman (Debbie Stewart), Regina Carrol (Lori Winters), T.A. King [Marilyn Joi] (Barbara), The Ritz Brothers (Themselves), Lon Bradshaw (Old Timer), Sheldon Lee (Chuck), Jerry Mills (Pilot), John Shank (Sheik), Nicole Riddell (Jackie), Carol Bilger (Chuck's girl), Leonard Geer, Jack Tyree, James Winburn (Passengers on plane).

Synopsis: Stewardesses Debbie and Lori visit the Los Angeles Zoo. Lori buys a gift for her boyfriend Chuck but later finds him in bed with another woman. When Debbie gets an invitation to Ben Brewster's dude ranch for a free two-week vacation, she, Debbie and Barbara, another stewardess, decide to accept. In exchange, they agree to work on a chartered flight to Brewster's Lucky Dollar Ranch.

There is plenty of hanky-panky on the flight. Debbie flirts with businessman Bob Travers; stewardess Jackie has sex with the copilot, and Jerry the pilot, who is drunk, comes on to Lori. Before they can consummate anything, Jerry falls into the plane's toilet, his head becoming stuck in the toilet seat. They finally get to the ranch where Ben introduces the stewardesses to Honey Morgan, madam of the brothel The Beehive. Honey hopes to lure them into her "trade."

Jimmy and Harry Ritz are hitchhiking along a desert road. They see a help wanted sign for the Lucky Dollar Guest Ranch and decide to head there. To stop a passing car, Harry does the bared leg routine made famous by Claudette Colbert in *It Happened One Night*. He also uses his rubbery facial expressions, rolls his eyes and finally lies down at the side of the road and twitches spastically.

In town, they see the stewardesses playing golf. Harry offers to "help" with their stances while taking the opportunity to run his hand up and down various limbs. When he tries to hit a golf ball, it is the club that goes flying. For some reason the Ritzes run off with the girls' golf clubs and the chase takes them to the rodeo.

There Jimmy and Harry are seen in the crowd yelling dubious encouragement to the rodeo riders. Later they are given jobs making hot dogs and hamburgers. Jimmy is asked by a customer to make a fried egg sandwich; he is reluctant but tries it. When he flips the eggs, they fly out of the pan and land on Harry's face. They later become ranch hands at the Lucky Dollar.

In a number cut from some versions of the film but included on the DVD release, the brothers break into one of their synchronized dances and are applauded by the rodeo crowd. They make their grand exit (by mistake?) into a ladies' room. The dance is a re-creation of one they had performed in their very first feature, *Sing, Baby, Sing*, in 1936.

Lori reveals that she has money troubles; Honey suggests that she work at the Beehive. Mike tells Lori that Honey uses people and then discards them, he having been one of her broken-hearted victims. Ben announces that gambling equipment is being trucked to his ranch and his casino will then have a grand opening. Mike, determined to prevent the opening, orders two hooded bandits to intercept the truck. He has previously used the thugs to attack Ben's ranch hands.

Mike is very jealous because Honey is attracted to Ben. He even punches him and throws him into a swimming pool; Ben does not retaliate. Mike is successful in having the gambling equipment stolen. Debbie and Barbara go to visit Lori, who has gone to work at the Beehive. Honey is orienting her new recruits, telling them that when a client is really drunk, they should substitute blowup dolls in their beds. Debbie decides to become one of Honey's girls; she follows her advice about the blowup dolls when her first client shows up drunk.

Mike and Honey meet secretly. It turns out that she is part of a plot to disrupt Ben's business. Unbeknownst to Ben, there is oil on his land, and they want to force him to sell. The thugs once again attack Ben's trucks, but this time he anticipates them with his own armed men. Ben catches Mike and makes him beg for mercy; Mike then signs a confession implicating Honey.

Ben shows the confession to Honey and demands that she make him a partner in the Beehive; she agrees. An Arab sheik, a guest at Ben's ranch, discovers the oil for himself. He has also discovered Lori, who calls him her new daddy. They pick up Debbie and Barbara in the sheik's limousine and drive back to Los Angeles, leaving Bob and Honey to fend for themselves.

* * *

The available versions of the film vary in length. There is indeed considerable padding which can be eliminated without harm to the story—such as it is. The zoo sequence at the beginning is one of them, as is some of the rodeo material, the parade sequence, plus the scenes of Honey on a shopping expedition. One reviewer actually suggested that this is the first movie that is *all* padding. If this is indeed an homage to the old-time singing westerns the producers forgot they were usually an hour or less in length.

The film begins with a title card which reads: "Dedicated to the Screen's unsung Directors, Performers, and Stuntmen of a bygone era—when Movies entertained with Simplicity and the World forgot its Cares." This might not be the sentiment that the film actually elicits with its smarmy plot. On its re-release to theaters, it was sometimes re-titled either *Cathouse Callgirls* or *Cathouse Cowgirls*.

Posters for the film played up the title's deliberate similarity to Mel Brooks' very successful 1974 western spoof *Blazing Saddles*: "Out-Blazing *Blazing Saddles*…. This Year's Mad, Mad World of Sheer Lunacy and Complete Insanity!" A variation on this had the secondary tagline read: "Sexy! … Zany! … Wild!"

Because it supposedly aims to parody the "B" singing cowboys, it features several songs: "Now the Game Is Over," "Lay It on Me One More Time," "Have I Lost the Thing I Found" and "Do You Want to Be with Me Tonight." At its heart it is like a "B" western (on steroids) with its masked bad guys, cowhands, forgettable songs and villains after some form of pelf.

The Ritz Brothers appear in the cast list as "Special Guest Stars: The Ritz Brothers, Harry and Jimmy Ritz." Their appearance has its humorous moments, but it is mostly a strained and juvenile attempt at humor. The deleted dance number is endearing but because they are in shorts in some scenes, rather than in one of their flamboyant costumes, their advancing age is only too apparent.

One reviewer unkindly called them "truly ancient." Another characterized them as "Two very old (VERY) men." These were overstatements; Jimmy was a year or so past 70, Harry had not quite become a septuagenarian. Their ages aside, another reviewer summed up what most viewers undoubtedly thought was the unfortunate truth: "What a comedown [the Ritz Brothers] and the rest had in doing this trash." One facetiously suggested that either the money was good, or the name actors had been blackmailed or coerced into doing the picture.

For Yvonne De Carlo, a sultry minor "A" film leading lady of the '40s, this continued a declining career that had begun with promise and hit its acme with the mid–1960s TV series *The Munsters*. A reviewer called her singing in this film "a criminal offense." Regina Carrol, who played Lori, was the wife of director Al Adamson, who one reviewer dubbed the worst director of all time. Another said that his direction of this film was "atrocious." A third said, "Like most of his movies, this is pretty much a complete mess."

Ex-cowboy star Don "Red" Barry came to prominence in a movie serial as cowboy hero Red Ryder and he worked up until the time of his death, with hundreds of movie and TV credits. Robert (Bob) Livingston had been in films since the silent days; this was to be his final role. Shortly before his death, cowboy star Gene Autry presented him with a Golden Boot award for his work in westerns.

Reviews

"The film's top performing honors go to the Ritz Brothers. Ignoring the smarmy script and clumsy direction, the Ritzes regale their old fans and win a few new ones by running through some of their classic routines." *Rotten Tomatoes* (which gave this film an abysmal 12 percent favorable rating).

"The worst here is the Ritz Brothers; never have [I] seen such an appalling spectacle. The grotesque pair appears on a number of occasions to deliver some of the worst 'comedy' routines I have ever seen. This easily ranks as one of the most clueless, incompetent and inept films I've ever worked my way through." Modern-day commentator.

"An awful Al Adamson movie with a bunch of Z list western actors … and the Ritz Brothers doing very unfunny comic 'relief'…. How the Ritz Brothers ended up in this 1970s T&A film is probably a more interesting story than the film itself. I didn't laugh more than two or three times during the film and none of them were because of the Ritz Brothers." Modern-day commentator.

Cameo Appearances

Ali Baba Goes to Town *(1937)*

The History

At the beginning of the talkie era, Eddie Cantor became a star for independent producer Samuel Goldwyn with the film adaptation of his hit Broadway musical comedy *Whoopee*. This was followed by other well-received films, like *The Kid from Spain* and *Roman Scandals*. His usual persona was the hapless schnook who becomes an accidental hero. He went back in time for the first time in *Roman Scandals* in 1933. By 1934, his movies were becoming less successful, perhaps because of the sameness of his characters and even because of the newly enforced Production Code. Cantor movies to that point had had their share of slyly racy material.

At 45 years of age in 1937, Cantor was not as convincing in his usual movie persona. *Strike Me Pink*, his 1936 effort and his final Goldwyn film, had not been a great success. An attempt was made to surround him with a strong supporting cast, but the muddled combination of comedy and crime melodrama set in an amusement park lacks a big quotient of laughs. It had been very unconvincingly advertised as "The Most Colossal and Most Stupendous Extravaganza Since the Epic!" (which "Epic" was uncertain).

The need for him to update his image was reflected in comments like that made by a small-town movie theater manager: "I kept looking for Cantor to change to blackface and do a song, but he never got around to that." Another said: "Cantor [is] not the draw he once was and the picture did no more than the average." To add to the woes of the film, its premiere at New York's Radio City Music Hall was impacted by severe cold weather.

At this point, Cantor needed a solid comeback vehicle. When he signed with Twentieth Century–Fox, that project was going to be the Damon Runyon horseracing story *Saratoga Chips*. Instead that became the Ritz Brothers' third starring film *Straight, Place and Show* two years later.

Cantor ended up in *His Arabian Nights*, released as *Ali Baba Goes to Town*. In an attempt to boost its chances of success, Cantor was backed up by sturdy supporting players, specialty acts, lavish settings, three-tone (copper, blue and orange) tinting, and footage of a batch of Fox stars including the Ritz Brothers going to a film premiere.

The film was reportedly budgeted at more than $1 million and a special 25-acre Old Baghdad set was constructed. On August 27, 1937, there were fatalities and injuries when the 1500-pound mechanism supporting the film's flying carpet collapsed during a test. A grip and a property man were killed; two other property men suffered injuries.

Cantor himself was supposedly bruised and skinned by kneeling on the coarse carpet when the wind machine blew up to 50 miles an hour in his flying scenes. This conceivably could have been studio publicity to mitigate the bad press after the fatal incident. A coroner's jury ruled the tragedy was accidental and affixed no blame.

The footage of the premiere, shot at Hollywood's Carthay Circle Theatre, was shot at the premiere of Shirley Temple's *Wee Willie Winkie* the preceding June. This explains the presence of Shirley's parents George and Gertrude in the film.

The Film

Directed by David Butler. In charge of production: Darryl F. Zanuck. Associate producer: Laurence Schwab. Screenplay: Harry Tugend and Jack Yellen. Story: Gene Towne, Graham Baker and Gene Fowler. Cinematography: Ernest Palmer. Editor: Irene Morris. Art director: Bernard Herzbrun. Set decorator: Thomas Little. Makeup (uncredited): Eugene Klum and Arthur Stone. Costume designer: Herschel McCoy and Gwen Wakeling. Hair styles: Gene Thomas. Sound: Alfred Bruzlin and Roger Heman. Music and lyrics: Mack Gordon and Harry Revel. Musical director: Louis Silvers. Music: Robert Russell Bennett and Walter Scharf. Dances staged by Sammy Lee. Dates of production: late July to early September 1937. Hollywood premiere, October 15, 1937; New York premiere, October 22, 1937. Released by Twentieth Century–Fox on October 29, 1937. 81 minutes.

Cast: Eddie Cantor (Aloysius Babson/Ali Baba/Himself), Tony Martin (Himself/Yusuf), Roland Young (Sultan Abdullah), June Lang (Herself/Princess Miriam), Louise Hovick [Gypsy Rose Lee] (Herself/Sultana), Raymond Scott and His Quintet (Themselves), John Carradine (Broderick/Ishak), Virginia Field

(Dinah/Deenah), Alan Dinehart (Boland), Douglass Dumbrille (Prince Musah). Maurice Cass (Omar the rug maker), Warren Hymer, Stanley Fields (Tramps), Paul Hurst (Captain), Sam Hayes (Radio Announcer), Sid Fields (Assistant Director), Ferdinand Gottschalk (Councilor), Charles Lane (Doctor), Peters Sisters [Ann, Mattie, Virginia], Jenni Le Gon, Pearl Twins (Specialties).

Among the uncredited cast members were Lynn Bari and Marjorie Weaver, future "B" movie leading ladies; Lee J. Cobb, destined to be a Broadway and cinema character star, and such old-time character actors as former Keystone Cop Hank Mann, Francis McDonald, Harry Woods and comic Eddie Collins. Also uncredited were the roster of Twentieth Century–Fox stars attending the fictional premiere, among them the Ritz Brothers, Phyllis Brooks, Dolores Del Rio, Douglas Fairbanks Jr., Jack Haley, Sonja Henie, Victor McLaglen, Tyrone Power, Cesar Romero, Ann Sothern, the Temple family (Shirley, Gertrude, George) and Michael Whalen.

Synopsis: Aloysius Babson, called Al, is a movie buff who heads for Hollywood on his vacation to hunt movie stars. In the California desert, he falls out of the boxcar in which he has been riding; fortunately he runs into a Fox movie company filming an Arabian Nights film. When he stumbles into an Arabian set, he gets tangled up with some of the film's horse riders and needs medical assistance.

Awakening in the Fox first aid room, Al is asked to sign a waiver to indemnify the studio against a damage suit. The nurse Dinah cautions him against signing, but given the chance to be an extra in the picture he does sign. He is given some pills for his pain. As an extra he plays one of the Forty Thieves, the one who wants to remain loyal to the sultan the other thieves plan to kill.

Instead of taking two pills at 12 o'clock as instructed, Al takes 12 pills at two. This causes him to dream that he is really in Baghdad 1000 years earlier, in 937. About to be executed as part of a rebellion against the sultan, Al tells them his name is Al Babson. His would-be executioners mistake it for Ali Baba and hail him as the son of their hero, the real Ali Baba. While having lunch at the sultan's palace, he convinces the potentate to invite all the starving people to lunch also. This generosity quells the rebellion and Al is made prime minister. He launches a series of projects clearly based on those of the 1930s New Deal. He also asks the sultan to disband the army, prompting the scheming Prince Musah and Sultana, one of the sultan's 365 wives, to plot his demise and a takeover of the country.

Al has by this time fallen in love with Deenah, daughter of Omar the rug maker. Yusuf, a champion of the oppressed peasants, and the princess are also in love, even though marriage between a commoner and royalty is forbidden. Al's solution is to convince the sultan to run for president instead of being a sultan. His campaign to elect Abdullah fails when he himself is elected. This angers the sultan who orders Al to be boiled in oil.

Al escapes, and veiled as a woman he goes to Musah's camp and dances for him. Then he ties up Musah with his veils and escapes. Omar the rug maker is experimenting with a magic carpet but he cannot get it to fly until Al says "inflation." Al and Musah, who has climbed aboard the carpet with Al, fight as it soars away followed by Musah's army. Both fall off.

This trauma causes Al to wake up in the present time and he is ejected from the Fox lot. He eagerly takes his autograph book to a premiere where actor Tony Martin is introducing the arriving celebrities, including the Ritz Brothers. The film ends with Al Babson looking on disapprovingly as the actual Eddie Cantor arrives and sings "Laugh Your Way Thru Life." As Cantor gets surrounded by autograph seekers, Al asks, rolling his eyes: "What's he got that I haven't got?" This may have been one impetus for giving Cantor a double role as himself and Joe Simpson in Warner Brothers' 1943 film *Thank Your Lucky Stars*.

* * *

Among the advertisements for this picture was one which unconvincingly claimed "Patrons storm theaters to see *Ali Baba Goes to Town*, shouting we want Cantor!" Another touted that the film had set an all-time attendance record in its second week, and boasted: "That's what you expect when Darryl F. Zanuck, your greatest maker of musicals, really goes to town with Eddie Cantor!" Despite the solid supporting cast, many ads just featured Cantor and Louise Hovick, now gaining fame as Gypsy Rose Lee. It was her second film. The same-year *You Can't Have Everything* with the Ritz Brothers had been her first.

Upon its release, Fox was sued for more than $1,000,000 by a writer who alleged the story had been plagiarized from one which he had submitted to them in 1936. It took two years to settle the case, which Fox won. The similarity of *Ali Baba Goes to Town* with Mark Twain's novel *A Connecticut Yankee in King Arthur's Court* was freely acknowledged by writer Gene Fowler and not lost on movie critics. The Twain story had been filmed by Fox as *A Connecticut Yankee* with popular Will Rogers in 1931.

Ali Baba garnered an Oscar nomination for Sammy Lee's choreography of the dance number "Swing Is Here to Sway." It did not win. A clip from the film was included in the 1975 film *The Day of the Locust*.

A *New York Times* critic thought this 1937 film was the first time "in which a studio has leveled satire and ridicule at the [Roosevelt] administration." Another critic noted Cantor's supposed burlesquing of Franklin Roosevelt's gestures and manner of speech. The film is clearly intended as a satire on the New Deal, something which might resonate with audiences. It was made despite Zanuck's often-stated distaste for satire.

The theater manager who was waiting for Cantor to don his familiar blackface in *Strike Me Pink* got his wish in this film: He does apply blackface to perform the song "Swing Is Here to Sway" with a large group of African-American extras in totally incongruous ersatz African native costumes. More incongruously, they are in front of a turbaned Middle Eastern crowd.

The solo female dancer in this number is Jenni Le Gon, who passed away in 2012 at age 96. Among the other tunes are the instrumental "Twilight in Turkey," performed by the Raymond Scott Quintet, "I've Got My Heart Set on You," "Vote for Honest Abe" and "Arabiana."

According to a well-respected biography of Dolores Del Rio who appears in the movie premiere scene, the sultry star called this film "a silly production in which practically everybody working as an actor around Fox appeared in one cameo or another." She considered doing this a big step downward in her career. Inherent in this observation is that Fox hoped to make this film a hit by surrounding Cantor with as much glitz and glamour as possible.

It is perhaps another sign that by itself, his name was no longer the draw it once had been. Cantor did not make another film until the indifferently received *Forty Little Mothers* (MGM, 1940). After that, his cinema career was sporadic. On radio, he helped jumpstart the careers of many young performers; he later worked in television. Both he and Gypsy Rose Lee were the subject of biopics. Lee's was the extremely successful *Gypsy*; Cantor's (*The Eddie Cantor Story*) was regarded as somewhat of an embarrassment.

Reviews

"A string of stale New Deal jokes that have been kicking around for the last couple of years…. If this picture was really an attempt at satire its main failure was that the story never got to the point where it could support itself." *World Film and Television Progress*, April 1937.

"A super spectacular hit." *Film Fun*, June 1937.

"The absence of Cantor seems to have whetted the interest of the fan public in seeing him…. Seems set to go to town in a popular way…. Because this essays something different it does not always hit the comedy bulls-eye. Now and again there are lines which fall flat…. But in a large way it is unusual entertainment and has been realized in the lavish manner." *Los Angeles Times*, November 4, 1937.

"There are glitter and flash, the spectacular and the glamorous elaborate sets … but the laughs are not as plentiful or spontaneous as might have been expected." *Motion Picture Daily*, November 7, 1937

"Nonsense of the sort that will appeal to those who want to forget reality [and] frolic in the world of make-believe…. The exuberance of the acting tides the story over a few weaknesses of plot." *Motion Picture Reviews*, December 1937.

"A dated comedy in many ways, but is valuable from a historical perspective. With its political satire and its glimpse of vintage Hollywood the movie is intriguing…." Modern-day commentator.

"The story is a bit thin and silly, kept afloat by the dialogue, some efficient pacing, and the songs, but more an excuse to string along musical numbers and comedy…. Eddie Cantor enjoys himself thoroughly and is enormous fun." Modern-day commentator.

Take It or Leave It *(1944)*

The History

According to cinema lore, the plot of the film version of *Take It or Leave It* was suggested by an incident which occurred on the popular radio quiz of the same name. (It ran from 1940 to about 1949, and originated the phrase "the $64 question"). A contestant mentioned that his wife was about to have a baby. The maximum $64 prize was increased for the first time ever. It was still wartime, and he was a sailor, a fighting man.

Contestants were picked at random from ticket stubs deposited in two glass bowls, one for men and one for women. During World War II, a third bowl was added to accommodate servicemen and women. The host's tagline was: "No prompting from the audience, please." When contestants opted to continue rather than take the money they had already earned, the audience would shout and drawl in unison: "You'll be soorrryyy!"

The show's first host, comedian Phil Baker, was known as "The Man with the $64 Question." A former vaudevillian, he had also been on Broadway and in a few films. A later host was Jack Paar, who was to become famous as a late night TV personality.

Baker's well-known trademark was the accordion he often had draped around his shoulders. It was reported that Fox had wanted to have the maximum prize increased in the film to something like $640, but the radio show's producers objected. They probably never dreamed that in decades to come, the show would morph into the popular but troubled TV series *The $64,000 Question*.

The plot idea for this film did not only spring from the radio show; it was a partial remake of an earlier Fox film, 1931's *Bad Girl*. That picture in turn was based on a Vina Delmar novel and a play of the same name. In 1940 came yet another version of the story, *Manhattan Heartbeat*. The working title for this 1944 version was *Movietone Follies*.

Producer Bryan Foy apparently wanted up-and-coming young actors William Eythe and Mary Anderson for the roles of Eddie and Kate Collins, but settled for the relatively unknown Edward Ryan and Marjorie Massow. (The latter later changed her name to the more glamorous Madge Meredith.) Vina Delmar declined to take any screen credit for this version.

The Film

Directed by Benjamin Stoloff. Produced by Bryan Foy. Music (uncredited): Cyril J. Mockridge. Cinematography: Joseph La Shelle. Editor: Harry Reynolds. Screenplay: Mac Benoff, Harold Buchman and Snag Werris. Art directors: Leland Fuller and Lyle Wheeler. Set decorator: Thomas Little. Costume designer: Kay Nelson. Sound: Jesse Bastian. Music director: Emil Newman. Makeup: Guy Pearce. Dates of production: March 20 to early April 1944. Released by Twentieth Century–Fox on July 12, 1944 (New York and Los Angeles premiere); July 17, 1944 (U.S. wide release). 68 minutes.

Cast: Phil Baker (Himself), Edward Ryan (Eddie Collins), Marjorie Massow [Madge Meredith] (Kate Collins), Stanley Prager (Herb Gordon), Roy Gordon (Dr. Preston), Nana Bryant (Miss Burke), Carleton Young (Program Director), Phil Silvers (Himself), Frankie Darro (Radio Listener), Earle Hagen (Musician), The Ritz Brothers, Lynn Bari, Borrah Minevitch and His Harmonica Rascals, Dixie Dunbar, James Dunn, Alice Faye, Billy Gilbert, Glenn Miller and His Orchestra, Betty Grable, Sonja Henie, The Ink Spots, Al Jolson, Buster Keaton, George Montgomery, Harry Morgan, Nicholas Brothers (Harold and Fayard), Jack Oakie, John Payne, Cesar Romero, Ann Rutherford, Shirley Temple, Fats Waller, The Wiere Brothers (Harry, Herbert, and Sylvester).

Among the uncredited actors who appear in the film are old character reliables like Renie Riano, Nella Walker, Tom Dugan, Frank Jenks and Ralph Sanford.

Synopsis: Eddie Collins and his buddy Herb Gordon, sailors on shore leave in New York, meet Eddie's expectant wife Kate. Concerned that she might have problems bearing the child, she wants to see Dr. Preston, one of the city's leading doctors. She is told that not only is he too busy but he charges fees ranging up to $1000. Eddie reassures Kate by telling her that Preston is definitely going to see her.

Eddie decides to try to raise money by going on the radio quiz show *Take It or Leave It*, although all he could hope to win is $64. Eddie is chosen and picks the category "Scenes from motion picture hits of the past"—all of them coincidentally being Fox pictures. He answers the first question correctly.

After Eddie reveals that his wife is pregnant, the show's host Phil Baker takes a liking to him and tries to help him by giving him broad hints. When the $64 limit is reached, Eddie is allowed to exceed it and keep going. Eddie mentions Dr. Preston, who happens to be listening. Preston was never told about Kate's visit to his office, but even so, his wife chastises him for over-charging. The annoyed doctor accuses the radio program of being a fake and insists that the Collinses are not even real people.

Eddie is up to $384 (every step being a multiple of $64) when Kate goes into labor and he must stop. As he leaves for the hospital, Eddie confesses to Baker that Dr. Preston will not really be attending her, but he had not wanted Kate to be worried. Mrs. Preston still attempts to get her husband to attend Kate but instead he leaves on a vacation, destination unknown.

Over the radio, Baker asks for Dr. Preston to help the couple; the doctor hears the plea in a taxi. He tells the driver to take him to the hospital, arriving to find that Kate has already given birth to a healthy boy—named Phil Baker Collins. Eddie's friend Herb tells them he has decided to marry his girlfriend; Phil laughingly tells him that he should announce his babies on the show as well.

* * *

In Brazil, the film was called *Calouros de Sorte*; in Portugal it was *O Grande Premio*; in Mexico it had a similar title, *El Premio Mayor*.

The clips shown in the film are from Twentieth Century–Fox productions made between 1934 and 1942: *Stand Up and Cheer, King of Burlesque, One in a Million, On the Avenue, Rose of Washington Square, Hollywood Cavalcade, Tin Pan Alley, The Great American Broadcast* and *Orchestra Wives*. The Ritz Brothers appeared in two of these: *One in a Million* and *On the Avenue*.

An advertisement for the film promised "27 Surprise Stars in the Big Musical.... The Cast's Star-rific.... Crowds, Crowds, Crowds as Far as the Eye Could See!" Another more simply read: "Surprise Hit with All Your Favorite Movie Stars." All featured a winking Phil Baker. Perhaps the major surprise came to audiences who expected to see all those stars in new footage, rather than in filmclips from old movies. There were theater tie-ins with the Eversharp Company, manufacturer of pens and pencils, which was the radio program's main sponsor.

This film is a reunion of sorts for Phil Baker and the Ritz Brothers since their joint appearance in *The Goldwyn Follies* six years earlier. This time only one of them is actually appearing live; the Ritzes are seen in the *On the Avenue* clip. In it, they perform their lively version of the Russian folk song "Otchi Tchorniya."

Another veteran of *The Goldwyn Follies*, Ella Logan was in the stage show that accompanied the opening of *Take It or Leave It* at New York's Roxy Theatre. It actually received a double premiere in New York and Los Angeles. The movie got a "B" rating from the Legion of Decency which signified that it was "Objectionable in part." This was presumably due to the pregnancy aspect of the plot.

As part of the film's publicity campaign, it was reported that Stanley Prager, who plays sailor Herb Gordon, had survived a rare heart ailment from which no one else in medical history had ever recovered. This was supposedly due to the administering of a rare drug. Whether or not this is true, Prager, who was later blacklisted, did pass away at age 55 from a heart ailment.

Far exceeding the onscreen drama was the real drama that was to come from the travails of the female lead Marjorie Massow. Following her name change to Madge Meredith, she became the client of a shady Hollywood character called Nicholas "The Greek" Gianaclis. After some serious interpersonal conflict, he accused the young actress of conspiring to have him kidnapped. Local newspapers featured headlines like: "Film Cinderella Sought for Kidnap Questioning."

Massow-Meredith was found guilty and sentenced to five years in prison. Humphrey Bogart and ZaSu Pitts began a letter-writing campaign; after two and a half years of imprisonment, Massow's sentence was commuted in 1951. Her innocence was established and she was able to resume a minor career. She passed away at age 96 in 2017.

Considering that *Take It or Leave It* only runs about 70 minutes, it is packed with music from all the filmclips. This leaves little time for the actual story, which was probably the general idea. Since Fox already owned the rights to all the filmclips, they did not have to hire expensive talent, although they did strive to obtain releases.

Al Jolson filed suit in August 1944 over the inclusion of his clip from the 1939 film *Rose of Washington Square*. He claimed that because he only had a one-picture deal with Fox, he was not under long-term contract. Therefore the studio did not have the specific right to reproduce his performance. Jolson was known as a litigious person but by this time in his career he had less clout.

Reviews

"The story itself is lightweight, but has been developed in so amusing a fashion that it keeps one laughing throughout. The spectator enjoys the quiz game." *Harrison's Reports*, July 17, 1944.

"Radio fans, especially admirers of the show, no doubt will take it. Others in quest of more substantial entertainment more than likely will leave it. The film is virtually nothing more than a photographed radio session. What little there is is hardly a master mental stroke. The budget has been kept down by the neat if simple process of trotting out excerpts from old Twentieth Century–Fox films. Going to the files may be one way of keeping production costs down, but it hardly makes for meritorious entertainment." *Film Daily*, July 17, 1944.

"Radio fans will be the chief customers for this film derived from the popular ether [i.e., radio] program." *Independent Film Journal*, July 22, 1944.

"We'd take it. There isn't much plot to carry, it has a pleasant scent, and besides it offers a lot of fun guessing. Judging from the construction of the story we'd say it cost about $64 to make." *Photoplay*, August 1944.

"Easy to take as light summer's entertainment.... Like the picture's obstetrical exigencies the pace is brisk.... The direction is gingersnappy." *Time*, August 21, 1944.

"Went over very well here and everyone seemed to like it." Manager, Koronis Theatre, Paynesville, Minnesota.

"Those who saw it found it very entertaining. Spoke well of it." Manager, Town Hall Theatre, Middlebury, Vermont.

Won Ton Ton, the Dog Who Saved Hollywood *(1976)*

The History

Lily Tomlin was originally a leading candidate to appear in a movie about Rin Tin Tin, the Warner Brothers dog star of the 1920s and early 1930s. Initially called *A Bark Is Born*, the title was changed to *Won Ton Ton, the Dog That Saved Warner Brothers* in deference to an upcoming Barbra Streisand remake of *A Star Is Born*. Rin Tin Tin movies actually did put Warner Brothers back on its feet, at least until *The Jazz Singer* came along. The dog was known as the mortgage lifter of the studio.

When Tomlin and Warner Brothers both withdrew from the project, Paramount picked it up and considered Cher and Bette Midler for the lead. Madeline Kahn was the final choice. Several silent film veterans were considered for cameos, and the list was whittled down to Carmel Myers, Dorothy Gulliver and Richard Arlen. Cy Howard, one of the writers, said he got the idea for the story several years earlier from Jack Warner, who said Rin Tin Tin was that studio's biggest star because "he never caused me any trouble."

A $2.5 million lawsuit was filed by the widow of Lee Duncan, owner-trainer of the original Rin Tin Tin, and Herbert Leonard, who owned the copyright for the 1950s television series *The Adventures of Rin Tin Tin*. The lawsuit demanded that no German shepherd be used in the film and that no connection be made with the original dog. Director Michael Winner actually claimed that he had never even heard of Rin Tin Tin so the film could have no connection with that canine.

The lawsuit failed and production proceeded. Anticipation for success was so high that two sequels were already considered: *Won Ton Ton, the Dog Who Saved Broadway* and *Won Ton Ton, the Dog Who Saved World War II*. In April 1976, an entire episode of *The Merv Griffin Show* was dedicated to publicizing the film, which was to open a month from then. Paramount sponsored a promotion with Milk Bone dog biscuits with a grand prize of a trip to Hollywood for a family of four *and* the family dog.

The Film

Directed by Michael Winner. Screenplay: Arnold Schulman, Jane Wagner and Cy Howard. Produced by David V. Picker, Arnold Schulman, Michael Winner and Tim Zinnemann. Music: Neal Hefti. Cinematography: Richard H. Kline. Editor: Bernard Gribble. Art director: Ward Preston. Set decorator: Ned Parsons. Makeup: Billy Laughridge, Phil Rhodes and Claude Diaz. Sound: Bob Post and Terry Rawlings. Dates of production: August 25 to November 12, 1975. Released by Paramount on May 26, 1976. 92 minutes.

Cast: The Ritz Brothers (Jimmy and Harry) (Charwomen), Augustus von Schumacher (Won Ton Ton), Dennis Morgan (Tour guide), Shecky Greene (Tourist), Phil Leeds, Cliff Norton (Dog catchers), Madeline Kahn (Estie Del Ruth), Teri Garr (Fluffy Peters), Romo Vincent, Keye Luke (Cooks), Bruce Dern (Grayson Potchuck), Sterling Holloway, William "Billy" Benedict, Dorothy Gulliver (Passengers on bus), William Demarest (Studio gatekeeper), Art Carney (J.J. Fromberg), Virginia Mayo (Miss Battley), Henny Youngman (Manny Farber), Rory Calhoun (Philip Hart), Billy Barty (Assistant director), Henry Wilcoxon (Silent film director), Richard Arlen, Ricardo Montalban (Silent film stars), Johnny Weissmuller, Jackie Coogan (Stagehands), Aldo Ray (Stubby Stebbins), Ethel Merman (Hedda Parsons), Yvonne De Carlo (Cleaning woman), Joan Blondell (Landlady), Andy Devine (Priest in dog pound), Broderick Crawford (Special effects man), Jack La Rue (Silent film villain), Dorothy Lamour (Visiting film star), Phil Silvers (Murray Fromberg), Nancy Walker (Mrs. Fromberg), Cyd Charisse, Janet Blair, Ann Miller, Gloria DeHaven (President's girls), Louis Nye (Radio interviewer), Stepin Fetchit

(Dancing butler), Ken Murray (Souvenir salesman), Rudy Vallee (Autograph hound), George Jessel (Awards announcer), Rhonda Fleming (Rhoda [sic] Fleming), Dean Stockwell (Paul Lavell), Dick Haymes (Dick Crawford), Tab Hunter (David Hamilton), Robert Alda (Richard Entwhistle), Eli Mintz (Tailor), Ron Leibman (Rudy Montague), Fritz Feld, Edward Ashley (Rudy's butlers), Kres Mersky (Girl in Arab Film), Jane Connell (Waitress), Dennis Day (Singing telegraph man), Mike Mazurki (Studio guard), Jesse White (Rudy's agent), Carmel Myers, Jack Carter (Journalists), Jack Bernardi (Fluffy's escort), Victor Mature (Nick), Barbara Nichols (Nick's girl), Army Archerd (Emcee at premiere), Fernando Lamas, Zsa Zsa Gabor (Stars at premiere), Huntz Hall (Moving man), Doodles Weaver (Man in Mexican film), Pedro Gonzales-Gonzales (Mexican projectionist), Eddie Le Vecque (Prostitute's customer), Edgar Bergen (Professor Quicksand), Ronny Graham (Mark Bennett), Morey Amsterdam, Eddie Foy Jr. (Custard pie stars), Peter Lawford (Slapstick star), Guy Madison, Patricia Morison (Stars at screening), Regis Toomey (Burlesque stagehand), Alice Faye (Secretary at gate), Ann Rutherford (Studio secretary), Milton Berle (Blind man), James Brodhead (Priest), John Carradine (Drunk), Walter Pidgeon (Grayson's butler).

    Among the uncredited performers in the film are old pros Douglas Fowley, Morgan Farley, Tom Pedi and Leon Belasco. Jimmy and Harry Ritz are also among the unbilled players, another sign that they had been relegated to the ranks of the mostly forgotten. Their brief cameo as charwomen harks back to 1937's *You Can't Have Everything* in which they dress as charwomen to get into an all-girls boardinghouse. The person they come to see in that film is Alice Faye, who also has a cameo in this film. Among the Ritzes' other former co-stars are Ethel Merman and Richard Arlen.

    This film marked the final cinema appearance of Jimmy Ritz, Stepin Fetchit, Rudy Vallee, George Jessel, Ann Rutherford, Andy Devine, Johnny Weissmuller and William Demarest. So many *Won Ton Ton* actors had died by the mid–1980s that a joke went around Hollywood that director Michael Winner had killed them all with his poor directing.

    Synopsis: A tour group stopping at the forecourt of Grauman's Chinese Theatre in Hollywood is told about Won Ton Ton, the famous dog star of silent film days. The German shepherd's story begins when he escapes from a dog pound and frees the other dogs. At the same time, aspiring actress Estie Del Ruth is hitchhiking to an audition because she cannot afford bus fare. To stop a ride, she sticks out her leg but causes four cars to collide. She hides behind a trash can in which the dog is "dining." When he emerges, he licks her face and they become friends.

    A juicy roast turkey falls off a catering truck and they both contend for it. All is forgiven when Estie cries. They head for New Era Pictures where she has her audition. Grayson Potchuck, a bus driver, arrives at the studio with a screenplay about a shark which attacks a New England town. A mogul scoffs at the idea and rejects it.

Estie arrives and the dog waits for her at the studio gate. She thinks her audition is with a director but he is actually a stagehand. The cad takes her into a back room and tells her to undress; she refuses unless he guarantees her a job, which he is in no position to do. The dog senses her peril, jumps the fence and rescues her. This is witnessed by studio executive J.J. Fromberg, who announces his intention to star the dog in a film. The bus driver has also seen this, and claims the dog is his.

The dog follows Estie home. She cannot have a dog in her apartment so she chains him up outside. The dog is nabbed by the dogcatcher but Grayson sees this and follows the dog to the pound where he barters his tour bus for the dog, thus rescuing him from being killed. He names him Won Ton Ton and claims he got the dog from a Chinese railroad worker. Fromberg hires Grayson as a writer-director; Grayson hires Estie as the dog's trainer and promises her a job as an actress as well.

She trains Won Ton Ton to do many stunts for which Grayson takes the credit. The dog's first film is a hit and he becomes a great star. Estie gets a role in one of his next pictures but trouble follows her. The dog attacks the leading man in a fit of jealousy; Estie is kicked off the picture because she "makes the dog nervous." Grayson presents her with a beachside mansion paid for with Won Ton Ton's earnings. He would like to move in with her but she rebuffs him, insisting on separate rooms. She does not believe that the dog will perform as well without her as his trainer.

Grayson tries to solve the problem of Estie's studio ouster by disguising her in various ways so she can get back in. On a night when she is disguised as a waitress, the dog wins an award and trots over to give it to her. Fromberg has her ejected again even though most of Hollywood knows that she is responsible for the dog's talent. Grayson promises he will try to reason with the mogul.

For his next film, *Custer the Brave,* Won Ton Ton gets actor Rudy Montague as his co-star. Unbeknownst to the studio, he is a cross-dresser. When he goes to a theater to watch his latest picture, he sees Estie in the crowd, overcome with emotion at his performance. At first he conceals his identity from her but realizes she is the one who made the dog a star. When she admits she would like to be an actress, he tells her who he is and promises to make her a star.

Grayson offers to direct Rudy's next film and accepts Rudy's suggestion to have Estie as his leading lady. During a press conference, Estie is revealed as the woman behind Won Ton Ton, leaving Rudy feeling upstaged. He is so upset that he hires Nick, a killer, to eliminate Estie, Grayson and the dog. Fortunately, Nick is incompetent. *Custer the Brave* is a failure and the dog, Estie and Grayson are reduced to sharing an apartment.

Grayson continues to write screenplays and the women resort to low occupations like pornography and prostitution. Desperate, Estie sells Won Ton Ton to Professor Quicksand, a dog trainer who is cruel to his animals, a fact of which she is unaware. Another director who has seen her in *Custer the Brave* thinks she will make a good slapstick comedienne because her acting in that film was so terrible.

She becomes a star and helps Grayson to get his own studio. They offer a reward to reclaim Won Ton Ton but do not find him; he has become a seeing eye dog. Estie and Grayson are going to be married; on their way to the ceremony, Won Ton Ton spots them and gives chase. He is unable to get into the church and is so despondent that he attempts suicide in various ways, including putting his head in an oven, lying in the middle of a road, putting his head in a noose and knocking the chair away, and finally running into the ocean surf in front of Estie's mansion. Estie and Grayson save him. Some reporters witness the rescue and ask if the dog is Won Ton Ton; Estie replies that he is just an ordinary dog.

* * *

Three German shepherds played Won Ton Ton, although it was claimed that the bulk of the heroics were performed by credited doggy star Augustus von Schumacher. One hopes that he was easier to work with than the original Rin Tin Tin. That dog had supposedly been found as an abandoned puppy by Lee Duncan on a World War I battlefield in 1918. He always remained a one-man dog. To others he was a surly biter, the bane of his co-stars. In addition he was not a very handsome looking dog, being a bit on the small side and of a color not favored by many shepherd lovers. Like all silent stars who made the transition to talkies, his "voice" was judged, one 1929 reviewer saying that "he barked huskily."

Reviews

"This project might have worked to a degree of whimsy, but the alchemy in the direction [of Michael Winner] has turned potential cotton candy into reinforced concrete." *Variety*, May 5, 1976.

"Sixty guest stars can't save [the film] from its unrelentingly crass tone and steady stream of unfunny jokes." *Los Angeles Times*, May 26, 1976.

"What saves the movie, a jumble of good jokes and bad, sloppiness, chaos, and apparently any old thing that came to hand, is Madeline Kahn.... The movie itself is an untidy, sometimes pleasant mess, a string of sight and situation gags strung along on a minimal plot." *New York Times*, May 27, 1976.

"A scattershot comedy that can't make up its mind whether to be a wholesome family entertainment or a smutty film industry in-joke. It goes both ways." *Chicago Tribune*, May 31, 1976.

"Michael Winner does not have Mel Brooks' frenzied gift for marshaling this kind of material; and to make matters worse the script attains a level of parody no higher than ... the mincing caricature of [Rudolph] Valentino." *The Monthly Film Bulletin*, August 1976.

"Is [this] the worst movie ever made? It's a comedy that has zero laughs.... It's a heartless film; every human being in it is worthless.... It's racist and homophobic, but the greater insult is to the whole of humanity." Modern-day commentator.

Silent Movie *(1976)*

The History

After defying tradition and shooting *Young Frankenstein* in black and white, Mel Brooks again defied conventional wisdom by pitching a silent movie. He wanted to make it completely silent but ultimately added sound effects and music. In a 2013 PBS interview, he also acknowledged that he wanted to give something back to Sid Caesar, on whose iconic early 1950s TV comedy series *Your Show of Shows* he had been a writer.

In *Silent Movie*, Caesar played a harried studio head and Brooks had his first starring role. He had appeared in several of his earlier films but only as an ensemble player. The cost of the film was reported to be in the range of $6,000,000. If the publicity was to be believed, such cameo players as Paul Newman, Liza Minnelli, Burt Reynolds and James Caan were only paid $138 a day.

The Film

Directed by Mel Brooks. Produced by Michael Hertzberg. Screenplay: Mel Brooks, Ron Clark, Rudy De Luca and Barry Levinson. Story: Ron Clark. Music: John Morris. Cinematography: Paul Lohmann. Editors: Stanford C. Allen and John C. Howard. Production designer: Albert Brenner. Set decorator: Rick Simpson. Costume designer: Patricia Norris. Makeup: William Tuttle. Sound: Don Hall. Dates of production: January 5 to March 5, 1976.

Produced by Crossbow Productions; distributed by Twentieth Century–Fox and released on June 30, 1976. 87 minutes.

Cast: Mel Brooks (Mel Funn), Marty Feldman (Marty Eggs), Dom DeLuise (Dom Bell), Sid Caesar (Studio chief), Harold Gould (Engulf), Ron Carey (Devour), Bernadette Peters (Vilma Kaplan), Carol Arthur (Pregnant lady), Liam Dunn (News dealer), Fritz Feld (Maitre d'), Chuck McCann (Studio guard), Valerie Curtin (Nurse), Yvonne Wilder (Secretary), Harry Ritz (Man Coming from Tailor Shop), Charlie Callas (Blind man), Henny Youngman (Man in restaurant), Arnold Soboloff (Acupuncture man), Patrick Campbell (Bellhop), Eddie Ryder (British officer), Al Hopson, Rudy DeLuca, Barry Levinson, Howard Hesseman, Lee Delano, Jack Riley (Executives), Inga Neilsen, Erica Hagen (Beautiful blondes), Robert Lussier (Projectionist), Burt Reynolds, James Caan, Liza Minnelli, Paul Newman, Anne Bancroft, Marcel Marceau (Guest stars).

Synopsis: Recovering alcoholic movie director Mel Funn and his two zany sidekicks Marty Eggs and Dom Bell (i.e., Dumbbell) pitch a silent movie to the head of Big Picture Studios, whose motto is "If It's a Big One We Make It Here." When presented with the idea, the boss parrots the conventional line: "Don't you know that slapstick is dead!" whereupon in the best slapstick tradition he slides across the floor and crashes into a wall.

Marty and Dom fear that such a rejection will cause Mel to relapse. But during the meeting, the boss learns that the greedy conglomerate Engulf and Devour plan to take over if the studio does not show a profit within a month's time. After Funn says he can land big stars, the boss agrees to greenlight the film.

Using various methods including dressing up as medieval knights, having a wheelchair race, and performing in a nightclub, they talk Burt Reynolds, James Caan, Liza Minnelli, Paul Newman and Anne Bancroft into appearing. The film simultaneously satirizes those very stars for their egotism. The only one to refuse is French mime Marcel Marceau, who naturally has the only word spoken out loud in the film: "Non!"

The studio boss, hospitalized, is almost killed when the goofy trio fools around with the machines he is plugged into. To stop production, the evil head of Engulf and Devour hires sultry singer Vilma Kaplan to vamp Funn. She succeeds in her plot until Funn is shown a large check made out to Vilma for "Pretending to be in love with Mel Funn." He resumes drinking, and when he falls off the wagon he really falls off! He staggers exaggeratedly around the streets, emerging from a liquor store with an enormously oversized bottle of booze. Vilma realizes she really does love Funn and quits her vamping job. They find a drunken Funn under a pile of down-and-out winos and pour him full of coffee. Amped up, he makes the film, and a preview is scheduled.

Just before the preview, the villains try to burn the film. They are foiled by someone snatching it from inside the fireplace chimney, but they do succeed in stealing the film and a car chase ensues. It is the film's final nod to silent comedy. The heroes fend off the villains by lobbing explosive Coke cans at them. Although Marty has entangled himself in the film in an attempt to rewind it, the projectionist manages to salvage it and the film is shown to the preview audience. They receive it rapturously.

* * *

Some of the foreign titles for this film included Brooks' name. In some Spanish-speaking countries, it was *La Ultima Locura de Mel Brooks*; the French had it as *La Derniere Folle de Mel Brooks*; in Italy, *L'Ultima Follia di Mel Brooks*, and the equivalent German *Mel Brooks Letzte Verruckheit*. In other words: *The Last Craziness of Mel Brooks*; or in Brooks Yiddish-speak: *Mishegoss*.

Because of its lack of dialogue and questions about how it would be received, the film was rolled out slowly. It played in limited release at first, supposedly earning $2 million in that initial release. It was then played in small movie houses which charged $1 admission, but Brooks felt it was being overexposed and these screenings were discontinued.

In this, his final film appearance, Harry Ritz is literally given only a few seconds onscreen, the very briefest of cameos. He is the man emerging from a tailor shop wearing a half-finished suit. If it were not known he was in the movie, his appearance might go totally unnoticed. This is almost true as well for Henny Youngman's jokey "There's a fly in my soup" appearance. Although Sid Caesar has a much more substantial role, he is regrettably absent from the entire middle part of the film.

Silent Movie features many referential nods to classic films, including the studio boss lighting two cigars at once (shades of Paul Henreid in *Now, Voyager*), but then smoking them both himself; the chariot race from *Ben-Hur* done with wheelchairs, and Rudolph Valentino's tango done as flamenco. Brooks dubs the big conglomerate out to take over the studio as Engulf and Devour (motto: "Our fingers are in everything"), surely a dig at Gulf and Western and other corporate conglomerates with little or no filmmaking experience.

Sid Caesar's eye rolls are very reminiscent of Harry Ritz's, perhaps intentionally done as a tribute, or merely part of the longtime shtick he acknowledged as a debt to Ritz. Sight gags include getting a foot crushed in a slammed door, a kiosk owner knocked down by a bundle of newspapers tossed from a delivery truck, and a swaying trailer. Less politically correct today is the repeated reference to supposed gay men as "fags," a word Harry Ritz often used himself in routines.

We also get a visible light bulb designating an idea; playing the video game Pong with a hospital monitor; corporate bigwigs praying to a dollar sign; the evil Engulf frothing at the mouth; serial slapping (*à la* the Three Stooges); a blind man mistaking the wrong dog for his guide dog; a pie in the face, and an encounter with a Murphy bed. In one scene, a huge Coca-Cola machine shoots out its contents willy-nilly. It may or may not be that funny, but it is surely a most blatant product placement.

A brief bit parodies a Fred Astaire-Ginger Rogers dance, something that has nothing to do with silent film. Even the final car chase, a great opportunity for building excitement, is oddly truncated. Marty Feldman seems be channeling silent comic Ben Turpin, which because of Feldman's strabismus condition was the intent.

What some would call bad taste has long been ignored by Brooks; this has frequently been what makes his greatest comedies great. He has always been fearless in pushing comedy to its extremes. This may not measure up to his very best work, although in at least one survey it was rated toward the top of his *oeuvre*.

The film received four Golden Globe nominations in 1977: Best Motion Picture in the Musical Comedy category; Best Motion Picture Actor in that same category for Mel Brooks; Best Motion Picture Actor in a Supporting Role for Marty Feldman, and Best Motion Picture Actress in a Supporting Role for Bernadette Peters.

In 2011, the French-made silent comedy-drama *The Artist* received rapturous reviews and multiple awards.

Reviews

"You might suspect that Mel Brooks' decision to make a contemporary silent movie starring himself as a director trying to make a silent movie was not the wisest thing he'd ever done, and you'd be right, but you can enjoy [the film] as a virtually uninterrupted series of smiles.... It is not the greatest movie Mr. Brooks has made ... but it could be one of the nicest things you'll see all summer." *New York Times*, July 1, 1976.

"Right from the opening seconds we all know that [the film] is going to be very silly indeed.... The trouble is it's the kind of silliness that's too strained and self-indulgent to be enjoyable.... Brooks himself combines frenzy with grace, and there are occasional moments of barmy splendor." *Time Out* (London).

"Mel Brooks will do anything for a laugh, anything. He has no shame.... [The film] is not only funny it's fun. It's clear at almost every moment that the filmmakers had a ball making it. The thing about Brooks' inside jokes is that their outsides are funny too." *Roger Ebert*, July 1, 1976.

"There are a huge amount of funny scenes offered in this flick. I almost laughed my lungs out." Modern-day commentator.

"A ridiculous film in many ways.... To a large extent [it] exists to enable a series of gags, mostly centered on various extended cameos." Modern-day commentator.

"[Brooks] is not just making us laugh through slapstick and pun-filled dialogue, he's also saying a lot of very intelligent things about the medium of film, as well as the relationship between film and reality." Modern-day commentator.

"It was presumptuous to think [Brooks] could make a silent movie. The comic situations he's thought up are just so elementary. It's just a disconnected series of gags sewed Frankenstein-style onto the skeleton of finding big-time stars to be in Mel Funn's movie." Modern-day commentator.

"I like Mel Brooks' broad slapsticky humor ... and while I admire his conceit in launching an almost literally silent movie it just doesn't come off. Perhaps the problem here is Brooks straining too much to emulate the silent masters." Modern-day commentator.

"It's one of his more brilliant and inventive ideas and it gets the wacky screen treatment you expect from Brooks.... It's full of the usual sight gags, everything that happened in a Keystone Cops comedy." Modern-day commentator.

The Short Subjects

Hotel Anchovy *(1934)*

The History

The Ritz Brothers were signed in March 1934 to appear in movie shorts for Educational Pictures, but because of heavy vaudeville commitments, their work on *Hotel Anchovy* had to be moved back. I could find no definitive record of whether they had previously been approached by any other movie studios.

In the aftermath of this film, both Educational and Warner Brothers announced that the Ritzes would be signed for additional shorts.

Educational publicized six additional shorts; Warners announced a program of 20 "Big V" comedies. Three of these were to star Canadian comic Ben Blue; two were to co-star Shemp Howard and Daphne Pollard, and two would star the Ritz Brothers. Oldest brother Al Ritz served as family spokesman to announce that no further shorts would be undertaken. In May 1934, both studios announced that decision as well.

The Film

Produced and Directed by Al Christie. Story: Art Jarrett and William Watson. Photographed: George Webber. Produced at Eastern Service Studios. Released by Educational Pictures, April 13, 1934. (Distributed by Fox Pictures.) An Educational Coronet Comedy. Production number 0315. 17 minutes.

Cast: Al Ritz (Al, hotel detective), Harry Ritz (Harry, hotel manager), Jimmy Ritz (Jimmy, bellboy), Doris Hill (Miss Whitney), Robert Middlemass (Mr. Kane), Harry Short (Mr. Pierce), Eddie Roberts (Suicidal guest).

Synopsis: Miss Whitney, owner of the Hotel Anchovy, is looking for a buyer for the hotel, which is in debt. In a last minute effort to save it, she hires the Ritz Brothers and tells them that for every guest who stays, they get $100; for every guest who leaves, they pay $100. The oft-repeated "Super service!" becomes their motto as they strive to please everyone.

This involves such antics as pouring water into the phone of a guest who has called asking for ice water, and helping a suicidal guest succeed in his quest by mixing a poisonous cocktail—which Harry samples without consequences. The guest keeps jumping out of his room window but always survives. Mr. Kane, a prospective buyer, arrives to make a very low bid. Another potential buyer, Mr. Pierce, is on his way but has not yet arrived.

To forestall the sale to Mr. Kane, or to get him to raise his bid, the Ritzes all dress like the supposed Mr. Pierce and thoroughly confuse Kane. At one point, all of them show up at the exact same time. When the real Pierce arrives, more pandemonium breaks out. Ultimately Pierce is so confused by the Ritz shenanigans that he offers Miss Whitney a very good price.

* * *

The motto of Educational Pictures was "The Spice of the Program," and its imaginative logo showed the studio name swirling out of an Arabian Nights magic lamp. Educational introduced the Ritz Brothers to the cinema in 1934. They emerge pretty much in their full glory, personas and routines already honed by a decade of performing their act. The credits list them with their name above the title as The Three Ritz Brothers, and the cast list in alphabetical order: Al, Harry, Jimmy Ritz.

The Brothers pretty much get equal screen time. Harry does at least a few of the bits he became known for, including looking sideways while counting the money in front of him, and the famous stumbling walk. More could have made of the gag where Harry drinks the poisoned cocktail; it would have been a perfect spot for his famous facial contortions.

They all do a brief tap dance and song, talents that they would elaborate upon in their features. Other shtick include turning several times in a revolving door with them grabbing at a brass ring as if it were a carousel, and house detective Al listening at doors with a stethoscope.

There is perhaps more than a passing resemblance to the first Marx Brothers film *The Cocoanuts* (1929) which also takes place in a hotel with Groucho as the manager, a role he was to repeat. Except for the Ritz Brothers' own tested routines, there is nothing really original about *Hotel Anchovy*. The gags are old but the Ritzes are new, and it is a creditable if not outstanding debut. They were all young then—Harry being only 27 at the time; the others in their early thirties.

An advertisement for Educational's Big Star Two Reel Comedies appeared in the *Motion Picture Herald* in 1934. Along with featuring the latest Buster Keaton short, it asked theater owners: "Have you played those nutty Three Ritz Brothers in *Hotel Anchovy*—they're a circus all by themselves." Because this film was released as part of the Coronet series, an ad touted: "Every new Coronet is a surprise and a rare laugh treat."

Another ad trumpeted: "Monotony is out of the show where Educational's short subjects add spice and variety to the program.... Always something new and different." One of the "new and different" things was "The screen debut of those popular 'nut' comics, The Three Ritz Brothers." It referred to *Hotel Anchovy* as "A fast and furious frolic of fun."

Educational was superior to some other lower ranking studios they could have worked with, having featured many talented people on their way up: Bing Crosby, Bob Hope, Bert Lahr, Joan Davis, Danny Kaye, June Allyson and Shirley Temple. There also were many talents on their unfortunate slide downwards: Roscoe "Fatty" Arbuckle (who directed for Educational under the pseudonym of William Goodrich), Harry Langdon, Louise Brooks and Buster Keaton. The latter made more than 15 shorts there before moving to Columbia.

The company was founded in the silent era as a distributor of instructional films for schools, hence its name. The production of comedies proved much more financially rewarding and through the silent years it did well. The

Depression brought major problems but it limped along through the 1930s. Much of its silent output is said to have been lost in a fire.

Hotel Anchovy was shot in Astoria, Queens, New York, where many early Paramount films were made. The Ritzes were fortunate to have the very experienced Al Christie as the director of their first film foray. Of course it always seemed questionable that the Ritz Brothers could be conventionally directed by anyone, a supposition fostered by their nihilistic brand of comedy.

Hotel Anchovy leading lady Doris Hill made one of her last film appearance in a brief role. Gruff-voiced Robert Middlemass was the best known of the supporting players; he made over 100 film appearances to 1947. He often played grumpy characters and was usually in small, sometimes uncredited supporting roles.

After the picture's release, Educational publicity said that the Ritzes were taken to the Roxy Theatre in New York where the film opened, to see if they laughed at themselves. The short was then booked to play on the entire RKO Metropolitan Circuit. Both that fact and the prestigious opening venue may have spoken to the perceived value of the Ritz Brothers brand. It was then that Educational announced that they had taken an option to sign the Ritzes for another six shorts.

Reviews

"The last laugh in looniness, and the first laugh and all the other laffs in between. So far as we are concerned there's nothing like 'em in pix. They pull their own brand of goofy nuttiness." *Film Daily*, April 26, 1934.

"One of the worst efforts we have played. Have failed to get any shorts from Fox [Educational Pictures' distributors] that had any laughs." Manager, Lync Theatre, Jefferson, Texas.

"I didn't hear much laughing on this." Manager, Eminence Theatre, Eminence, Kentucky.

"The Ritzes almost remind me of three Grouchos in their characterization…. They're probably most famous today for not being the Marx Brothers…. That doesn't mean I don't think they're funny." Modern-day commentator.

"The film's maniacal pacing combined with Ritz Brothers fancy 'hoofing,' their rapid fire wisecracking, their uncanny ability to move as one … somehow blended smoothly and gave us a sort of figurative 'Stooges on speed' farce." Modern-day commentator.

"I have never understood why the Ritz Brothers were considered a comedy team. At least the Marx Brothers and the Three Stooges made you laugh…. I have never heard anyone under 90 mention the Ritz Brothers." Modern-day commentator.

"Of all the comedy teams that ended up in the movies in the 1930s, the Ritz Brothers were probably the most unrestrained ever and are probably not as appreciated as a result…. This is probably where Sid Caesar and Mel Brooks got their inspiration, so for that we fully thank them." Modern-day commentator.

Broadway Highlights, #6: High Spots of the Main Stem *(1936)*

The History

Broadway Highlights was a short-lived series of one-reel short subjects produced by Paramount Pictures. The first one was released on May 17, 1935, with the subtitle *Paramount Varieties*. The series ended with Number 8 in December 1936. The introduction at the beginning of each: "Adolph Zukor Presents Broadway Highlights: Intimate News of the Great White Way." As the title indicates, each segment looked at current Broadway shows and prominent Big Apple personalities. Zukor was the founder and longtime head of Paramount.

The Film

Directed by Fred Waller. Editors: Fred Waller, Milton Hocky and Carl Timlin. Narrated by Ted Husing. Released by Paramount on April 20, 1936. 9 minutes.

Cast includes: The Ritz Brothers, Robert Ripley, Rube Goldberg, Jimmy Walker, Edward G. Robinson.

Synopsis: The Ritz Brothers do an imitation of once-famous bandleader Ted Lewis.

* * *

This is one of the Ritz Brothers' very first film appearances after their debut in the 1934 short *Hotel Anchovy*. It precedes the release of their first feature *Sing, Baby, Sing*, which opened in August 1936. Their segment may have been captured on film while they were doing their nightclub act. The Ted Lewis imitation was repeated in their 1942 Universal film *Behind the Eight Ball*.

Among the other personalities in this short subject are Robert Ripley, known for his long-running feature *Believe It or Not*, a radio, newspaper, film and TV phenomenon; Rube Goldberg, the cartoonist famous for his complex wacky inventions, and Jimmy Walker, the dapper former mayor of New York City.

Ted Husing was a well-known radio personality who narrated scores of film shorts and who was best known for his sports analysis. The term "Main Stem" that appears in the subtitle of this film was one of the many appellations applied to that part of Broadway which housed the theater district.

Cinema Circus (1937)

Directed by Roy Rowland. Produced by Louis Lewyn for Louis Lewyn Productions. Written by John Krafft. Technicolor cinematography by Aldo Ermini. Technicolor color director, Natalie Kalmus. Released by MGM on January 27, 1937. 19 minutes.

Cast: Lee Tracy (Ringmaster), The Ritz Brothers, The California Collegians, The Marcus Show Girls, The Fanchonettes, The Gay Boys, Gladys Ahern, Will Ahern, Baby Le Roy, George Barbier, Rex Bell, Leo Carrillo, Chester Conklin, Cliff Edwards, Alice Faye, James Gleason, William S. Hart, Chic Johnson, Ole Olsen, Boris Karloff, Hank Mann, Charlie Murray, Mickey Rooney, Fred Stone, Ben Turpin, Dixie Dunbar, Bob Burns, Allan Jones, Pert Kelton, Jack La Rue, Billy Lee, Martha Raye.

Synopsis: Whistle-blowing ringmaster Lee Tracy introduces several circus acts, an acrobat wedding and a parade of circus animals. Some movie stars do their own acts in a tent. Other stars watch, sometimes interacting with the circus performers. In the stands, Alice Faye holds a baby chimpanzee in her arms and suave Jack La Rue sits among his adoring lady friends.

The Ritz Brothers do an imitation of the Three Stooges; Mickey Rooney shows up in a gorilla suit at the finale with Olsen and Johnson; Cliff Edwards, in coonskin cap and buckskins, rides into an Indian village in a covered wagon and does a "Ukulele Ike" number complete with falsetto; Pert Kelton and other shapely ladies dance as skimpily dressed Indian maidens; Fred Stone and old-time cowboys William S. Hart and Rex Bell do rope tricks; professional hillbilly Bob Burns plays his bazooka; and silent comics Ben Turpin, Hank Mann and Chester Conklin sing a music hall song. The parade of animals is led by performers wearing giant cartoonish heads of famous movie stars who are not there: Clark Gable, Jimmy Durante, Wallace Beery, Joe E. Brown and Eddie Cantor.

* * *

This film is shot in an attractively muted pastel-like Technicolor with a cast of silent comics, current comedy stars, dancers and actual circus performers. The occasional serious actor can also be glimpsed including ringmaster Lee Tracy, the epitome of fast-talking and fast-hustling newspapermen, agents and others of that ilk in 1930s comedies and melodramas.

Despite all of the recognizable stars, an MGM advertising poster printed in the muted colors of the film only publicizes the names of cinematographer Aldo Ermini and the omnipresent Technicolor supervisor Natalie Kalmus. The background is dominated by the instantly recognizable towers of the iconic 100,000 square foot Pan Pacific Auditorium where the film was shot. The Auditorium, with its four arched towers and tall flagpoles, opened in 1935. It was home to sporting events, circuses and other events until it closed in 1972. Its famous art moderne exterior was seen in many motion pictures even after its closing. It was eventually listed as a historic landmark, but neglect caused it to deteriorate and it burned down in 1989.

The popularity of *Cinema Circus* in 1937 was probably because short subjects had only begun to be shot in the expensive Technicolor process a few years earlier. They were still relatively rare, especially in the pastel color of this film. Upon release, it garnered positive feedback. However, modern eyes may regard it differently. In an ultimate example of damning with faint praise, one modern-day reviewer states that in the context of this "drunken miscellany churned out with obvious contempt for audience and performers alike," even the Ritz Brothers seem normal!

Reviews

"Swell. A very elaborate and gorgeous circus production … and 25 screen stars taking part." *The Film Daily*, March 6, 1937.

"Blending circus atmosphere with caricatured film personalities, and with the audience composed of varied performers, this two-reel novelty done in Technicolor unreels as first-rate entertainment." *Motion Picture Daily*, March 9, 1937.

"[William S. Hart] has finally come out of his retirement and made a picture. Bill is his old self in it and bearing his years well. He does a little riding and roping, the sort you have craved to see him in, you oldtimers." [Hart made his last full-length film in 1925.] *Hollywood Magazine*, April 1937.

"An entertaining hodgepodge…." *National Board of Review Magazine*, April 1937.

"This elaborate Technicolor short merits marquee billing and can very well replace the second feature on [double bills]. [It's] a veritable 25-star circus." *Boxoffice*, April 17, 1937.

"Two reels packed full of entertainment. Once again we say Metro should pattern all their two-reel musicals after this type." *Motion Picture Herald*, August 1937.

"[It] was well received. Our patrons like pictures of this type." Manager, Star Theatre, Bay Springs, Nebraska.

"A very good color film of a circus, with many interesting movie folks. Should be popular for the kids." Manager, Plaza Theatre, Tilbury, Ontario.

"There's an annoying segment with the Ritz Brothers aping the Three Stooges (and not very well).... Overall there's not much to it." Modern-day commentator.

"Practically plotless.... It's a bizarre circus.... You see mostly B- and C-list stars like the Ritz Brothers, Olsen and Johnson.... A strange collection of acts and a really weird finale." Modern-day commentator.

"I've seen quite a few of these 'show off the stars' shorts, and there's no question that this one here is the most boring. Yes, it was fun seeing the stars and yes, the Technicolor looks amazing, but this is really all there is. ...I was deadly bored." Modern-day commentator.

"Big top performers trot out their tricks in brief visual bits, watched by earnestly faking-it 'stars,' few remembered in the contemporary pantheon: The Ritz Brothers, Olsen and Johnson, Leo Carrillo.... Allows for only the most disappointing kind of entertainment.... MGM's idea of how to use silent comedians has not improved since they ruined Buster Keaton." Modern-day commentator.

Screen Snapshots

The History

The Ritz Brothers together or separately appear in a few of the *Screen Snapshots* short subjects produced by Columbia between 1922 and 1958. These mostly one-reel films purport to show celebrities being "real" at work and play. These little films do not only spotlight those people under Columbia contracts; talent from any studio might be featured in a *Screen Snapshots*. Most of these shorts were in numbered series up to 1949, after which they also received subtitles. As many as 20 or 25 were produced annually. Various websites contain descriptions of some of them; one purports to be a complete listing (see Bibliography).

Columbia had a very active short subjects program that employed several well-known comic actors; the Three Stooges were especially prolific and probably are the best-known today. By the time production ceased on the *Screen Snapshots* series, several hundred of them had been produced. As time went on, stock footage from earlier shorts was inserted in many of the later ones. Some of the later ones were shot in Eastman Color.

Originally these shorts were produced under the aegis of Jacob "Jack" Cohn, the younger brother of martinet Columbia boss Harry Cohn. The earlier films were narrated by Eddie Lambert. In the 1930s, their production was put into the hands of Harriet Parsons, daughter of columnist Louella Parsons. When she became a full-time producer at Republic in the early 1940s, the ongoing *Screen Snapshots* series was completely taken over by Ralph Staub. He did yeoman duty, often even doing the camerawork and appearing in many. The deep smooth voice of actor Art Baker can often be heard as narrator.

The Films

The *Screen Snapshots* in which one or all of the Ritz Brothers appear are listed below in chronological order.

Screen Snapshots Series 17, #6 *(1938)*

Produced, directed and written by Ralph Staub; executive producer (uncredited): Harriet Parsons. Released by Columbia on February 4, 1938. 10 minutes.

Cast: The Ritz Brothers, Jack Benny, Joan Crawford, Danielle Darrieux, James Gleason, Lucile Gleason, Fernand Gravey, Mary Livingstone, Gene Morgan, Barbara Stanwyck, Franchot Tone.

Synopsis: The Ritz Brothers put their feet into the cement of Grauman's Chinese Theatre; several stars attend a premiere of Samuel Goldwyn's *The Hurricane* at the Carthay Circle Theatre in Los Angeles; James Gleason brings some film fans to his home and introduces them to stars; a football film is being shot on the campus of Pomona College; French actors Danielle Darrieux and Fernand Gravey arrive at the Pasadena train station.

* * *

The Ritz Brothers' footage is recycled from a *Fox Movietone News* short which captured a publicity appearance at the Chinese Theatre to advertise their first starring film *Life Begins in College* in 1937. It was seen yet again in a 1950 *Screen Snapshots* film. For a full account of the Ritz Brothers' antics at the Chinese Theatre forecourt, see the *Life Begins in College* entry.

This short features three married acting couples: Jack Benny and Mary Livingstone, James and Lucile Gleason, and Joan Crawford and Franchot Tone. The latter couple's nuptial bliss was to end in divorce the following year.

Fernand Gravey was also known as Fernand Gravet. The former spelling was devised to help people who did not speak French to correctly pronounce his surname. Danielle Darrieux, who was about 21 in 1938, had a career that lasted through eight decades. She died at the age of 100 in 2017.

Screen Snapshots, Series 22, #5 *(1942)*

Produced, written, and directed by Ralph Staub. Released by Columbia on December 25, 1942. 10 minutes.

Cast: The Ritz Brothers, Jimmy Durante, George Raft, Xavier Cugat, Marlene Dietrich, Sabu, Constance Moore, George Jessel, James Ellison, Bill Henry, Leo Carrillo, Chris-Pin Martin, Broncho Billy Anderson, Cesar Romero, Richard Ney, Gig Young.

Synopsis: Hollywood personalities are seen during a USO tour to entertain the troops. They are a very eclectic group of performers, from old-time western star Broncho Billy Anderson to new Hollywood talent like Richard Ney and "Elephant Boy" Sabu.

Screen Snapshots, Series 22, #8: Seeing Hollywood *(1943)*

Produced, written and directed by Ralph Staub. Narrated by Alan Mowbray. Released by Columbia on March 26, 1943. 10 minutes.

Cast: The Ritz Brothers, Gene Autry, The Marx Brothers (Chico, Harpo, Groucho), Lou Holtz, Tyrone Power, Annabella, Kay Kyser, Ish Kabibble, Brian Aherne, Ingrid Bergman, Adolphe Menjou, Pat Paterson, Charles Boyer, Irene Rich, Claire Trevor, Jinx Falkenburg, Arthur Lake, Glenn Ford, Christy Mathewson Jr., Michele Morgan, Marjorie Tidesdale, Lee Krieger, The Three Stooges.

Synopsis: Gene Autry leads a tour of Thunderbird Field and Brian Aherne goes to Falcon Air Field; both were Army Air Force bases in the Southwest. The Ritz Brothers, the Marx Brothers and Lou Holtz sell war bonds at the Orpheum Theatre; Tyrone Power and his wife, French actress Annabella, hold a party at their home for Hollywood's Free French contingent with several celebrity guests; Irene Rich visits the Women's Auxiliary Ambulance Corps; bandleader Kay Kyser and his comic sidekick Ish Kabibble are seen selling bonds at Victory House, and the Three Stooges and others visit the Corona Naval Hospital.

Review

"Fans should derive considerable pleasure out of the latest of the series." *Film Daily*, March 31, 1943.

Screen Snapshots, Series 29, #11: Hollywood's Famous Feet (1950)

Produced, directed and written by Ralph Staub. Narrated by Al Jolson. Released by Columbia on July 20, 1950. 8 minutes.

Cast: Ralph Staub, Al Jolson, The Ritz Brothers, Gene Autry, Edgar Bergen, Sid Grauman, The Marx Brothers (Chico, Groucho, Harpo, Zeppo), Tom Mix, Ken Murray, Donna Reed, Shirley Ross, John M. Stahl, John Wayne.

Synopsis: This short tells the story behind the famous forecourt of Sid Grauman's Chinese Theatre in Hollywood. The signatures, hand- and footprints (and sometimes other body parts) of stars (human and otherwise) from the silent era onwards are preserved there in concrete. The Ritz footage from the *Fox Movietone News* is once again recycled in this short. Al Jolson died on October 23, 1950, three months after the release of this short and not long after returning from entertaining American troops in Korea.

Screen Snapshots, Series 31: Memories of Famous Hollywood Comedians (1952)

Produced, directed and written by Ralph Staub. Narrated by Joe E. Brown. Released by Columbia on January 24, 1952. 10 minutes.

Cast: Joe E. Brown, The Ritz Brothers, Bud Abbott, Lou Costello, Gracie Allen, George Burns, Roscoe "Fatty" Arbuckle, Mischa Auer, Jack Benny, Mary Livingstone, Milton Berle, El Brendel, Smiley Burnette, Charles Butterworth, Charles Chaplin, Charley Chase, Andy Clyde, Jerry Colonna, Chester Conklin, Clyde Cook, Bing Crosby, Joan Davis, Jimmy Durante, Louise Fazenda, W.C. Fields, Trixie Friganza, Billy Gilbert, Oliver Hardy, Stan Laurel, Bob Hope, Ole Olsen, Chic Johnson, Kay Kyser, The Marx Brothers (Chico, Harpo, Groucho), Alan Mowbray, Ken Murray, Jack Oakie, Joe Penner, ZaSu Pitts, Martha Raye, Ben Turpin.

Synopsis: Comic actor Joe E. Brown narrates a compilation of filmclips and behind-the-scenes footage of famous movie comedians from the early silent film days to the 1950s.

Screen Snapshots: Hollywood's Invisible Man (1954)

Produced, directed and written by Ralph Staub. Released by Columbia on June 10, 1954. 10 minutes.

Cast: William Lundigan, Ralph Staub, Harry Ritz, Bob Hope, Jerry Colonna, Burgess Meredith, Roy Rogers.

Synopsis: Actor William Lundigan is the guest of producer Ralph Staub as they visit a Hollywood restaurant, The Pirate's Den. There they encounter an eclectic group of male celebrities.

Screen Snapshots: The Great Al Jolson *(1955)*

Produced, directed and written by Ralph Staub. Released by Columbia on June 18, 1955. 10 minutes.

Cast: Al Jolson, Ralph Staub, The Ritz Brothers, The Marx Brothers (Chico, Harpo, Groucho), Gene Autry, L. Wolfe Gilbert, Sidney Clare, M.K. Jerome, Sammy Fain, Harry Ruby, Jean Schwartz, Benny Davis, Isham Jones, Jimmy McHugh, Sid Grauman, Tom Mix, Ken Murray, John Wayne.

Synopsis: A group of film composers and actors pay tribute to the late Al Jolson. The Ritzes and Marx Brothers are together in the same film, but apparently the Marxes appeared in new footage while the Ritz Brothers' appearance was via archival footage.

Hollywood Hobbies *(1939)*

Directed by George Sidney. Produced by Louis Lewyn. Original story and screenplay: Morey Amsterdam. Editor: Tom Biggart. An MGM Miniature. Released by MGM on May 3, 1939. 9 minutes.

Cast: Truman Bradley (Narrator), Joyce Compton, Sally Payne (Tourists), William "Billy" Benedict (Tour guide), The Ritz Brothers, Clark Gable, Allan Jones, Robert Young, Irene Hervey, James Stewart, George Murphy, Reginald Denny, Cesar Romero, Joan Davis, Spencer Tracy, Virginia Bruce, Joe E. Brown, Buster Keaton, James Cagney, Milton Berle, John Boles, Mary Pickford, Arthur Lake, Buddy Ebsen, Tyrone Power, Jane Withers, Carolyn Cagney, Jack Durant, Frank Mitchell, Dick Powell, Nat Pendleton.

Synopsis: Two ditzy female tourists hire a bored tour guide to take them around Hollywood in a jalopy to find stars. First they follow Clark Gable's station wagon to his farm in Encino, where they spy on him making whitewash for the barn.

While lurking at the Bel Air stables owned by Allan Jones and Robert Young, they almost get trampled when the horses jump over the hurdle they have hidden behind. (A sign says "Robert Young, I'm the Pres.; Allan Jones, I'm the Vice.") Irene Hervey (Mrs. Allan Jones) brings out a new colt to show her husband. Reginald Denny is briefly spotted standing outside his model airplane shop.

The two ladies wind up at a celebrity baseball game with the comedians playing against the leading men. The players include Buster Keaton, John Boles, Joe E. Brown, the Ritz Brothers, Milton Berle and Buddy Ebsen. Mary Pickford is shown throwing out the first ball. Harry Ritz gives comic Joe E. Brown a smooch on the lips, while Al and Jimmy Ritz do a little dance with each other.

Arthur Lake, whom the game announcer calls Daggy because of his role as the movies' Dagwood Bumstead, does an amusing play-by-play. Other celebrities are very briefly visible in the crowd. The tourists look for their favorite stars James Stewart and George Murphy, not realizing they are standing right in back of them. When the actors offer to give them autographs, the women think they are mashers; they faint when they finally realize who the men are.

* * *

MGM's in-house publication *Metro-Goldwyn-Mayer Short Story* described *Hollywood Hobbies* as a film "that looks behind the klieg lights and discovers just what the city is like when it lets its hair down." It is likely that a short such as this would have been intended mainly for those less discerning small town and rural moviegoers. They may have more readily believed that this was a candid look at some of their favorite celebrities.

Besides Wrigley Field where the baseball game was shot, the Los Angeles locations seen in this film include the Café Trocadero; the tony neighborhood of Bel Air; West Hollywood and the Sunset Strip. There were also typical local Hollywood joints like the Coffee Cup Café and the Pup Eat 'n' Sup.

Most of the scenes—in fact, probably everything that does not involve either the tourists or their guide—were recycled from other shorts. The celebrities who are momentarily glimpsed in the crowd seem to be at the horse races rather than a ball game. The only actual contact between the two women and the stars is that with James Stewart and George Murphy. Neither of the men was then the star he was later to become.

Joyce Compton made an entire career, lasting from the silent days, playing an eternally dumb redhead in numerous films. Sally Payne had a respectable career beginning in the mid–1930s, but ultimately made little splash in the Hollywood talent pool. William Benedict also had a lengthy career with more than 300 roles to his credit.

George Sidney finally got out of directing shorts like this one and became a feature director in the early 1940s, helming *The Harvey Girls, Anchors Aweigh* and *Kiss Me Kate*. He directed prestige films into the 1960s. Morey Amsterdam became best known for playing the irrepressible comedy writer Buddy Sorrell on the popular 1960 sitcom *The Dick Van Dyke Show*.

The baseball game footage was shot during one of the annual Hollywood celebrity games, this one possibly being from 1937. A modern-day blogger commented, "[T]he Ritz Brothers laugh team wears outfits more indicative of jailbirds than their reputed position of umpires." They played on both sides, took tickets, umpired and "shot" crooner Dick Powell as he stole second base.

The comic kiss on the lips between Harry Ritz and "The Mouth" Joe E. Brown, and the shot of Al and Jimmy Ritz waltzing with each other, is typical of their humor. In their nightclub appearances and feature film specialties, they frequently incorporated what might be termed gay references. *Variety* had years earlier criticized their nightclub act for what the publication called too much "pansy stuff." For the Ritz Brothers, this kind of shtick could have been meant as mockery of homosexuality in those less politically correct days, or more than likely was simply thought of as being humorous.

Reviews

"Just a lot of hokum, which the fans seem to like." Manager, Star Theatre, Hay Springs, Nebraska.

"Pretty good, but I couldn't make my patrons believe that a new-born colt could be so frisky." Manager, Princess Theatre, Lincoln, Nebraska.

"This type of short will please on any program. Don't pass this one up." Manager, Plaza Theatre, Lyons, Nebraska.

"Outstanding. Why is it that Metro's shorts are so much better than any other company?" Small town theater manager.

"[This] pretty good 'let's show off our stars' short from MGM is cheaply made, but we at least get to see countless A-list stars.... The actual 'plot' of this short is silly, but that's to be expected as the main goal is to show as many Hollywood stars as possible, and this film certainly does that." Modern-day commentator.

"It's an amusing film, a must for stargazers." Modern-day commentator.

"At least the baseball segment which makes up the last half of this short is more riveting than watching the paint dry on Clark Gable's barn." Modern-day commentator.

"The quality of this short is pretty poor.... The film seems to be promoting stalking! ... Most of the 'meetings' with celebrities are obviously nothing but stock films and publicity films poorly spliced into the movie. It just made the whole thing look cheap and like a big lie.... It's all a very staged series of photo ops all strung together with a plot that isn't very convincing." Modern-day commentator.

Meet the Stars, #6: Stars at Play *(1941)*

Produced by Harriet Parsons. Cinematography: Robert Tobey. Released by Republic on May 24, 1941. 9 minutes.

Synopsis: Former child star (and now somewhat awkward adolescent) Jane Withers is shown celebrating her fifteenth birthday at her home with a group of teenage friends, including Jackie Hughes and Buddy Pepper. She entertains them with archery, jitterbug dancing and drinks (nothing but innocent sodas, of course).

Also featured is Cesar Romero, seen playing backgammon with "B" picture leading lady and later Broadway star Patricia Morison. Rita Hayworth, on the cusp of major stardom, oversees the construction of her swank new home. A very large group of Hollywood personalities are at the Santa Anita racetrack for the San Antonio Handicap, among them Harry Ritz *sans* brothers.

Cast: Harriet Parsons, Harry Ritz, Jane Withers, Cesar Romero, Patricia Morison, Rita Hayworth, Annabella, Desi Arnaz, Gene Autry, Lucille Ball, Binnie Barnes, Judith Barrett, Joe Brown Jr., Joe E. Brown, June Collyer, Bing Crosby, William Demarest, Stuart Erwin, Virginia Field, Jack Holt, Tim Holt, Bob Howard, Jackie Hughes, Roscoe Karns, Andrea Leeds, Edmund Lowe, Tony Martin, Mary McCarty, Constance Moore, J. Carrol Naish, Gail Patrick, Buddy Pepper, George Raft, Robert Riskin, Randolph Scott, Lana Turner, Fay Wray.

This was one of a short-lived series of *Meet the Stars* short subjects issued by Republic from March 1940 to July 1941. They were all produced by Harriet Parsons (1906–1983), daughter of columnist Louella Parsons. Similar to Columbia's long-running *Screen Snapshots* series, they were intended to showcase Hollywood celebrities at work and play. Although supposedly showing the stars and other film folk in a more causal and candid way, they were as carefully protective of Hollywood reputations as studio publicity people could make them.

Jane Withers and Harry Ritz are here reunited, or at least they appear in the same film separately. They had been seen more directly opposite each other in the Ritzes' final Twentieth Century–Fox film, 1939's *Pack Up Your Troubles*. In that disappointing comedown for the Brothers, the precocious 13-year-old Withers was top-billed, clearly a punitive move against the Ritz Brothers who fell to a credit below the title.

Reviews

"Those legions who are chronically as well as betimes interested in the doins' of the film colonies personalities will like this reel, which is well devised and photographed. The Harriet Parsons commentary is crisp and interest-riveting." *Film Daily*, June 8, 1941.

"Entertains and fascinates those who are naturally entertained and fascinated by the off-screen activities of their favorite players, and there are many such fans." *Showmen's Trade Review*, June 14, 1941.

"Entertaining reel." Manager, Paramount Theatre, Dewey, Oklahoma.

Show Business at War *(1943)*

The History

The March of Time issued a new newsreel approximately every four weeks. Given its subject matter, it is possible that this short was more widely reviewed by media outlets than most of them. Because of its propaganda value, it was supplied to movie theaters gratis. *The March of Time* was played as a radio series from 1931 to 1946, and as a theater series from 1935 to 1951. With the advent of TV, most short subjects dealing with world news proved less profitable and were gradually rendered obsolete.

The *March of Times* dramatic narrations were usually supplied by the deep plummy voice of Westbrook van Voorhis. The de Rochemont brothers, Louis and Richard, were almost always credited as directors and/or producers. The films were Oscar-nominated several times.

The Film

Directed and produced by Louis de Rochemont for Time, Inc. Distributed by Twentieth Century–Fox. *The March of Time* (1942–1943 Season), Number 10; AKA Volume 9, Number 10. Released on May 21, 1943. 18 minutes.

Cast: The Ritz Brothers, Carole Lombard, Walt Disney, John Ford, Darryl F. Zanuck, Irving Berlin, Alfred Lunt, Ballet Russe de Monte Carlo, Jack Benny, Mary Livingstone, Olivia de Havilland, Marlene Dietrich, Deanna Durbin, Hedy Lamarr, Al Jolson, Eddie "Rochester" Anderson, Carole Landis, Louis Armstrong, Phil Baker, Ethel Barrymore, Jackson Beck, Robert Benchley, Edgar Bergen, Beverley Sisters, Joe E. Brown, James Cagney, Lawrence Cowan, Bing

Crosby, Michael Curtiz, Linda Darnell, Bette Davis, Irene Dunne, W.C. Fields, Errol Flynn, Glenn Ford, Kay Francis, Clark Gable, Claire Gagnier, John Garfield, Bert Glennon, Joan Ham, Rita Hayworth, Alfred Hitchcock, Bob Hope, Brenda Joyce, Kay Kyser, Dorothy Lamour, Gertrude Lawrence, Anatole Litvak, Myrna Loy, Fred MacMurray, Victor Mature, Mitzi Mayfair, George Murphy, Eugene Ormandy, Tyrone Power, The Radio Rascals, Martha Raye, Ginger Rogers, Mickey Rooney, President Franklin D. Roosevelt, Eddie Russell, Ann Rutherford, Frank Sinatra, Penny Singleton, Kenneth Thomson, Gregg Toland, Lana Turner, Hal Wallis, Jack Warner, Orson Welles, Don Wilson, Loretta Young.

Synopsis: A *March of Time* newsreel that celebrates the contributions of Hollywood personalities, including stars, directors, executives and technicians to the war effort. Studio moguls Walt Disney, Jack Warner, and Darryl F. Zanuck are portrayed in a rather self-congratulatory way. In his military uniform, Zanuck is seen shooting film in what appears to be a European combat zone.

Hollywood cameramen teach their craft to military personnel. The show business publication *Daily Variety* is highlighted with its ongoing feature of the same name as this film. Hollywood performers are shown mostly in uncredited and silent snippets interpolated from other films and radio programs. Some are entertaining the troops overseas and some in home front canteens.

The Ritz Brothers are among the few celebrities actually heard onscreen. They are standing before a microphone and "conversing" in nonsense French syllables, with Harry leading the way as usual. Others heard onscreen are Jack Benny jousting with wife Mary Livingstone; Edgar Bergen doing the same with Charlie McCarthy, and bandleader Kay Kyser broadcasting a quiz on the radio.

Musical numbers, all partial, include Irving Berlin singing his Army anthem "Oh, How I Hate to Get Up in the Morning" in his reedy voice; Eugene Ormandy conducting the Philadelphia Symphony Orchestra in "Du und Du"; a trio of Black performers doing "Oh Dem Golden Slippers"; Al Jolson pouring his heart into "Mammy," and a band playing "This Is the Army, Mr. Jones."

* * *

As effective as this two-reel short may have been in bucking up home front and overseas military audiences, the reviews perceptively indicate that it was also effective propaganda for the industry. Altruism went only so far in Hollywood.

The film opened at Radio City Music Hall in New York City on May 21, 1943, as one of the short subjects accompanying the main feature. There were various posters issued for the film, all bearing the same legend: "Over 75 Entertainers in a Riot of Spontaneous Fun as They Do Their Part in Canteen and

Front Line Outposts to Keep Our Boys' Spirits High."

Reviews

"A very interesting résumé of the many contributions the picture industry is making to the war effort by entertaining the armed forces, supporting canteens, selling war bonds, and giving trained personnel to important [military] technical services. It is entertaining and informative." *Motion Picture Reviews*, May 1943.

"Because of the timeliness and morale-building value to its exhibitors in its interpretation of the contribution of stage, screen and radio to the war effort, it will be made available to all theaters whether they have other issues of *The March of Time* under contract or not." *Showmen's Trade Review*, May 1943.

"Unquestionably the all-time tops for cast name power and as an institutional ballyhoo in behalf of show biz. It's a gem in less than 20 minutes, kaleidoscopically in montage and pithy commentary.... Periodically punctured by audience applause." *Variety*, May 15, 1943.

"Tops. The film industry stands to profit heavily from the glowing tribute accorded to show business." *Film Daily*, May 1943.

"Was thoroughly enjoyed, especially the scene wherein the G.I. backed away from a chance to kiss Hedy Lamarr. A guy like that oughta be court-martialed. I got a special kick outta this two-reeler.... A marquee attraction, one which will do the industry a lot of good and one which should be given the most intensive backing." *The Exhibitor*, June 1943.

"Excellent, a tribute to a great industry. [I] was proud to show this short." A soldier stationed overseas, Summer, 1944.

"Very good two-reeler." Manager, Paramount Theatre, Dewey, Oklahoma.

Brooklyn Goes to Las Vegas *(1956)*

Directed and written by Arthur Cohen. Released by Universal-International on April 18, 1956. 9 minutes.

Cast: Phil Foster (Narrator), The Ritz Brothers, Jeff Chandler, Joe E. Lewis, Marilyn Maxwell.

Synopsis: The well-traveled character who calls himself Brooklyn makes another trip, this time to Las Vegas, Nevada. He sees the sights and sounds of the city, and then takes in a nightclub performance given by the Ritz Brothers.

* * *

These one-reel short subjects do not actually show the character of Brooklyn; he was the narrator who took the audience through a dizzying montage of the sights of each city.

The film series that followed the character of Brooklyn visiting various locations in the U.S. and Europe began with the short subject *Brooklyn Goes to Beantown* [i.e., Boston] in 1951. The others in the series are *Brooklyn Goes South, Brooklyn Goes to Chicago, Brooklyn Goes to Philadelphia, Brooklyn Goes to Rome, Brooklyn Goes to Cleveland, Brooklyn Goes to Paris, Brooklyn Goes to San Francisco* and the last in the series, *Brooklyn Goes to Detroit*, released in 1957.

Sources differ about the credited director-writer Arthur Cohen, about whom there seems to be little reliable biographical information. Was there really such a person, or was that actually a pseudonym for Phil Foster himself; or, as an outlier or two speculate, Phil Foster's birth name?

According to most sources, Foster was born Fivel Feldman in Brooklyn in 1913, and first took the professional name of Phil Brooks. He was active in most forms of show business and was seen often in the early days of TV, including on *The Four Star Revue*, working with Tallulah Bankhead. He became most famous for playing the role of Frank de Fazio on the television series *Laverne and Shirley*.

Live Television

The following are the known television appearances of the Ritz Brothers from 1949 to 1977, listed according to broadcast date. It is possible there were others. The Ritzes tended to limit such appearances because they did not want to be overexposed, saving their material for their club performances.

To that end, their television appearances from the latter 1960s onward were on talk shows on which they would not need to do their full routines. By that time, oldest brother Al had passed away. At the time of writing, some of these shows are available for viewing on YouTube or other delivery systems.

Toast of the Town, *September 11, 1949 (Season 1, Episode 65) (CBS)*

Before it officially became *The Ed Sullivan Show* in 1955, *Toast of the Town* was the name of the popular variety show. On this last episode of the first season, the other guests included tough-guy actor George Raft, the Harmonicats, comedian Buddy Lester, Spanish dancers Herrero and Vasquez, and singer Alan Dale.

The Ritz Brothers briefly appear on what may have been their first television show. They pretend to gang up on host Sullivan, who then is "rescued" by George Raft. The actor, who was originally a dancer, shows his skill in that area. A female whistler and a male unicyclist also have their moments in the limelight.

The All-Star Thanksgiving Show, *November 24, 1949 (NBC)*

The opening credits read: *Elgin-American Presents the All-Star Thanksgiving Show*. It was actually the eighth such show since it began in 1942 on the

Armed Forces Radio Service, and was the first one to be televised. Its initial purpose was to spread cheer among the troops overseas, so far from home. This 1949 version was simulcast on the Armed Forces Radio to the military personnel still overseas.

Produced by Max Liebman, this 90-minute show reunited the Ritz Brothers with singer Frances Langford, the leading lady of their final feature, 1943's *Never a Dull Moment*. Others who appeared included host George Jessel, Milton Berle, dancer Rod Alexander, singers Phil Regan and Virginia Gibson, and the comic acrobatic act of the Swiss couple Ruth Mata (Meta Krahn) and Eugene Hari (Otto Ulbricht). Telecast in the era of live television, the show produced its share of boners, as the review below indicates.

Review

> "Elgin-American will have a whole year to mull over the mistakes committed. Insufficient rehearsal, its major boner, led to most of the others. George Jessel, the emcee, introduced one wrong act; the station break came in the middle of a production number; the commercials cut another number; the show ended before still another production number was finished…. The comedy of the Ritz Brothers was more successful [than that of Milton Berle]. Their 'Continental Sentimental Gentlemen of Song,' interspersed with mimicry of Harry Richman, [Maurice] Chevalier and others was good fun. However their parody of *Snow White* was nonsensical and added up to nothing more than idiotic farce." *The Billboard*, December 3, 1949.

All Star Revue, *May 17, 1952 (Season 2, Episode 37)* (NBC)

The *All Star Revue* began on television in October 1950 as *Four Star Revue*. Its original format was a rotating roster of four hosts: Ed Wynn, Jimmy Durante, Jack Carson and Danny Thomas. Each episode featured well-known performers singing, telling jokes or whatever it was they did best, and the host performing his own material. The ratings were not high, which in turn caused sponsors to drop out.

To give the *Revue* more staying power, the show evolved into *The All Star Revue* with revolving hosts who included popular performers Martha Raye, Ole Olsen and Chic Johnson, George Jessel and Tallulah Bankhead. The latter had hosted the last big radio variety program *The Big Show*, which did not succeed in prolonging radio as a viable alternative to television. The writers included some who would raise television comedy to new levels: Nat Hiken, Larry Gelbart and Norman Lear.

Toward the end of its second season, it was the Ritz Brothers' turn. They fill their hour with skits, dancing, singing and jokes; in other words, they give a full-out Ritz Brothers performance. They are the whole unadulterated show and are only interrupted by commercials of sponsors like Snow Crop Orange Juice and Kellogg Cereal.

The show begins with a comic scene outside the studio where they try to convince a studio cop that they are actually in the show. Besides their usual vigorous dancing (one done to the tune of "Tiger Rag") and singing, they enact several skits, one of them a supposed Revolutionary War song while dressed as the famous fife and drum trio. They had done this routine in more than one film.

Another is a sketch in which they are three gypsies by the names of Sasha, Misha and Goss. The last two names are a play on the Yiddish word "mishegoss" which means craziness. Others include bits as diners and a waiter in a Paris restaurant; as French singers, and a clever parody of the then-popular police procedural series *Dragnet* ("Just the facts, ma'am").

The last skit is performed by the brothers in pantomime and narrated by *Dragnet* star Jack Webb. The "dead body" which the brothers keep tripping over turns out to be actor John Payne, who says nary a word.

Other bits include the Ritzes lying down in front of a studio light as if it were a sunlamp, causing chaos in the control room, and hanging underwear on the cable of a microphone boom. In an extended commercial for Snowcrop Orange Juice, they play three runners whose shirts offer a sly dig at their old rivals: "This space rented by Groucho, Chico, Harpo."

The All Star Revue continued to be low-rated with competition like *The Jackie Gleason Show* and was on the verge of cancellation more than once. It was temporarily saved by Sid Caesar's *Your Show of Shows* moving to a format of three weeks out of every four. It then filled in the fourth week. It ended its run in December 1953 and morphed into *The Martha Raye Show*. It had been one of the most expensive shows to produce and could not survive the loss of sponsors.

Olympic Fund Telethon, *June 21, 1952 (CBS-NBC)*

Supposedly the first nationally televised telethon, this 14½-hour event was hosted by Bob Hope and Bing Crosby. There had been locally aired telethons before; one hosted by Milton Berle in 1949 was one of the earliest. This one raised

$350,000, an enormous sum in those days, for the benefit of the athletes bound for the Helsinki Olympics. It was broadcast from Hollywood's lavish El Capitan Theatre to an estimated 50,000,000 viewers (that figure seems inflated for 1952).

Its roster of stars was unparalleled, everyone from Bud Abbott to Johnny Weissmuller. Among that stellar pack were the Ritz Brothers. Others contributing their time (and perhaps their money) were June Allyson, Edgar Bergen, Eddie Cantor, Joan Crawford, the Three Stooges, Tab Hunter, Dean Martin, Jerry Lewis (perhaps he got his own later telethon idea from this one), Marilyn Monroe, Edward G. Robinson, Frank Sinatra and many others.

It was reported that Bing Crosby departed when Jerry Lewis arrived. Apparently, or so the gossip grapevine said, he was afraid the zany young comic would pull off his (Crosby's) toupee as a gag. In between the jollity, there was much talk about how sending our athletes to Finland would be a blow to Red Russia in those Cold War days.

All Star Revue, *November 22, 1952 (Season 3, Episode 12) (NBC)*

The Ritzes returned to host in the third season, some five months after their previous appearance. Their celebrity guests were opera singer Mimi Benzell, actor John Ireland, dancer Bill Skipper, and Lou Bring and his orchestra. The brothers spoof the arrival of the *Mayflower* (it was a Thanksgiving show); *Snow White and the Seven Dwarfs* and *Ivanhoe*. *Variety* called it a funny show.

The Colgate Comedy Hour, *February 22, 1953 (Season 3, Episode 22) (NBC)*

For most of its six-year run, *The Colgate Comedy Hour* was one of TV's more popular variety shows. Beginning in 1950, it went head to head with Ed Sullivan's *Toast of the Town* and held its own for a long while. A spin-off from *The Four Star Revue*, it was heavy in comedy sketches.

Among the numerous stars who were guests or hosts were Frank Sinatra, Dean Martin and Jerry Lewis, Bud Abbott and Lou Costello, Eddie Cantor, Ethel Merman, Bob Hope, Fred Allen and Jimmy Durante. It may have been the first series to be telecast live from coast to coast and among the first to be shot in color. It gradually lost its star roster and in 1955, its final year, it was renamed *The Colgate Variety Hour*.

The Ritz Brothers appeared about midway through its run. They hosted the show with Jack Webb, with whom they had done *The All Star Revue*. The guests included singer Kay Starr and actresses Coleen Gray and Corinne Calvet. The actresses presumably assisted in the Ritzes' sketches. These include a send-up of the current film *Moulin Rouge*, with Harry doing a Toulouse-Lautrec imitation. Harry also had fun as a nearsighted umpire (something the Ritzes had done in movie short subjects), and there is a sketch showing how 3-D would work on television.

Max Liebman Presents, *January 2, 1955 (Season 1, Episode 9) (NBC)*

Broadway producer-director Max Liebman is best known today for introducing Sid Caesar to TV audiences via *Your Show of Shows*. A good judge of talent, he was responsible for recruiting writers Mel Brooks and Neil Simon, and comic performers Carl Reiner, Imogene Coca and Howard Morris.

Dubbed "The Ziegfeld of Television," Liebman staged television "spectaculars." The Ritz Brothers appeared on the episode called "Good Times." Humorist Steve Allen hosted; other guest stars included Judy Holliday, comic Dick Shawn and dancer Timmy Everett. Neil Simon was one of the writers.

Pontiac Star Parade: The Ginger Rogers Show, *October 15, 1958 (CBS)*

CBS-TV's *Pontiac Star Parade* consisted of a series of one-hour specials from about 1958 to 1960. Among the featured celebrities were Carol Lawrence, Tony Randall, Gene Kelly, Perry Como and Donald O'Connor. By the time of this special, Ginger Rogers was no longer a major movie star and she had increasingly turned to TV and the stage. Her guests were the Ritz Brothers and Ray Bolger, with actor Elliott Reid and dancer Dante DiPaolo providing support. Nelson Riddle and his orchestra furnished the music and Nick Castle did the choreography.

Rogers performed two dance numbers, one of which was her interpretation of the moods of nighttime Manhattan. The other was a reprise of several of the songs and dances she had performed in the movies. Bolger and Rogers did a song-and-dance routine to the tune of "Carolina in the Morning" in a county fair setting. The Ritz Brothers and Bolger mugged their way through a satire on westerns. For the finale, all the stars got together for an homage to vaudeville.

Jackpot Bowling, Starring Milton Berle, *January 23, 1961 (NBC)*

This show was a comedown for Milton Berle, who hosted celebrity guests and champion bowlers on each episode. The Ritz Brothers were invited to bowl for their favorite charity, the Campers Scholarship Fund for Children. After some comic discussion about the brothers' athletic ability and who was going to throw the bowling ball (Harry pleaded, "Don't holler, please don't holler!"), Harry was selected.

He slid halfway down the alley with the ball and still got a strike, winning $1000 for the charity. His brothers seemed genuinely delighted at his prowess. They were now off to perform at the Roosevelt Hotel in New Orleans, where in 1965 Al suffered his fatal heart attack.

What's My Line?, *March 12, 1961 (Season 12, Episode 28: Series Episode 555) (CBS)*

The title of the panel show *What's My Line?* summarizes its simple premise. That premise proved so entertaining that the show ran from 1950 to 1967. Each week, several guests with unusual occupations appeared, and celebrity panelists questioned them and tried to figure out what they did. The last guest (or guests) was always a celebrity; in these segments, the panelists wore blindfolds. They asked questions, trying to deduce the celebrity's identity.

The gimmick was that the guests usually did not look like the stereotype of that occupation. On this March 12, 1961, episode, the first contestant, a burly, heavily mustachioed Englishman, was a rose grower, the second a petite Englishwoman who was a circus clown. The panelists did not guess their occupations and they walked off with the grand prize of $50 each.

The long-serving host was suave, tuxedoed South African John Charles Daly. Permanent panelists were publisher Bennett Cerf, actress Arlene Francis and columnist Dorothy Kilgallen. The fourth panelist on this episode is stand-up comic Joey Bishop, an auxiliary member of Frank Sinatra's famous Rat Pack. When the mystery guest segment is announced, Bishop recuses himself because he has accidentally learned the the guests' identity. (The Ritz Brothers appeared on Bishop's talk show some years later.)

That mystery guest this time is *three* people: the Ritz Brothers. They emerge to great audience applause and with linked hands they all sign in on the blackboard simultaneously. Al sits next to Daly, the others stand behind him, a gesture of respect for their eldest brother. They do not attempt to disguise their voices (which mystery guests usually did) and their identities are guessed almost immediately by Bennett Cerf after he inquires whether there is a famous hotel that bears their name.

Again, seemingly as a mark of respect from his younger brothers, Al Ritz does all the talking. He mentions that they have returned to perform in New York for the first time in five years and are proud that the landmark Lindy's Restaurant is going to throw a party for them. There seems to be an air of almost rueful nostalgia about the now aging trio but an enduring closeness as well.

Here's Hollywood, *October 2, 1961 (Season 2, Episode 21) (NBC)*

Running for two seasons over three years, from September 1960 to December 1962, this was a 30-minute afternoon show in which hundreds of celebrities were interviewed, often at home. Among the hosts were Dean Miller, Jack Linkletter (son of TV star Art Linkletter), Joanne Jordan and former band singer Helen O'Connell. This episode features the Ritz Brothers.

The Ed Sullivan Show, *October 19, 1961 (Season 14, Episode 7) (CBS)*

The famously stone-faced Ed Sullivan was in his fourteenth season with his top-rated variety show when the Ritz Brothers guested for the first time since their 1949 appearance. The show began in 1948 and had a phenomenal 23-year run. George Gobel, the pint-sized humorist, guest-hosted this episode as Sullivan was ailing. The usual array of name talents includes the singing Everly Brothers, Robert Goulet and Dorothy Loudon.

During the course of the show, Gobel reads some comic poems and sings; the Everly boys sing their hit "Bye Bye Love," among other tunes, and Goulet does *West Side Story*'s "Maria" and a medley of songs popularized by Fred Astaire. The vivacious Loudon performs a comic singing act. The Ritzes, on toward the end, clown their way through something called the Moisyeu Ballet. This presumably is meant as a comic homage to the famed Moiseyev Ballet Company founded by Igor Moiseyev. The Ritz Brothers being excellent dancers, the skit was expertly executed.

The Joey Bishop Show, *December 13, 1967 (Season 2, Episode 60) (ABC)*

This was one of the many talk shows that came and went on late night TV in failed opposition to the powerful Johnny Carson. It was co-hosted by the smooth, ever-smiley Regis Philbin and featured the music of Johnny Mann's orchestra. Bishop (*née* Joseph Gottlieb) had had his own eponymous sitcom on which he played a television host and had several movie and many TV roles to his credit. A few of his roles were in Rat Pack pictures, including the popular Las Vegas heist film *Ocean's 11*.

The night that Jimmy and Harry appeared, the other guests were actress Janice Rule and actor-singer John Davidson.

The Joey Bishop Show, *July 4, 1969 (Season 3, Episode 216) (ABC)*

The return of the two Ritz Brothers to the Bishop show came in the final year of its run. Regis Philbin and the Johnny Mann Orchestra were still with the show. Another guest on this episode was the squeaky-voiced actor Pat Buttram, best known as the comic sidekick of oater star Gene Autry in his later films and for his role on the rural comedy *Green Acres*. The singer-composer Curtis Mayfield was also there with his group The Impressions.

The Merv Griffin Show, *March 3, 1970 (Season 7, Episode 140) (Syndication)*

When the Ritz Brothers made their initial appearance with genial host Merv Griffin, it was toward the beginning of that talk show's amazing run of 4855 episodes. Having made the first broadcast in 1962, Griffin saw it through to 1986 with only a small break. His gift was getting his guests to talk about themselves at length, which often took a good deal more time than most chat shows gave their guests. He was nominated for many daytime Emmys and won some.

Griffin's sidekick was the tall, long-faced actor Arthur Treacher, who had played many a stereotypical English butler in the movies. He did not accompany the show when it relocated from New York to Los Angeles, supposedly because he did not want to move to a "place that shakes." The Mort Lindsey Orchestra supplied the music.

Other guests on this episode with the Ritz Brothers were blonde baby-voiced ingénue Connie Stevens, comic Marty Allen of the Allen and Rossi team, and singer–champion golfer Don Cherry. The comedy team of Pepper Davis and Tony Reese rounded out the guest roster.

A shrewd businessman, Griffin went on to create game shows, including the hits *Jeopardy!* and *Wheel of Fortune*, in the process gaining fabulous wealth. This was not bad for a basically ordinary singer whose big hit was "I've Got a Lovely Bunch of Coconuts."

The Merv Griffin Show, *January 7, 1971 (Season 8, Episode 80) (Syndicated)*

By that time Harry and Jimmy Ritz returned to chat again with Griffin, Arthur Treacher had left; Mort Lindsey and his music remained. The Ritzes were in the company of distinguished character actor Jack Albertson, actress Lisa Todd (*Green Acres*) and a ragtag bunch of actors with some interesting movie credits: Dyanne Thorne (*Wam Bam Thank You Spaceman* and *Swinging Barmaids*), Irving Benson (*Scanty Panties*) and Roger Ray (*There's Always Vanilla*). One wonders what the conversation was about that afternoon. Even the irrepressible Harry might have been nonplussed. Years later, Jimmy and Harry did *Blazing Stewardesses*, a film in the same category as the above novelties.

The Mike Douglas Show, *June 2, 1971 (Season 10, Episode 188) (Syndicated)*

Before he attained his talk show fame, Mike Douglas (*née* Michael Dowd Jr.) had been a singer with big band leader Kay Kyser and had recorded a few popular standards. His first talk show was a local one in Cleveland; from there he gradually became better known and went into national syndication in 1962 with a daytime show that lasted until 1981.

Douglas had an engaging but rather bland personality and he always had a well-known co-host. When Harry and Jimmy Ritz came to the show, journeyman western actor Dale Robertson was sharing the hosting gig. The Joe Harnell Sextet provided the music. Sharing the stage with the Ritzes were country singer Lynn Anderson and basketball star Walt Frazier.

The Merv Griffin Show, *November 2, 1971 (Season 9, Episode 40) (Syndicated)*

The Ritzes' third Griffin outing was in an episode originating from Caesar's Palace. They were joined by the lively comedienne Totie Fields, musician Louis Prima, comic Jan Murray (who 15 years later officiated at the Ritzes' induction to the Hollywood Walk of Fame), and Heidi Bruhl, German actress-singer.

The Merv Griffin Show, *August 3, 1972 (Season 9, Episode 210) (Syndicated)*

The last *Merv Griffin Show* for the brothers also featured well-known dancers Ann Miller and Gene Nelson, stars of many a Hollywood musical. Sandra Dee was also present, along with dancers Jerry Antes and Skip Cunningham.

Texaco Presents Bob Hope in "Joys" (A Comedy Whodunit), *March 5, 1976*

This is one of Bob Hope's 90-minute specials, a TV tradition beginning in 1950 and lasting until 1996 for a total of 252 such programs. The title of this one, *Joys*, is a play on *Jaws*, the blockbuster film that had premiered a year earlier. The plot concerns a so-called human shark devouring the comedians gathered at Hope's house for a party. Bob hires television detectives Mannix, the Police Woman (Angie Dickinson), Kojak, Ellery Queen, Fish (from *Barney Miller*) and Harry O. to solve the mystery. Harry Ritz keeps repeating his tagline "Don't holler, please don't holler!"

Cast: Harry Ritz, Don Adams, Jack Albertson, Marty Allen, Steve Allen, Desi Arnaz, Rona Barrett, Billy Barty, Milton Berle, Foster Brooks, George Burns, Red Buttons, Pat Buttram, John Byner, Sid Caesar, Sammy Cahn, Glenn Campbell, Jack Carter, Charo, Jerry Colonna, Mike Connors, Scatman Crothers, Bill Dana, Angie Dickinson, Phyllis Diller, Jamie Farr, George Gobel, Jim Hutton, David Janssen, Alan King, George Kirby, Don Knotts, Fred MacMurray, Dean Martin, Groucho Marx, Jan Murray, Wayne Newton, Freddie Prinze, Don Rickles, Telly Savalas, Phil Silvers, Larry Storch, Abe Vigoda, Jimmie Walker, Flip Wilson.

The Dick Cavett Show, *October 12, 1977 (Episode 3)* (PBS)

The Ritz Brothers were the sole guests on this episode, which was just the third one that Cavett did on PBS after his years-long run on ABC. The first two PBS shows featured show business legends Alfred Lunt and Rudolf Nureyev.

At least one source states that Jimmy and Harry Ritz appeared on the short-lived 1970–1971 television version of the old radio panel show *Can You Top This?* The author was not able to uncover definitive evidence of the brothers' participation.

Archival Appearances: Films and Television

The Sound of Laughter *(1963)*

The History

This film was probably an attempt to cash in on the great success of comic Harold Lloyd's two recent documentaries *World of Comedy* (aka *Harold Lloyd's World of Comedy*, 1962) and *Funny Side of Life* (1963). Producer Robert Youngson had been releasing compilations of silent and talkie comedy clips for many years, including *The Golden Age of Comedy*, *When Comedy Was King*, and *Days of Thrills and Laughter*.

One of the differences with this compilation is that it only highlights clips of comedians' work in features and short subjects made in the 1930s. Also included are a few performers not ordinarily considered comics but who are presumably captured in comic moments, like Roy Rogers, Shirley Temple and the singing Pickens Sisters.

The Film

Directed by John O'Shaughnessy. Produced by Irvin Dorfman, Dick Randall and Barry B. Yellen. Writer: Fred Saidy. Music: Robert Waldman. Editor: Elliot Geisinger. Educational Films Corporation of America; distributed by Union Film Distributors. Released on December 17, 1963. 72 minutes.

Cast: Ed Wynn (Narrator), The Ritz Brothers, Buster Keaton, Danny Kaye, Bing Crosby, Bob Hope, Bert Lahr, Shirley Temple, Milton Berle, Imogene Coca, Lillian Roth, Will Mahoney, Joan Davis, F. Chase Taylor (aka Colonel Lemuel Q. Stoopnagle), Budd Hulick, Myra Keaton, Roy Rogers, The Pickens Sisters (Jane, Helen, Patti), Charlotte Greenwood, Snub Pollard, Andy Clyde, Edgar Kennedy, Joe Cook, Harry Gribbon, Vernon Dent, Doris Hill, Billy Gilbert, Vince Barnett, George J. Lewis, William Irving, Lloyd Ingraham,

John Ince, Harold Goodwin, Dewey Robinson, Lona Andre, Leah Ray, Sally Starr, The Cabin Kids, Harry Langdon.

Synopsis: Comedian Ed Wynn ("The Perfect Fool") supplies the narration for these filmclips from the 1930s. The Ritz Brothers and Doris Hill appear in a clip from the Ritzes' first film, the Educational Pictures short subject *Hotel Anchovy* (1934).

* * *

Posters advertising this film all carried the caption "A Star-Studded Parade of the Classic Clowns More Hilarious Than Ever!"

Reviews

"The funniest thing about *The Sound of Laughter* is to see how ridiculously dated and unfunny most of its comedy is…. You might think it would have an eternal good humor quality, no matter how sketchy it may be. But it doesn't, not by a long shot. What it has is a sense of strain and routine mechanical contrivance that approaches the absurd…. A sequence in which the Ritz Brothers do a vaudeville skit is sheer horror." *New York Times*, December 18, 1963.

"Since most of the material in this awkward compilation of comedy clips from the early 1930s has been seen with frequency on kiddie TV programs, it will have difficulty in securing even second feature billing. There's precious little laughter in the fleeting glimpses one gets…. The Ritz Brothers are dragged in for a long, unfunny routine…." *Independent Exhibitors Film Bulletin*, December 23, 1963.

Hollywood and the Stars: The Funny Men, *Part 2* (1963) (NBC)

Directed by Jack Haley Jr. Produced by Jack Haley Jr., Julian Ludwig, Al Ramrus, Irwin Rosten and David L. Wolper. Writer: Irwin Rosten. Music: Ruby Raksin and Elmer Bernstein. Editor: Melvin Shapiro. Sound: Morton Tubor. Released to television by Wolper Productions and United Artists Television on December 16, 1963. 30 minutes.

Cast: Joseph Cotten (Narrator), The Ritz Brothers, Bud Abbott, Lou Costello, Mischa Auer, Lucille Ball, Robert Benchley, Edgar Bergen, Milton Berle, Joe E. Brown, Sid Caesar, Eddie Cantor, Jack Carson, Charles Chaplin, Jimmy Durante, Leon Errol, W.C. Fields, Billy Gilbert, Sid Grauman, Jack Haley, Hugh Herbert, Judy Holliday, Bob Hope, Edward Everett Horton, Danny Kaye,

Edgar Kennedy, Dorothy Lamour, Jerry Lewis, Dean Martin, Shirley MacLaine, The Marx Brothers (Chico, Harpo, Groucho), Frank McHugh, Donald Meek, Ethel Merman, Victor Moore, Chester Morris, Jack Norton, Jack Oakie, Franklin Pangborn, Joe Penner, Martha Raye, Will Rogers, Mickey Rooney, Charles Ruggles, Jane Russell, Rosalind Russell, S.Z. Sakall, Dick Shawn, Phil Silvers, Red Skelton, Arthur Treacher, Mae West, Bert Wheeler, Robert Woolsey, Jonathan Winters, Ed Wynn, Keenan Wynn, Henry Bergman, Peter Bull, Elise Cavanna, Si Jenks, Marjorie Kane, Edna Purviance, John Rand.

Synopsis: NBC's *Hollywood and the Stars* was a weekly 30-minute TV series that ran a full season, from September 30, 1963, to May 4, 1964, for a total of 31 episodes. Jack Haley Jr. produced and the suave actor Joseph Cotten served as the narrator. The first episode was titled "The Man Called Bogart." Each subsequent show highlighted a major star (Al Jolson, Paul Newman, Bette Davis, etc.), film genre (westerns, horror, romance, etc.), particular films (*The Cardinal, The Night of the Iguana*, etc.) or even a significant time span. The final show was titled "The Wild and Wonderful Thirties." The first of the "Funny Men" episodes was broadcast on December 9, 1963. The episode featuring the Ritz Brothers material came one week later.

Review

> "Part Two of this series is much like the first in that they didn't put any effort into researching their subject…. Most of the comedians here are nothing but a lightning-fast few frames, enough to cover the length of time their names can be spoken. Hal Roach and his productions go unmentioned…. Roach or many other sources would charge for their use so they didn't make the cut. The footage used is mostly public domain material." Modern-day commentator.

Hollywood: The Gift of Laughter *(1982) (ABC)*

Directed and written by Jack Haley Jr. Produced by Michael Bloom, Jack Haley Jr., Julian Ludwig and David A. Wolper. Music: Billy Goldenberg and Fred Karlin. Editor: David Blewitt, Bea Dennis, Lawrence Saltzman, Vic Lowrey and Sol Weisel. Production designer: Ron Talsky. Released to ABC-TV by David Wolper Productions, Jack Haley Productions and the Motion Picture Association of America on May 6, 1982. 180 minutes (original version), 135 minutes (edited version).

Cast: Carol Burnett, Jack Lemmon, Walter Matthau, Burt Reynolds, Dom DeLuise, Richard Pryor (Narrators), The Ritz Brothers, Mischa Auer, Bud

Abbott, Lou Costello, Eddie Acuff, Judith Allen, Woody Allen, Eddie "Rochester" Anderson, Roscoe "Fatty" Arbuckle, Asta (the dog), Baby LeRoy, Lucille Ball, Anne Bancroft, Our Gang (Matthew "Stymie" Beard, Robert Blake, Darla Hood, Joe Cobb, Jackie Cooper, Scotty Beckett, George "Spanky" McFarland, Carl "Alfalfa" Switzer, Billie "Buckwheat" Thomas), Louise Beavers, Wallace Beery, John Belushi, William Bendix, Jack Benny, Edgar Bergen, Henry Bergman, Billy Bevan, Ward Bond, Eileen Brennan, Lou Breslow, Lloyd Bridges, Mel Brooks, Edward Brophy, Joe E. Brown, Nigel Bruce, Peter Bull, Tommy Bupp, Sid Caesar, James Cagney, Eric Campbell, John Candy, Dyan Cannon, Eddie Cantor, Philip Carey, Ron Carey, Art Carney, Leslie Caron, Nancy Carroll, Charles Chaplin, Chevy Chase, Tommy Chong, Cheech Marin, Berton Churchill, Jill Clayburgh, Chester Clute, Charles Coburn, Peter Coe, Claudette Colbert, Jerry Colonna, Chuck Connors, Tim Conway, Jackie Coogan, Bill Cosby, Broderick Crawford, Joseph Crehan, Bing Crosby, Ken Curtis, Tony Curtis, William B. Davidson, Mildred Davis, Harold Lloyd, Doris Day, Evelyn Del Rio, Melvyn Douglas, Lesley-Anne Down, Marie Dressler, Jan Duggan, Margaret Dumont, Eddie Dunn, Irene Dunne, Minta Durfee, Clint Eastwood, Zedna Farley, Marty Feldman, Sally Field, W.C. Fields, The Three Stooges, James Finlayson, Henry Fonda, Bernard Fox, Kay Francis, William Frawley, Clark Gable, Greta Garbo, James Garner, Teri Garr, Betty Garrett, John Gielgud, Billy Gilbert, Jack Gilford, Burton Gilliam, Jackie Gleason, Paulette Goddard, Thomas Gomez, Leo Gorcey, Huntz Hall, Betty Grable, Dorothy Granger, Cary Grant, Reed Hadley, Julie Haggerty, Jack Haley, Margaret Hamilton, Oliver Hardy, Stan Laurel, Jean Harlow, Goldie Hawn, Robert Hays, Audrey Hepburn, Katharine Hepburn, Gregory Hines, Judy Holliday, Bob Hope, Kathleen Howard, Trevor Howard, Mary-Margaret Humes, Glynis Johns, Chic Johnson, Ole Olsen, Allan Jones, Madeline Kahn, Carol Kane, Danny Kaye, Buster Keaton, Diane Keaton, Grace Kelly, Percy Kilbride, Don Knotts, Harvey Korman, Kris Kristofferson, Bert Lahr, Arthur Lake, Penny Singleton, Dorothy Lamour, Harry Langdon, Jerry Lewis, Dean Martin, Cleavon Little, Perry Lopez, Sophia Loren, Edmund Lowe, Myrna Loy, Marjorie Main, Hank Mann, Marion Marshall, Steve Martin, ZaSu Pitts, The Marx Brothers (Chico, Harpo, Groucho), Elaine May, John Miljan, Marilyn Monroe, Colleen Moore, Dudley Moore, Joe Morrison, Zero Mostel, Jack Mulhall, Bill Murray, Mildred Natwick, Leslie Nielsen, Mabel Normand, Donald O'Connor, Jack Oakie, Franklin Pangborn, Cecil Parker, Slim Pickens, William Powell, Bill Quinn, Jessie Ralph, Basil Rathbone, Martha Raye, Ronald Reagan, Tracy Reed, Lee Remick, Debbie Reynolds, Thelma Ritter, Ginger Rogers, Gilbert Roland, Mickey Rooney, Rosalind Russell, Tiny Sanford, George C. Scott, Vito Scotti, Peter Sellers, Mack Sennett, Red Skelton, Alison Skipworth, Walter Slezak, Robert Stack,

Barbara Stanwyck, Graham Stark, Ford Sterling, Barbra Streisand, Mack Swain, Gloria Swanson, Kenneth Tobey, Lily Tomlin, Spencer Tracy, Ben Turpin, Murvyn Vye, Sam Wanamaker, Mae West, Gene Wilder, Robert J. Wilke, Esther Williams, Hal Williams, Grant Withers, Cora Witherspoon, Harry Woods.

Synopsis: This film features filmclips of comedy performances from the silent era to the early 1980s with the greatest emphasis on the comedies contemporary to the production of this program. Several hosts introduce the segments in the film, which begins with the late Zero Mostel singing "Comedy Tonight" from the musical comedy *A Funny Thing Happened on the Way to the Forum*. The music from the song is reprised throughout. The prologue reads: "This film is dedicated to the thousands of filmmakers, craftsmen, and technicians who accomplished the most difficult job in motion pictures: They made people laugh."

* * *

Early in the film, the Ritz Brothers appear in three very brief clips. In one they do a synchronized dance (possibly from *Sing, Baby, Sing*); in the second they reprise the wheezy old "walk this way" gag with Franklin Pangborn from *Never a Dull Moment* (1943), and in the third they emphatically tell another character how to spell "Ritz."

This made-for-television movie was originally broadcast in three one-hour segments and was later edited down and shown at 45 minutes per segment. (At the time of writing, it was available on YouTube in its abbreviated format.) It was nominated for two Emmy Awards: Bruce Bryant and James Castle for Outstanding Individual Achievement in Informational Programming, and Jack Haley Jr. for Outstanding Informational Special. This kind of programming would now probably fall within the Emmy's Documentary/Nonfiction category.

Director–co-producer–co-writer Jack Haley Jr., scion of a well-known show business family, was a multiple award-winning producer and director; one of his best-known films was the very successful compilation *That's Entertainment!* (1974). When asked what he personally thought was the funniest bit in this documentary, he referenced the scene from the comedy *Play It Again, Sam* in which the Woody Allen character haplessly prepares for a blind date.

Most of the clips are not identified as to title. Many excerpts are so brief that they give unfamiliar viewers little idea of why the performers had been popular. As *People* magazine flippantly reported: "To keep out the Mongol hordes the Chinese built the Great Wall; to counter NBC's *Marco Polo* juggernaut ABC has called up this comedy special featuring nearly everyone who has ever said anything funny in front of a camera." *Marco Polo* was a star-studded U.S.-Italian co-production which ran for nine hours over several nights.

Review

"One of those programs that just couldn't miss, a warm, nostalgic very, very funny retrospective of the great moments in screen comedy." *Los Angeles Times*, May 15, 1982.

Classic Comedy Teams *(1986)*

Directed by David Bergman. Produced by Paul Harris. Editor: Sandy Oliveri. Makeup: Carolyn Brandon. Sound: Sandy Bull. Bergman-Harris/Movietime; distributed by Goodtimes Home Video, 1986. 108 minutes.

Cast: Steve Allen (Host-Narrator), The Ritz Brothers, Stan Laurel, Oliver Hardy, The Marx Brothers (Chico, Harpo, Groucho, Zeppo), George Burns, Gracie Allen, Dorothy DeBorba, The Three Stooges (Moe Howard, Larry Fine, Curly Howard, Shemp Howard, Joe Besser, Joe DeRita), Ted Healy, Bud Abbott, Lou Costello, Dean Martin, Jerry Lewis, Our Gang (Shirley Jean Rickert, Carl "Alfalfa" Switzer, George "Spanky" McFarland, Billie "Buckwheat" Thomas, Darla Hood, Eugene "Porky" Lee, Jackie Cooper, Douglas Greer, Buddy McDonald, Mary Ann Jackson, Allen "Farina" Hoskins, Norman "Chubby" Chaney, Joe Cobb, Donald Haines, Ernest Morrison), Clifton Young, June Marlowe, The East Side Kids (aka the Dead End Kids, the Bowery Boys) (Leo Gorcey, Huntz Hall, Gabriel Dell, Billy Halop, Bobby Jordan), Amos 'n' Andy (Charles Correll, Freeman Gosden), Bert Wheeler, Robert Woolsey, Paul McCullough, Bobby Clark, Edgar Bergen, Ole Olsen, Chic Johnson, Bob Hope, Bing Crosby, the Keystone Cops, Tons of Fun, Frank Albertson, Eve Arden, Alexander Asro, Clyde Beatty, Noah Beery, Bonnie Bonnell, Betty Mae Crane, Beverly Crane, Vernon Dent, Douglass Dumbrille, Margaret Dumont, Cliff Dunstan, Fritz Feld, John Garfield, Anita Garvin, Betsy Gay, Percy Helton, Doris Houck, Bert Hunn, Virginia Hunter, Gloria Hurst, Bud Jamison, George Jeske, Allan Jones, Eddie Kane, Danny Kaye, Isabelle Keith, Patsy Kelly, Edgar Kennedy, Margaret Kerry, Walter Woolf King, Dorothy Lee, Henry "Spike" Lee, Edward LeSaint, George J. Lewis, Alyn Lockwood, Bela Lugosi, Donald MacBride, June MacCloy, Gloria Mackey, Barton MacLane, Judy Malcolm, Hank Mann, Charles Middleton, Rube Miller, Polly Moran, James C. Morton, Mabel Normand, Virginia O'Brien, Robert Emmett O'Connor, Dorothy Oelze, Bennett Parker, Rosemary Portia, Roger Pryor, Andy Samuel, Nancy Saunders, Fritz Schade, Harry Semels, Ronald Sinclair, Harold Switzer, Ben Taggart, Ben Turpin, Laura June Williams, Ed Wynn.

Synopsis: This compilation was made as a VHS production for home consumption and features television personality Steve Allen as narrator and host. Using filmclips, it presents many of the famous comic teams of the silent and sound eras.

Reviews

"A pretty good documentary. It's the first to show all the classic comedy teams from the '20s to the '70s. The problem is that some [sequences] were too long and other things were too short ...." Modern-day commentator.

"A fun little video compilation ... a straight-up glimpse at almost all of the popular comedians of the day. The main complaint is that the clips are generally of very poor quality. However, the wealth of talent portrayed is remarkable.... [It's] guaranteed to raise a chuckle for classic comedy fans." Modern-day commentator.

20th Century–Fox: The First 50 Years *(1997)*

Directed by Kevin Burns. Produced by Di Barker, Kevin Burns, Michele Farinola, Shelley Lyons and Jeff Scheftel. Editor: Craig Colton and David Comtois. Camera: Robert Truitt. Van Ness Productions/Foxstar Productions/Twentieth Television/American Movie Classics. Distributed by American Movie Classics and released to television on January 21, 1997. 150 minutes (television version); 129 minutes (DVD version).

Cast: James Coburn, Julie Andrews, David Brown, Red Buttons, Alice Faye, Mel Gussow, Frances Klamt, Roddy McDowall, Don Murray, Sheree North, Debbie Reynolds, William Reynolds, Robert Wagner, Eli Wallach, Robert Wise, Jane Withers, Richard Zanuck, The Ritz Brothers, Gregory Peck, Elizabeth Taylor, Lowell Thomas, Lauren Bacall, Irving Berlin, Pat Boone, Ralph Bunche, Theodore Case, President Calvin Coolidge, Wally Cox, Mark Damon, Cesare Danova, Ray Danton, Olivia de Havilland, Irene Dunne, Fabian, Jimmy Fidler, Anthony Franciosa, Kay Francis, Betty Grable, Edmund Gwenn, Oscar Hammerstein II, Howard Hawks, Rita Hayworth, David Hedison, Audrey Hepburn, Bob Hope, Carole Landis, June Lang, Al Lichtman, Charles Lindbergh Jr., Myrna Loy, Rouben Mamoulian, Joseph Mankiewicz, Jayne Mansfield, Fredric March, E.G. Marshall, Herbert Marshall, Chris-Pin Martin, Dean Martin, James Mason, Victor Mature, Dorothy McGuire, Nina Mae McKinney, Barbara McLean, Stephen McNally, Beryl Mercer, Gary Merrill, Sal Mineo, Carmen Miranda, Cameron Mitchell, Thomas Mitchell, Robert Mitchum, Tom Mix, Marilyn Monroe, Terry Moore, Agnes Moorehead, Harry Morgan,

Alan Mowbray, Herbert Mundin, Ken Murray, Alan Napier, Patricia Neal, Gene Nelson, Ruth Nelson, Lloyd Nolan, Tommy Noonan, Edmond O'Brien, George O'Brien, Arthur O'Connell, Una O'Connor, Maureen O'Hara, Frederick O'Neal, Jack Oakie, Warner Oland, Robert Osterloh, Patricia Owens, Debra Paget, John Payne, Millie Perkins, Jean Peters, Walter Pidgeon, Ezio Pinza, Sidney Poitier, Wiley Post, Dick Powell, Tyrone Power, Elvis Presley, Vincent Price, Edmond Purdom, Anthony Quinn, Tony Randall, Basil Rathbone, Michael Rennie, Anne Revere, Dick Rich, Roy Roberts, Jay Robinson, Richard Rodgers, Will Rogers, Barbara Rush, Jane Russell, George Sanders, Tommy Sands, Maximilian Schell, Joseph Schildkraut, David O. Selznick, Al Shean, Ann Sheridan, Anne Shirley, Jean Simmons, Russell Simpson, Frank Sinatra, Walter Slezak, Howard Smith, Robert Stack, Rod Steiger, James Stewart, Dean Stockwell, George E. Stone, Russ Tamblyn, Don Taylor, Shirley Temple, The Three Stooges, Lawrence Tibbett, Gene Tierney, Spencer Tracy, Arthur Treacher, Tom Tryon, Lana Turner, Rudy Vallee, Evelyn Varden, Diane Varsi, Helen Walker, Henry Wallace, Henry B. Walthall, Harry Warner, Jack Warner, Ethel Waters, John Wayne, Orson Welles, Stuart Whitman, Richard Widmark, Michael Wilding, Shelley Winters, Natalie Wood, Joanne Woodward, Ed Wynn, Dana Wynter, Diana Wynyard, Loretta Young, Robert Young, Blanche Yurka, Darryl F. Zanuck.

Synopsis: Hungarian immigrant William Fox, like the other great Hollywood pioneer moguls, began in a lowly station in life. By the early 1910s, he owned a chain of movie theaters, and by 1914, he was also making movies, the first notable one being *Life's Shop Window*. The next year in *A Fool There Was*, he introduced the prototype of the female vampire, popularly shortened to vamp, a woman who toyed with men and then destroyed them. Theda Bara was the actress who sensationalized this type of predatory woman, and she set Fox's studio on the road to great success. Cowboy star Tom Mix was another early draw.

Supposedly using more than 100 clips, *20th Century–Fox: The First 50 Years* celebrates the studio from 1915 to 1965. It did not become Twentieth Century–Fox until 1935 when Fox merged with Twentieth Century Pictures. William Fox himself did not long outlast the early years of the Great Depression as the head of his studio: The brash Darryl F. Zanuck became the company's long-serving production chief. The producers could not resist the temptation to stray outside of the chronology to plug more recent Fox films.

＊ ＊ ＊

The advertising tagline for this film was "Step Inside a Hollywood Dream Factory." Ritz Brothers co-stars Alice Faye and Jane Withers were among those interviewed for this documentary.

Reviews

"A veritable feast for cinephiles.... The good times and the bad, the classics and the box office duds, are all here for the taking in this exhaustive, highly informative documentary.... Much more than a history lesson; it's a homage to Hollywood's illustrious past, and a celebration of all that cinema has to offer." Modern-day commentator.

"[The film] is interesting and entertaining, though a little long. The producers could have dug a little deeper for unusual clips and paid a little more attention to the clips that were shown." Modern-day commentator.

"It's almost like a time machine and gives you the feel of old Hollywood.... Old movie junkies will love this!" Modern-day commentator.

Hidden Hollywood II: More Treasures from the 20th Century–Fox Vaults *(1999)*

Directed by Shelley Lyons and Kevin Burns. Produced by Brian Anthony, Kevin Burns, Michi Jones, Stephanie Keane, Shelley Lyons, Erika Schroeder and Kim Egan. Writers: Brian Anthony, Kevin Burns, Shelley Lyons and Michael Matessino. Editors: Lisa Citron and Poppy Das. Released to television by Foxstar Productions on July 20, 1999.

Cast: Joan Collins (Host), Darrilyn Zanuck DePineda, The Ritz Brothers, Margaret Dumont, Alice Faye, Ronald J. Fields, W.C. Fields, Billy Gilbert, Kay Francis, Robert Gitt, Betty Grable, Sonja Henie, Danny Kaye, Buster Keaton, Carole Landis, Mitzi Mayfair, Carmen Miranda, The Nicholas Brothers (Fayard, Harold), Martha Raye, Ginger Rogers, Abby Schwarzwalder, Phil Silvers, Anthony Slide, Fidel Castro, Joe DiMaggio.

* * *

This made-for-television movie was a sequel to 1997's *Hidden Hollywood: Treasures from the 20th Century–Fox Vaults*. A poster promised: "A Cavalcade of Stars in Complete Long Lost Musical Numbers!" and "See Rare Hollywood Footage Rescued from the Cutting Room Floor!"

Synopsis: Darrilyn Zanuck DePineda, daughter of longtime Twentieth Century–Fox production chief Darryl F. Zanuck, provides some context, as do film historians Robert Gitt and Anthony Slide. The Ritz Brothers are seen in clips from three films. They are shown dancing in their first feature *Sing, Baby, Sing* (1936), and in scenes which had been deleted from *One in a Million* (1936) and *On the Avenue* (1937).

Reviews

"Takes up where *Hidden Hollywood* left off, deleted musical numbers and some newly found scenes.... This included film preservationists showing how nitrate film can turn into dust, and color in film restored with computer techniques.... I think this sequel better than the first." Modern-day commentator.

"Studios interested in nostalgia started digging into their archives, and this led to many of the Fox outtakes being brought together for two different segments of *Hidden Hollywood*, both glorious and necessary viewing for fans of old films.... The Ritz Brothers get a few moments to show their somewhat dated style, perfectly acceptable to those who understand the humor of the 1930s.... The great Alice Faye proves to be a great sport ... having been one of those stifling a laugh during the antics of the Ritz Brothers in *On the Avenue*." Modern-day commentator.

Don Ameche: Hollywood's Class Act *(1999)* *(A&E)*

Directed by Steven C. Smith. Produced by Hayley Briana, Kevin Burns, Michael Cascio, CarolAnne Dolan, Kerry Jensen, Sonja Nelson, Lydia O'Neil and Steven C. Smith. Editor: Bryan Richert. Sound: Gerard Byrne.. Season 8, Episode 62 of *Biography*. Released to A&E Television on October 1, 1999. 44 minutes.

Cast: Peter Graves (Narrator), The Ritz Brothers, Don Ameche, Don Ameche Jr., Rita Ameche, Alice Faye, Ron Howard, John Landis, Frances Langford, Leonard Maltin, The Nicholas Brothers (Fayard, Harold), Carol Ameche Nicholson, Jim Ameche, Annabella, Ralph Bellamy, Edgar Bergen, Irving Berlin, Alice Brady, Klaus Maria Brandauer, Wilford Brimley, Tom Brown, Eddie Cantor, Cher, Charles Coburn, Laird Cregar, Hume Cronyn, Brian Dennehy, Alfred Drake, Denholm Elliott, W.C. Fields, Henry Fonda, James Garner, Janet Gaynor, Betty Grable, Steve Guttenberg, Sonja Henie, Jean Hersholt, William Hickey, Hildegrad Neff, Robert Loggia, Tina Majorino, Joe Mantegna, Tony Martin, Robert Morse, Eddie Murphy, Ornella Muti, J. Carrol Naish, Tyrone Power, Tyrone Power Jr., P. Jay Sidney, Sylvester Stallone, Maureen Stapleton, June Storey, Jessica Tandy, Shirley Temple, Gene Tierney, Gwen Verdon, Jon Voight, John Wallace, Tahnee Welch, Loretta Young, Darryl F. Zanuck.

Synopsis: This episode of the A&E series *Biography* highlights the ups and downs of the long career of suave actor Don Ameche. He went from a humble childhood as the son of an Italian immigrant to Hollywood stardom, helped along by his iconic 1939 role as inventor Alexander Graham Bell. After a lengthy period in career doldrums, Ameche's comeback and an Oscar came in the 1980s. The Ritz Brothers appeared with Ameche in the Fox pictures *One in a Million, You Can't Have Everything* and *The Three Musketeers*.

Modern-Day Commentators; or, "We Don't Get No Respect"

(WITH APOLOGIES TO THE LATE, GREAT RODNEY DANGERFIELD)

The Ritz Brothers are a comedy team whose work most contemporary audiences do not know. "Zany" was a word often associated with them; unfortunately, "forgotten" also is a word associated with them. The last feature film starring all three of the Brothers, *Never a Dull Moment*, was made in 1943. They remained a big draw in clubs for decades so they did continue to have an audience for almost 30 years thereafter.

As their movies become more accessible, they are being written about again, and often not in neutral terms. The author of a 1980s book on comedy teams made this the very first line in the chapter about the Ritzes: "Either you love them or you hate them." Modern-day commentators often seem to lean toward the latter.

One non-fan blogged: "I just don't get their silly wigs, dancing in drag, and simple slapstick. They make the Marx Brothers seem Shakespearean. To me the Ritz Brothers are why they invented 'fast forward.'" The blogger's reference to Shakespeare ignores the fact that the Bard had many such characters in his plays, even the tragedies. The Ritz routines may actually be very much in the mode of Shakespearean clowns.

One such blog headed "The Appeal of the Ritz Brothers" starts out somewhat ominously: "This is not a blog about what I hate [but] I wanted to ... write about the Ritz Brothers, a comedy act I do not like. I never understood their appeal through the years and I still don't." It goes on to say: "The only film I saw them in was *On the Avenue* ... and I thought they slowed down the whole movie."

The blogger may not realize that such specialty acts were routinely interpolated into films of the era, and—yes—they could have been edited out without anyone knowing they had been in the film. That was not because the acts were bad; they were there to spice up what otherwise could have been a dull picture. They could be deleted for another reason: Black specialty performers were often excised when films were shown in the Deep South.

The writer then concedes: "[O]bviously [they] had a lot of appeal in the 1930s and 1940s *and still do today* [italics mine].... The brothers had a large following and some fans compare them to the Marx Brothers." Then he goes on to repeat an often stated complaint: "[T]he Ritzes did not play contrasting characters like the Marxes did ... making it harder to tell them apart." This is certainly true, although Harry Ritz did look somewhat different than his older brothers who were undeniably very much alike. The fact is that the brothers did not base their comedy on being different from each other. That was a conscious career choice they made.

One of the blog's readers, while agreeing that the Ritz Brothers were "an acquired taste," also said with some acumen, "They never got the scripts or movies that could have or would have shown their talents or brand of comedy in the best possible way." In a tip of the hat to both of the famous 1930s trios, the comment was wittily signed "Long live Ritzmarxism!!!" A similar idea was expressed by another blogger: "Too often the Ritz boys were not allowed to just let loose and run away with a picture like other comedy teams of the time." It might be added that they did not have the benefit of the very talented writers furnished to the Marx Brothers at MGM or that studio's production values.

Another blogger said of the brothers: "They could sing, dance and make faces, but as for portraying characters in a narrative film the Ritz Brothers might have as well have been three trained mules.... I find calling the Ritz Brothers a 'comedy team' problematic. It's a comedy team in which all three members are the same guy." In another post he commented: "[They make] a lot of random, aimless contortions to little effect. Rarely have so many faces been pulled in the production of so little laughter."

For a final example of those who dislike the Ritzes: "I've seen about a half-dozen of the Ritz movies and have tried hard to like them, with no success.... Perhaps if I see more I'll grow to like [them] or I'll become suicidal!" One respondent to a blog may have summed up the negative views of some who dislike their type of humor when he said: "[A] theory I've begun to believe in more and more [is] that anyone who was loved by primarily New York audiences usually sucks to the rest of the world." That comment is reflective of a sensibility that many urban audiences seem to develop toward certain types of humor, not necessarily shared by those with dissimilar experiences.

The fact is that the Ritz Brothers were very successful for decades and still have their avid defenders, sometimes in the most unexpected places. In a February 11, 1967, *New Republic* article, "Tourist in the City of Youth," film critic and iconoclast Pauline Kael (1919–2001) wrote about attending a performance of the famous French mime Marcel Marceau. First she mocked the audience for "applauding its own appreciation of beauty and culture." Then she took a contrarian view of Marceau's art:

> It had been bad enough when [Charlie] Chaplin or Harpo [Marx] pulled this beauty-of-pathos stuff.... It just wouldn't do to say something like "I prefer the Ritz Brothers" (though I do, I passionately do).... If I tried to talk in terms of Marceau's artistry versus Harry Ritz's artistry it would be stupid because "artist" is already too pretentious a term for Harry Ritz, and so I would be falsifying what I love him for.

In a December 1978 *New Yorker* review of a science fiction film, Kael says of one of the characters: "She spins her eyeballs, like the great Harry Ritz." In yet another essay, she contrasts the female impersonation done by Cary Grant in *I Was a Male War Bride* with that of Harry Ritz in *On the Avenue*.

Among their chief advocates were some of the most celebrated comics of the modern day who freely acknowledge their debt to the brothers, particularly Harry. More or less echoing the sentiments of Kael, Mel Brooks is quoted in a 1976 *Esquire* article as saying: "As far as I'm concerned there was no intellectualizing with [Harry Ritz]. You just hoped there were no pointy objects in the room when he was working 'cause you were down on the floor, spitting, out of control, laughing your brains out. Harry Ritz always put me away. Always."

Some 40 years later on Conan O'Brien's late night TV show, Brooks was still praising the Ritz Brothers. He speculated their comedy was ultimately based on Jewish historical misfortunes in Europe. When O'Brien asked why they were not better known, Brooks suggested that their films needed to be re-released. He reiterated that contemporaries like Sid Caesar and Jerry Lewis also owed much to the Ritzes. Brooks called Harry "the sire of [comedy] mugging." He is quoted as saying that when he was a kid growing up in Brooklyn, he preferred Harry over Charlie Chaplin.

In the 1976 article, Sid Caesar and Jerry Lewis spoke for themselves. "This man gave comedy a whole new dimension," said Caesar. "Harry was the great innovator. His energy and his sensibility opened things up for all of us. He had to be the funniest man of his time." It has been rumored that when Caesar was doing his popular 1950s television show, just before show time he would repeat to himself, "Tonight I'm Harry Ritz." If true, it seems to have succeeded as a great psych-up line, because Sid Caesar was often brilliant.

Lewis was even more expansive. "Harry was the teacher. He had the extraordinary ability to deny himself dignity on the stage ... that the only thing that mattered was getting a laugh—whether you did it with a camel or two rabbis humping a road map. Harry spawned us all. We all begged, borrowed and stole from him, every one of us. Without him, we wouldn't be here."

In a wide-ranging 1982 *Playboy* interview, George Carlin offered: "I don't know why the Ritz Brothers weren't more popular. It's my belief that Milton Berle and many other successful Jewish comics got their schtick from Harry Ritz. That man invented the moves for a whole generation." It was a tip of the hat from one humorist who broke boundaries to another.

That same year, the highly praised comedy film *My Favorite Year* looked back almost three decades to a time in the 1950s when comic King Kaiser (obviously based on Sid Caesar) reigned supreme on television. The character of writer Benjie Stone enthuses: "On the funny side, there's the Marx Brothers, except Zeppo, the Ritz Brothers, no exceptions, both Laurel and Hardy, and Woody Woodpecker."

Films like *Pretty Woman* and *Mr. Saturday Night* also mentioned them. On the long-running Korean War–era television dramedy *M*A*S*H*, the character Hawkeye Pierce raises his glass in a toast: "Let's drink to something important: To the Ritz Brothers." The television shows *The Simpsons* and *Soap* also gave them a nod. Finally, Norman Lear, legendary creator of many groundbreaking TV shows, gave all the Brothers their poetic due: "[Harry Ritz] was a jewel in a glorious setting and his brothers were the setting,"

In Jerry Lewis' encomium may actually lie one of the reasons the Ritzes are not popular with some viewers. The idea of denying one's dignity may be just the thing they do not understand in the same way comedians do. The Ritzes' willingness to make fools out of themselves may seem more embarrassing to them than brave. The conventional view of proper behavior is violated. In more psychological terms, some viewers simply have no way of identifying with the characters played by the Brothers.

The reaction of another blog respondent may also explain why the Brothers' differences from some other comedy teams irk some viewers: "Every two-person act I can think of uses this same basic premise: with a comic and straight man. But all the Ritzes did the same schtick at the same time." But other three-man acts also did that. All of the Three Stooges and the Marxes had their share of the comedy, always excepting poor Zeppo when they were a foursome. (In real life, Zeppo was reputed to be the funniest of the brothers.)

It was useful for comedy teams to have a memorable tagline that fans always associated with them. Some examples:

Laurel and Hardy: "Here's another fine mess"
Wheeler and Woolsey: "Whoaah!"
Fibber McGee and Molly: "T'ain't funny, McGee"

Modern-Day Commentators; or, "We Don't Get No Respect" 193

Marx Brothers: "Why a duck?"
The Three Stooges: "I'll moider you!"
Rowan and Martin: "Blow in my ear, I'll follow you anywhere"
Amos and Andy: "Holy mackerel, Kingfish!"
Ritz Brothers: "Don't holler, please don't holler!"

The analysis of an actual admirer of Al, Jimmy and Harry has a novel—or at least colorful—slant on the negative reaction of some Ritz watchers:

> To modern viewers [the Ritz Brothers] look like a trio of Huntz Halls [the "dumb" member of the Bowery Boys, Dead End Kids and their other iterations], or three Danny Kayes on drugs. Since they don't look weird (unlike the Stooges or the Marxes) their brand of zaniness seems forced. Audiences think, "They look OK, so what's the problem?" If you look like Curly or Harpo, there's a reason for havoc.

This is an interesting, if debatable, analysis because there are some who think the Ritzes do look "weird," particularly when they are dressed in drag or in one of the other outre costumes they seemed to favor.

There will always be many opinions, pro and con, about the team. Perhaps it all boils down to an individual's sense of humor—or sense of the ridiculous. "Funny" *will* always be, and *should* always be, in the eye of the beholder.

Appendix One:
The Ritz Brothers' Co-Stars

Don Ameche (Dominic Amici), 1908–1993

He was talented as a singer and actor, and had a pleasant enough persona, to have a worthy career without ever becoming a really top star. Don Ameche had his first screen credit in 1936, the same year the Ritz Brothers made their first feature. During the war years he headlined the popular musicals *Down Argentine Way*, *Moon Over Miami* and *That Night in Rio*, all in lush Technicolor, and did some dramas, but then could not sustain his starring career.

Ameche's essential blandness as an actor did not resonate in the grittier postwar era. Television, radio and the stage kept him before the public, and in the 1980s he had a surprising comeback (via *Cocoon*) and won a Best Supporting Actor Oscar. He then was able to work up to the time of his death.

With the Ritz Brothers: *One in a Million, You Can't Have Everything, The Three Musketeers*

LaVerne Andrews, 1911–1967

Although strong-featured LaVerne Andrews sometimes seemed to be in the shadow of her younger siblings, she was the one who encouraged them to persevere until they achieved fame. Their path to popularity began to ascend in 1937 after they were signed by Decca Records. Their recording of "Bei Mir Bist Du Schon" was the number one seller in the country. In some ways, their recordings, especially in the World War II era, were symbolic of America's spirit. Songs like "Don't Sit Under the Apple Tree (with Anyone Else But Me)" and "Boogie Woogie Bugle Boy" became emblematic of the home front.

Maxene Andrews, 1916–1995

Known as the "pretty one," Maxene contributed the high harmony to the trio's songs. She was with her sisters throughout their movie careers in the 1940s when they made a series of peppy "B" musicals for Universal, including *Private Buckaroo* and *Swingtime Johnny*. They sold war bonds and went on numerous tours to entertain the troops. Maxene seemed to be the odd woman out during the group's quarrelsome times but they kept up appearances. She ultimately became a college administrator, proving her bow had more than a single string.

Patricia (Patty) Andrews, 1918–2013

The youngest of the Andrews, Patty was given the most to do as a performer apart from her singing as the lead soprano. She was about 14 when the sisters began their act and she went on to have the longest career. Patty sometimes expressed annoyance at the fact that the trio was always treated as a single entity, saying, "We're not glued together." She need not have worried; she was recognized as the vivacious comic talent of the sisters' act.

With the Ritz Brothers: *Argentine Nights*

Kenneth (Kenny) Baker, 1912–1985

In the mid–1930s, melodious youthful tenor Kenny Baker hit the big time, beginning a four-year stint as the singer on Jack Benny's popular radio show. It gave him the recognition to go from uncredited movie bits to minor leading man status, including in the Marx Brothers film *At the Circus*, *The Goldwyn Follies* and the film version of *The Mikado*. He departed the Benny show in 1939 under unclear circumstances.

Several years later he claimed that he had grown to dislike his persona on the Benny show as the comic butt of jokes. His successor Dennis Day apparently did not mind being portrayed as a dunderhead. Although Baker appeared in a few "B" films in the early 1940s, his career did not continue to prosper. He was in a supporting role in *The Harvey Girls* in 1946, but not too long thereafter left show business.

With the Ritz Brothers: *The Goldwyn Follies*

Donald (Red) Barry (Donald De Acosta), 1912–1980

Donald Barry started in films around 1933, playing uncredited and small roles. He took a big step up the ladder with his casting in the western serial *Adventures of Red Ryder* in 1940. He gained the nickname of Red, which he was to use off and on for the rest of his career. *Red Ryder* led to a long series of "B" westerns and scores of other movie roles that generally diminished in size as time went on. Television provided the source of his working life in the last decades of his life.

With the Ritz Brothers: *Blazing Stewardesses*

Phyllis Brooks (Phyllis Seller), 1915–1995

Pretty former model Phyllis Brooks ("The Ipana Toothpaste Girl") was like many another "B" movie actress. She was competent enough but ultimately left little mark on cinema history in her ten-year career. Among her better-known films were *Little Miss Broadway* and *Lady in the Dark*, as well as some entries in the *Charlie Chan* series. She was one of the first actresses to tour military bases during the war and at the end of that conflict retired from filmmaking. Marriage to a future Congressman who was a former roommate and continuing good friend of John F. Kennedy became a more satisfying occupation.

With the Ritz Brothers: *You Can't Have Everything, Ali Baba Goes to Town, Straight, Place and Show*

Carol Bruce (Shirley Levy), 1919–2007

A husky-voiced band singer and Broadway performer, winsome Carol Bruce made only a handful of films. She is probably best-known today for her role as the overbearing TV station owner Lillian "Mama" Carlson in the comedy series *WKRP in Cincinnati*. (She took over the role from Sylvia Sidney.) Besides co-starring with the Ritz Brothers, she made the film *Keep 'Em Flying* with the *other* Universal comedy team, Bud Abbott and Lou Costello.

With the Ritz Brothers: *Behind the Eight Ball*

Eddie Cantor (Isidor Iskowitch), 1892?–1964

One of the great theatrical talents of the first half of the twentieth century, Eddie Cantor developed a unique style of singing and a memorable persona. These virtues made "Banjo Eyes" a Broadway star in the *Ziegfeld Follies* and the musical shows *Kid Boots* and *Whoopee*. He became a radio and TV personality as well.

Cantor was somewhat of a pioneer in talking pictures, having appeared in an experimental sound short in 1923. By 1930, his film career had taken off but after mid-decade he had lost some of his star luster. The lavish *Ali Baba Goes to Town* was meant to restore that shine. Although he continued to make films thereafter, it was in other media that his continuing fame came. He was known for generously fostering the careers of many young performers.

With the Ritz Brothers: *Ali Baba Goes to Town*

Madeleine Carroll (Edith Carroll; some sources say O'Carroll), 1906–1987

One of Alfred Hitchcock's icy blonde heroines, Madeleine Carroll attained stardom after starring in Hitch's 1935 spy thriller *The 39 Steps*. She had been in British films for several years before that and Hollywood beckoned afterwards. Among her popular 1930s films were *The Prisoner of Zenda, Lloyds of London* and *On the Avenue*, in which she may have been miscast. For a time she was the highest paid actress in Hollywood.

Serious drama was her forte but one of her better remembered roles was the eponymous leading lady of the 1942 Bob Hope film *My Favorite Blonde*. Carroll returned to London to contribute to the war effort and was recognized for that work with a French Legion of Honor.

With the Ritz Brothers: *On the Avenue*

Yvonne De Carlo (Margaret Middleton), 1922–2007

Hollywood turned Canadian chorus girl Yvonne De Carlo into an "exotic" from places like Morocco, Java, Spain and Arabia. She even played a Native American. It was her sultry brunette looks that landed her in films like *Salome, Where She Danced, Slave Girl, Scheherazade, The Desert Hawk* and *Casbah*. She also had the acting chops for gritty works like *Brute Force* and *Criss Cross*.

After doing a couple of prestige movies in the 1950s, *The Ten Commandments* and *Band of Angels*, De Carlo was seen in some less than major westerns. She may have been only a middling Hollywood success but she was a bigger one on television in *The Munsters*, and then in the Broadway musical *Follies*. In her later movie career, she did some films she may have come to regret, including the one she made with the Ritz Brothers.

With the Ritz Brothers: *Blazing Stewardesses, Won Ton Ton, the Dog Who Saved Hollywood*

Alice Faye (Alice Leppert), 1915–1998

Her low voice and perfect phrasing enabled Alice Faye to put over romantic songs like few other singers. With her blonde hair and blue eyes, she was easy to look at, and her acting was always up to par. She quickly rose from chorus girl to star at Fox. Starting in the mid–1930s, she made a string of musicals and dramas which kept her at the top. Among them were *Alexander's Ragtime Band, In Old Chicago, Lillian Russell, Weekend in Havana* and *The Gang's All Here*.

Faye seemed made for Technicolor and remained popular through much of the World War II era. At some point she decided that family life looked more appealing and announced her retirement in 1943. Fox continued to dangle offers in front of her, and she wanted to essay more dramatic roles, so Faye returned for the 1945 film noir *Fallen Angel*. Many of her scenes were cut and that was the end of her time at Fox. She did not make another film until 1962, and then rarely thereafter.

Faye returned to Broadway, briefly appearing in a revival of *Good News*. Her radio comedy shows with husband Phil Harris were also popular. Any lasting fame Alice Faye may have comes mainly from her unique way of putting over such romantic ballads as "You'll Never Know" and "No Love, No Nothin'."

With the Ritz Brothers: *Sing, Baby, Sing, On the Avenue, You Can't Have Everything, Won Ton Ton, the Dog Who Saved Hollywood*

Dick Foran (John Foran), 1910–1979

With his fine singing voice, red-haired Dick Foran (known as Nick in private life) could have had a career like his Warner Brothers contemporary Dick Powell. Since Warners already had Powell, Foran did his warbling in a series of "B" westerns in 1936 and 1937. Warners' resident singing cowboy, he was meant to rival Gene Autry and others of that ilk. He apparently did not catch fire but did go on to sing in occasional movies like *Ride 'Em Cowboy* at Universal.

Foran worked steadily in Hollywood from about 1934 until the mid–1940s. He appeared in some prestigious Warner productions: *The Petrified Forest, Dangerous* and the *Four Daughters* series. At Universal, he was a leading man in a few horror films such as *The Mummy's Hand* and in other "B" films. He spent the 1950s and '60s making frequent TV appearances and an occasional film. Six-foot-three, with a deep, commanding voice, he was an imposing guest artist.

With the Ritz Brothers: *Behind the Eight Ball*

Jane Frazee (Mary Jane Frehse), 1915 [some sources say 1918]–1985

When sisters Ruth and Mary Jane Frehse were still children, they had a vaudeville act that featured their precocious singing and dancing. In the 1930s, both went into the movies. Ruth did not pass muster with the studios, but Jane did: Following a series of musical shorts with Ruth, she made her first solo "B" feature musical, *Moonlight and Melody* (1940). For the next ten years, she was seen frequently, singing in similar "B" films like *What's Cookin'*, *She's a Sweetheart* and *Swingin' on a Rainbow*. She later did some musical westerns with Roy Rogers in which she was always billed *after* Trigger.

With the decline of such films, Frazee's feature career effectively ended, but the peppy actress went on to be seen as the long-suffering wife of Joe McDoakes in the *Behind the Eight Ball* comedy shorts. She is perhaps best-remembered for her role in Abbott and Costello's *Buck Privates*.

With the Ritz Brothers: *Hi'Ya Chum*

Sonja Henie, 1912–1969

She was small (5'1") but mighty, at least in a business sense. Sonja Henie parlayed a talent for the ice skating she learned in her native Norway to careers as a popularizer of ice skating, ice show entrepreneur, and movie star. In the process, she made a fortune. The winner of gold medals in the Olympic Games of 1928, 1932 and 1936, she was also a six-time European champion. To sign her at Fox, Darryl Zanuck agreed to all of Henie's sharp business demands. It was not a bad deal for either one.

Henie made her first film, 1936's *One in a Million*, a big hit; by 1938, she was the movies' third-most popular star. Her 11 starring films also included *Thin Ice*, *Wintertime* and *Sun Valley Serenade*. She was admittedly no actress and eventually her film career began to fade. Henie retired from skating in 1956. Her showmanship on the ice had earned her the sobriquets of "Ice Queen of Norway" (although the "ice" part had a double meaning), and for her business acumen "Little Miss Moneybags."

With the Ritz Brothers: *One in a Million, Ali Baba Goes to Town*

Doris Hill, 1905–1976

A 1929 Wampas Baby Star, Doris Hill was the Ritz Brothers first leading lady. She began appearing in films in the silent era and had her biggest opportunity in the 1929 talkie *His Glorious Night*, playing Hedda Hopper's daughter; but that was a disaster for almost everyone involved. The red-haired Hill was more or less reduced to "B" westerns for the rest of her career. Given her weak speaking voice and indifferent acting ability, she had shown little aptitude for a lengthy talkie career.

With the Ritz Brothers: *Hotel Anchovy*

Patsy Kelly (Bridget Kelly), 1910–1981

Although raucous Patsy Kelly was technically only a supporting player in *The Gorilla*, she was given equal screen time with the nominal stars, the Ritz Brothers. Her role had been built up to express Darryl Zanuck's displeasure with the Ritzes. With the aid of her trademark wisecracking and screaming, she even managed to outshine them. Kelly also had been in their first feature *Sing, Baby, Sing*, in which she had had the better billing.

Kelly honed her comedy skills in a long series of comedy shorts with Thelma Todd in the 1930s and had many movie roles dating back to the early 1930s, always with the same aggressive persona. She had also been on Broadway, and returned to the Great White Way in the 1970s, winning a Tony Award for Best Featured Actress in the musical comedy *No, No, Nanette*. Kelly's well-publicized (and scandalous in those days) personal life, including heavy drinking, impacted her movie career. In 1943, she dropped out of films but returned decades later for a few small roles, including one in *Rosemary's Baby*.

With the Ritz Brothers: *Sing, Baby, Sing, The Gorilla*

Frances Langford (Frances Newbern), 1913?–2005

Possessed of a low singing voice figuratively dripping with honey, Frances Langford was more or less discovered by crooner Rudy Vallee and offered a job on his popular radio show. Her theme song was "I'm in the Mood for Love"; one of her nicknames was "the Florida Thrush."

Besides offering her singing talents, she was a competent enough actress, appearing in more than 25 movies from the mid–1930s. Most of the films were programmers but she was seen in a few big musicals like *Broadway Melody of 1936*, *Born to Dance* and *Yankee Doodle Dandy*. She was the leading lady in the last feature film to star all three of the Ritz Brothers, *Never a Dull Moment*. It was during the war years, especially in her tireless touring of military bases with Bob Hope, that Langford made her greatest contribution. She gained another nickname, "Sweetheart of the Fighting Fronts." Her radio program *The Bickersons*, co-starring Don Ameche, brought her additional popularity.

With the Ritz Brothers: *Never a Dull Moment*

Andrea Leeds (Antoinette Lees), 1913–1984

These days, if Andrea Leeds is known at all, it is for one film, 1937's *Stage Door*. In it, she held her own against an ensemble of actresses that included strong screen personalities Katharine Hepburn, Ginger Rogers, Lucille Ball and Eve Arden. Her more subdued screen persona was just right for her role as a doomed actress, and she was nominated for a Best Supporting Actress Oscar.

In 1933, Leeds had begun working in films under her real name in uncredited and small roles. *Come and Get It* (1936) marked the beginning of a wider recognition of her talents. Her Hollywood days were brief; she made her final film in 1940. Viewed though a modern-day lens, she lacked the charisma that major Hollywood stars require. Perhaps she recognized that talent alone was only going to elevate her to a certain plateau and she did not find that acceptable.

With the Ritz Brothers: *The Goldwyn Follies*

Anita Louise (Anita Fremault), 1915–1970

It may be a coincidence but almost immediately after doing *The Gorilla*, Anita Louise's film career began to decline rapidly. By that time she had reached her apogee with such prestige 1930s films as *A Midsummer Night's Dream*, *Anthony Adverse*, *The Story of Louis Pasteur* and *Marie Antoinette*. She had begun acting in the silent cinema as a child of six or so.

A delicate-looking blonde with a swanlike neck, she seemed mainly suited to roles as a fragile heroine. Only 25 at the beginning of the 1940s, Louise's image was perhaps not gritty enough for the changes the decade wrought in the cinema. She continued to appear in "B" pictures; nevertheless, it was a comedown from the previous decade. She eventually turned to TV to sustain her career and found steady work in that medium.

With the Ritz Brothers: *The Gorilla*

Tony Martin (Alvin Morris), 1913–2012

Tony Martin and the Ritz Brothers both came to feature films at about the same time, in the mid–1930s, and he was to become their most frequent cast-mate. He also co-starred with the Marx Brothers in *The Big Store*, during which he performed the grandiose "Tenement Symphony." His other films included *Ziegfeld Girl*, *Hit the Deck*, *Casbah* and *Two Tickets to Broadway*. Sometimes billed as Anthony Martin, he was never a major star, but his mellow baritone enabled him to have a lengthy career. With an occasional non-musical role, Martin's leading man days lasted until the mid–1950s. He also had many hit recordings, among them "I Get Ideas," "Tonight We Love" and "Fools Rush In." Upon Martin's passing at the great age of 98, a musician friend paid tribute to him as "the ultimate crooner who outlasted all his contemporaries."

With the Ritz Brothers: *Sing, Baby Sing, You Can't Have Everything, Life Begins in College, Ali Baba Goes to Town, Kentucky Moonshine*

Adolphe Menjou, 1890–1963

For many decades, Adolphe Menjou alternated successfully between comic and dramatic roles. He could play hammy and harried and he could play suave and villainous. This versatility was a major reason that his cinema career, which began in the mid–1910s, became a starring one in the 1920s and continued into 1960. He was in many prestigious silent films including *The Sheik*, *A King on Main Street* and *The Three Musketeers*. His manic Oscar-nominated performance in *The Front Page* (1931) firmly established him as a presence in talkies.

In the 1940s, both Menjou's film output and the quality of his films began to decline. He had always been known for his sartorial splendor. In the late 1940s, he was also to be known for a strident anticommunism that some believed adversely affected his career. After many indifferent films, he played a noteworthy part as an incompetent French general in the much-praised World War I story *Paths of Glory* (1957). It was a worthy if brief comeback and a fitting send-off for an actor who had for so long been an important part of Hollywood.

With the Ritz Brothers: *Sing, Baby, Sing, The Goldwyn Follies*

Ethel Merman (Ethel Zimmermann), 1908–1984

Composer Cole Porter compared Ethel Merman's singing to "a brass band going by." The critics at the opening night of her first Broadway show, George Gershwin's *Girl Crazy* (1930), agreed. It launched her on a storied, decades-long stage career. Less storied was her film career. On Broadway, she was a notorious scene-stealer; in Hollywood, she proved too oversized for the motion picture screen.

Merman was rarely asked to recreate her stage roles for the movies. Her appearance with the Ritz Brothers was her last one (except for making one cameo appearance) for the next 15 years. In one of her final major movie roles, in *It's a Mad Mad Mad Mad World*, she literally screamed her way though most of it. However, such Great White Way successes as *Anything Goes*, *Du Barry Was a Lady*, *Annie Get Your Gun* and *Gypsy* well served to honor her considerable talents.

With the Ritz Brothers: *Straight, Place and Show, Won Ton Ton, the Dog Who Saved Hollywood*

Pauline Moore, 1914–2001

It was emblematic of pretty Broadway actress and model Pauline Moore's brief movie career that she went directly from the prestige film *Young Mr. Lincoln* (she was Ann Rutledge) to the programmer *Charlie Chan in Reno*. Except for the occasional "A" film like *Heidi*, she made her career in "B" fare like the Chan series and in westerns with Roy Rogers.

Moore entered films in 1937 and by 1941 she had left them. Two of her more popular efforts were *Charlie Chan at Treasure Island* and the serial *King of the Texas Rangers*, which starred football hero "Slingin'" Sammy Baugh. When she was the sole female performer in a film, she proved to be an adequate leading lady. When cast in a film in which there was a strong female character (like Binnie Barnes' scheming Milady de Winter in *The Three Musketeers*), she was a rather colorless performer. Moore was sporadically seen in the movies during the 1950s and she did some TV as well.

With the Ritz Brothers: *The Three Musketeers*

Robert Paige (AKA David Carlyle) (John Paige), 1910?–1987

Considering the large number of films made by Robert Paige in the 1930s and '40s, one is hard-pressed to find even a few well-known titles. Although blandly handsome, an appealing actor and possessed of a good singing voice, he perhaps was not outstanding enough in any of those talents. Paige was one of a large number of interchangeable leading men who never achieved any real stardom. He did appear with such Universal luminaries as Deanna Durbin and Abbott and Costello but it was not in their better vehicles.

Paige began in films as an uncredited player about 1934; when he did receive billing, it was as David Carlyle. As he became better known, he re-assumed his own surname. Among the films that have some recognition today are *Son of Dracula*, *Hellzapoppin'* and his very last, *Bye, Bye, Birdie*.

With the Ritz Brothers: *Hi'Ya Chum*

Nat Pendleton, 1895–1967

It was often the case in Hollywood that an actor's physical appearance, voice or some other easily identifiable attribute determined his casting opportunities. In Nat Pendleton's case, his wrestler's bulk resulted in an intelligent and well-educated actor being generally cast as dumb, comic or nasty thugs and law officers. His role in the Ritz Brothers' *Life Begins in College* gave him a rare chance to play a heroic leading man, even if it was as a stereotypical Native American.

After a few silent films, Pendleton launched a career in the early 1930s as a character actor and amassed more than 100 credits by the time he left the screen. He actually had been a medal-winning Olympics wrestler and played several in the movies, as well as strongman Sandow in *The Great Ziegfeld*. His best-remembered work may be in the *Thin Man* and *Dr. Kildare* series, and his harried Sgt. Collins in Abbott and Costello's first hit film *Buck Privates*. He repeated the role in his very last film, 1947's *Buck Privates Come Home*.

With the Ritz Brothers: *Life Begins in College*

Dick Powell, 1904–1963

Very few actors have managed as successful and radical a transition in their screen image as did Dick Powell: from innocuous round-faced crooner to hardboiled, hard-faced hero. Starting off as a band and radio singer, he broke into the movies in 1932 and almost immediately found success at a time when screen musicals were making their comeback at Warner Brothers. He had roles in *42nd Street*, *Gold Diggers of 1933* and *Footlight Parade*.

Powell was already approaching 30 so sustaining a long-term career as a "juvenile" (in the musical comedy sense) would become harder and harder. An occasional non-musical role came his way but Powell became increasingly unhappy. He was 40 when he tried for the role that Fred MacMurray got in *Double Indemnity*.

Finally in 1944, man and perfect role came together: He played Philip Marlowe in the very successful film noir *Murder, My Sweet*. In the following years, more hardboiled roles in films and radio followed. Eventually Powell turned to producing and directing, and became a very successful TV entrepreneur.

With the Ritz Brothers: *On the Avenue*

Gloria Stuart (Gloria Stewart, later Finch), 1910–2010

She was no vacuous, albeit beautiful starlet but a thoughtful woman who grew to denigrate her movie career as an ingénue, calling it "stupid and clichéd." Designated a Wampas Baby Star in 1932, the year she entered films, Gloria Stuart worked for Universal and Fox through the 1930s. The studio bosses were not thrilled with her outspokenness, which was very unusual for that time. Movie buffs probably best remember her for a couple of films with Shirley Temple and roles in *The Invisible Man* and *Gold Diggers of 1935*. After a few movies in the 1940s, Stuart departed Hollywood for private life, reappearing on TV almost 30 years later.

In the 1980s, she played a few movie bits including a cameo in *My Favorite Year* (1982). It was therefore a surprise when she suddenly showed up in one of the most successful and profitable films of the modern era: 1997's *Titanic*. For her performance as the 101-year-old Rose in the framing story, she was nominated for both a Best Supporting Actress Golden Globe and an Oscar, the oldest actress to be so nominated. Two more film assignments followed in 1999, making Gloria Stuart Hollywood's oldest working actress. She passed on at age 100, almost as old as the fictional Rose of *Titanic*.

With the Ritz Brothers: *Life Begins in College*, *The Three Musketeers*

Marjorie Weaver, 1913–1994

After a few uncredited roles, pert Marjorie Weaver was destined for a career as a supporting player in "A" films and a leading lady in bottom-of-the-bill fare such as the *Charlie Chan* series. She was seen onscreen until the mid–1940s, occasionally top-billed. Her one prestige film role was as Mary Todd in 1939's *Young Mr. Lincoln*. This was apropos, as she was a Kentuckian like the historic Mary Todd Lincoln. Weaver displayed little to differentiate her from the scores of pretty actresses who could fill a role competently but forgettably.

With the Ritz Brothers: *On the Avenue*, *Life Begins in College*, *Ali Baba Goes to Town*, *Kentucky Moonshine*

Jane Withers, born 1926

She came to moviegoers' attention as the little girl you loved to hate, the mean nemesis of Shirley Temple in 1934's *Bright Eyes*. Soon Jane Withers became the little girl you loved to love when Fox cast the multi-talented youngster in a series of films, including

Ginger, *Pepper* and *Checkers*. She was always the spunky can-do girl, a persona which fit her fast-developing physical attributes. On the cusp of her teen years, Withers had already matured quite a bit.

Although she was still active during the early 1940s, like most former child stars her career inevitably faded. If Withers is known to modern-day movie audiences, it is perhaps for her role as Vashti Snythe in the popular 1956 film *Giant* in which she was fifth-billed. Her last feature was *Captain Newman M.D.* in 1963. She did many TV shows and was still doing voiceovers into the twenty-first century. Most likely it is her long-running series of television commercials as the hearty Josephine the Plumber that people remember.

With the Ritz Brothers: *Pack Up Your Troubles*

Appendix Two: Ritz Brothers Miscellany

This section contains Ritz items that do not easily fit in the other categories into which this book is arranged. They are chronologically arranged.

Hollywood Hotel *(radio broadcast). 1936.*

An episode of the popular hour-long radio program, hosted by columnist Louella Parsons. This was captured on film for publicity purposes by Twentieth Century–Fox. Guests were the Ritz Brothers, Alice Faye, Sonia Henie, Darryl F. Zanuck and Dick Powell.

The Autograph Hound *(cartoon). Walt Disney Company, 1939.*

Donald Duck seeks autographs from some big stars; a policeman tries to keep Donald from annoying them. Among those Donald pursues are Greta Garbo, Mickey Rooney, Sonja Henie, Shirley Temple and the Ritz Brothers. The brothers finally agree to sign, and they do—on Donald's rear end. They are cleverly caricatured with pointy chins and their antics are unmistakably Ritzian. When the stars realize it is Donald Duck, they all scramble to get *his* autograph.

Lasker-Schuler, Else. IchundIch: eine theatralische Tragodie *(Play). 1941.*

A play within a play, translated into English as *I and I*, this is a parody of National Socialism and classical German culture. The setting is a rehearsal directed by famed impresario Max Reinhardt. There are characters from the Bible and *Faust* plus modern-day figures including the Ritz Brothers. In the play, the Biblical trio of Saul, Solomon and David act as the serious counterweights to the antics of the Ritzes. The characters ruminate on current events and the meaning of eternity while the Nazis attempt to conquer Hell as they have conquered the world.

Life Can Be Crazy in Balmy Florida—Gin Rummy Helps! *Introduced by Lew (Schneider) Lehr. Newsreel excerpt. Fox Movietone News, distributed by Twentieth Century–Fox, 1946.*

The Ritz Brothers dressed as lifeguards are playing gin rummy beside a pool in Miami Beach, and quibbling about the cards. A girl falls into the pool and appears to be drowning. The brothers ignore her plight as bystanders yell at them to rescue her. As one of the Ritzes announces he has gin, Harry asks what happens if the girl goes down for a third time. "She drowns," his brothers reply.

This was probably taken at a time when the Ritz Brothers were performing at a Miami Beach nightclub. Lew Lehr was a comic and writer known for his catch phrase "Monkeys is the cwaziest [sic] people."

Hilarity in Hollywood *(recording). Hilarity Hi-Fi Records, 1958.*

Along with such diverse performers as Sophie Tucker, Skinnay Ennis and his Band, and the Ben Yost Royal Guards, Harry Ritz recorded four tracks on an LP record. With a group called the Bon Vivants, he performs "Hilarity/Don't Holler" and "Rockabilly Wedding Day"; as a soloist he performs "What the Little People Say" and "Who's Got Troubles?" It was recorded in Hollywood in July 1958.

The Beanes of Boston *(television series pilot). Paramount Television, 1979.*

The British television comedy series *Are You Being Served?* ran from 1972 to 1985. Set in the fictional Grace Brothers Department Store, and featuring a cast of eccentric store employees, it was very popular in Britain as well as in the U.S. It was perhaps inevitable that an American equivalent would be attempted. On May 5, 1979, an unsold pilot called *The Beanes of Boston* aired. Based on the original series' April 3, 1975, episode "German Week," it features the talented actors Tom Poston, John Hillerman, Morgan Farley, Charlotte Rae and Alan Sues.

Some filmographies also list Harry Ritz in the cast as Mr. Beane. If he was actually considered for or cast in the pilot, it would probably have been as one of the elderly founding Beane brothers. (Some sources say his character was to be named Uncle Fred.) In any case, he does not appear in the completed pilot. Perhaps he dropped out because of poor health?

Women in Film Oral History Interview *(recording). University of California, Los Angeles, Center for Oral History Research, October 11, 2001.*

Actress Gloria Stuart (1910–2010) is interviewed by Bobbi Frank about her life and career. Among the numerous actors whom she discusses are the Ritz Brothers, with whom she appeared in *Life Begins in College* and *The Three Musketeers*.

Appendix Three:
Versions of The Three Musketeers

It is doubtful that many, if indeed *any*, stories have been retold in the cinema more than *The Three Musketeers*. There have been famous versions, obscure ones, serious ones, comic ones, musical ones, parodies, silents, talkies, 3-D, even cartoons.

It has been remade in many lands and in many languages, a noteworthy record for a novel originally written in 1844. It has never gone out of print. Another of Alexandre Dumas' swashbucklers, *The Count of Monte Cristo*, is also no slouch in the cinema department. Below is a list of a few of the versions of this seemingly evergreen story.

The Stage

There have been at least two Broadway musical versions of *The Three Musketeers*. The first one, an operetta, opened in 1921 and closed after five performances. Richard Temple wrote the lyrics, book and music and played D'Artagnan.

The second version, a musical comedy subtitled *A Musical Adventure*, opened in 1928 and ran for over 300 performances. Rudolf Friml was the composer; Flo Ziegfeld, the producer; one of the lyricists was humorist P.G. Wodehouse of *Jeeves* fame. Among the cast members was deep-voiced Douglass Dumbrille, portrayer of many a movie villain. He was also in the Ritz version, playing Athos. English actor Reginald Owen and operetta stars Dennis King and Vivienne Segal were also featured. It was briefly revived in the 1980s.

Films

A reviewer of the 3-D film version made in 2011 joked about the plenitude of *Three Musketeers* adaptations by saying: "Given that Hollywood did a film with the title characters played by the cult comedy team the Ritz Brothers, is there any version that can still shock us?" He makes the common mistake: The Ritzes do *not* actually play the Musketeers, but their inept substitutes.

The motion picture and made-for-TV versions of *The Three Musketeers* are too numerous to list even if limited to those in the English language. World productions date back to near the dawn of the silent era, possibly to a 1903 French version. Besides the 1939 Ritz film, the better known American versions are: 1921, Douglas Fairbanks (he had made an earlier comedy called *A Modern Musketeer*); 1935, Walter Abel; 1948, Gene

Kelly; 1973, Michael York; 1993, Charlie Sheen; 2011, Logan Lerman. There have also been some *Four Musketeers* films.

Among the more unusual film versions:

The Three-Must-Get-Theres (1922)

One of French comedian Max Linder's few full-length American features, this is a parody of the Douglas Fairbanks film. Linder's character is known as Dart-in-Again; another is called L'il Cardinal Richie Loo.

The Three Musketeers (1933)

A serial version starring pre-fame John Wayne, and updated to the French Foreign Legion in modern-day North Africa.

The Three Mesquiteers (1936 to 1943)

A lengthy series of more than 50 "B" westerns, starring Robert (Bob) Livingston, Ray Corrigan, John Wayne and others as the series progressed. Livingston appeared with Jimmy and Harry Ritz in *Blazing Stewardesses*.

The Two Mousketeers (1952)

One of the entries in the long-running *Tom and Jerry* cartoon series. Two mice, Jerry and Nibbles, raid the king's feast. Tom, the cat, has been assigned to guard the food but as usual is easily bested.

Other cartoon versions include: *Three Blind Mouseketeers* (1936) and *Mickey, Donald, Goofy: The Three Musketeers* (2004).

Barbie and the Three Musketeers (2009)

In this animated version, fashion doll Barbie plays Connie D'Artagnan, who dreams of becoming a musketeer like her father. Even her cat wants to be a mus-cat-eer!

Bibliography

Books

Allen, Steve. *The Funny Men.* New York: Simon & Schuster, 1956.
Ashbery, John. *Breezeway: New Poems.* New York: Ecco, 2015.
Berg, A. Scott. *Goldwyn: A Biography.* New York: Knopf, 1989.
Bordman, Gerald. *American Musical Theatre: A Chronicle.* New York: Oxford University Press, 1978.
Brant, Marley. *Happier Days: Paramount Television's Classic Sitcoms, 1974–1984.* New York: Billboard Books, 2006.
Crick, Robert Alan. *The Big Screen Comedies of Mel Brooks.* Jefferson, NC: McFarland, 2002.
Cullen, Frank, et al. *Vaudeville, Old and New: An Encyclopedia of Variety Performers in America.* New York: Routledge, 2007.
Dauber, Jeremy. *Jewish Comedy: A Serious History.* New York: Norton, 2017.
Dietz, Dan. *The Complete Book of 1920s Broadway Musicals.* Lanham, MD: Rowman & Littlefield, 2017.
Epstein, Lawrence J. *Mixed Nuts: America's Love Affair with Comedy Teams.* New York: Public Affairs, 2004.
Erickson, Hal. *From Radio to the Big Screen: Hollywood Films Featuring Broadcast Personalities and Programs.* Jefferson, NC: McFarland, 2014.
Flinn, Caryl. *Brass Diva: The Life and Legends of Ethel Merman.* Berkeley: University of California Press, 2009.
Hall, Linda. *Dolores Del Rio: Beauty in Light and Shade.* Stanford, CA: Stanford University Press, 2013.
Hedges, Inez. *Framing Faust: Twentieth Century Cultural Struggles.* Carbondale: Southern Illinois University Press, 2007.
Kael, Pauline. *The Age of Movies: Selected Writings of Pauline Kael.* New York: Library of America, 2011.
Krefft, Vanda. *The Man Who Made the Movies: The Meteoric Rise and Tragic Fall of William Fox.* New York: Harper, 2017.
Lasker-Schuler, Else. *Three Plays: Dark River; Arthur Aronymous* [sic] *and His Ancestors; I and I.* Evanston, IL: Northwestern University Press, 2005.
Library of Congress. Copyright Office. *Catalog of Copyright Entries: Works of Art...* 3rd Series. Washington, D.C.: 19--.
Liebman, Roy. *Broadway Actors in Films, 1894–2015.* Jefferson, NC: McFarland, 2017.
_____. *From Silents to Sound: A Biographical Encyclopedia of Performers Who Made the Transition to Talking Pictures.* Jefferson, NC: McFarland, 1998, 2009.
_____. *The Wampas Baby Stars: A Biographical Dictionary, 1922–1934.* Jefferson, NC: McFarland, 2000, 2009.
Maltin, Leonard. *Movie Comedy Teams.* Revised and updated ed. New York: New American Library, 1985.
McGilligan, Patrick. *Funny Man, Mel Brooks.* New York: HarperCollins, 2019.

Medved, Harry, with Randy Dreyfuss. *The Fifty Worst Films of All Times; And How they Got That Way.* New York: Popular Library, 1978.
Mordden, Ethan. *Make Believe: The Broadway Musical in the 1920s.* New York: Oxford University Press, 1997.
Parish, James Robert, and William T. Leonard, with Gregory W. Mank and Charles Hoyt. *The Funsters.* New York: Arlington House, 1979.
Price, Ira. *A Hundred Million Movie-Goers Must Be Right.* Cleveland, Ohio: Movie Appreciation Press, 1938.
Robinson, Jeffrey. *Teamwork.* New York: Proteus, 1982.
Sforza, John. *Swing It! The Andrews Sisters Story.* Lexington: University Press of Kentucky, 2000.
Slide, Anthony. *Encyclopedia of Vaudeville.* Reprint ed. Jackson: University Press of Mississippi, 2012. Originally published: Greenwood Press, 1994.
Trav S.D. [i.e., Travis Stewart]. *No Applause, Just Throw Money, or The Book That Made Vaudeville Famous.* New York: Farrar, Straus & Giroux, 2005.
Watz, Edward. *Wheeler & Woolsey: The Vaudeville Comic Duo and Their Films, 1929–1937.* Jefferson, NC: McFarland, 1994.

Periodicals

Periodicals and newspapers were mostly consulted via online databases. Many were useful resources for reviews, opinions, commentary, information, speculation, and gossip about the Ritz Brothers.

Box Office Digest
Boxoffice
Boy's Cinema
Broadcasting
Business Screen Magazine
Cinema Progress
The Educational Screen
Exhibitor
Exhibitors Herald
Exhibitors Herald and Moving Picture world
Exhibitors Herald World
Film Daily Yearbook
Film Fun
FilmIndia
Glamour of Hollywood
Harrison's Reports
Hollywood
Hollywood Motion Picture Reviews
Hollywood Reporter
Hollywood Spectator
Independent Exhibitors Film Bulletin
Independent Film Journal
International Photographer
Los Angeles Examiner
Los Angeles Times
Modern Screen
Motion Picture and the Family
Motion Picture Daily
Motion Picture Herald
Motion Picture News
Motion Picture Reviews
Movie Classic
Movie Makers
Movies…and the People Who Make Them
National Board of Review Magazine
NBC Transmitter
New York Times
Paramount International News
Philadelphia Exhibitor
Photoplay
Picture Play Magazine
Radio and Television Mirror
Radio Annual and Television Yearbook
Radio Daily
Radio Mirror
Screenland
Showmen's Trade Review
Silver Screen
Swing
TV Radio Mirror
20th Century–Fox Dynamo
Variety
World Film and Television Progress

DVDs

Classic Musical Shorts from the Dream Factory. 4 discs. Warner Archive, 2010. Contains the 1937 short *Cinema Circus.*

Hollywood's Classic Comedy Teams: 12 Legendary Laugh-Making Teams. 5 discs. North Hollywood, CA: Passport, [undated]. Includes selected features or short films of twelve comedy teams, ranging from John Bunny and Flora Finch in 1912 to Dean Martin and Jerry Lewis in 1950. The Ritz Brothers appear on disc number four in *The Gorilla*. Other comedy teams include Olsen and Johnson, Wheeler and Woolsey, The Marx Brothers, Amos and Andy, Laurel and Hardy, The Three Stooges, Abbott and Costello, and the rarely seen Clark and McCullough.

Television

Mel Brooks: Make a Noise. American Masters for Thirteen (PBS), 2013. 90 minutes.

Selected Online Sources

ancestry.com
archive.nytimes.com
columbiashortsdept.weebly.com/screen-snapshots
ibdb.com
imdb.com
latimes.newspapers.com

mediahistoryproject.org
playbill.com
proquest.com
worldcat.org
youtube.com

20th Century–Fox Archives

Cinematic Arts Library, the University of Southern California. Progressive versions of scripts for all the films the Ritz Brothers made for 20th Century–Fox; budget proposals; casting suggestions; conference minutes; memoranda; publicity; production data; handwritten notes by Darryl F. Zanuck.

Index

Numbers in **_bold italics_** indicate pages with illustrations

Ali Baba Goes to Town 130–135
All Star Revue 168–170
All-Star Thanksgiving Show 167–168
Ameche, Don 34, 61, 93, 187–188, 195
Ames, Walter 1
Andrews Sisters (LaVerne, Maxene, Patricia "Patty") **_38_**–39, 108–109, 112–113, 195–196
Argentine Nights 38–39, 108–115, **_110_**
Autograph Hound 205

Baker, Kenny 76, 196
Baker, Phil 135, 137
Barry, Donald "Red" 41, 126. 129, 196
Barrymore, John 31, 43, 45–46
Bat 96–97, 102
Beanes of Boston 206
Behind the Eight Ball 40, 115–118, **_117_**
Berle, Milton 9–10, 172
Berlin, Irving 53
Blazing Stewardesses 25, 41, 125–130
Bob Hope in Joys see *Texaco Presents Bob Hope in Joys*
Boys from Syracuse 37, 108
Broadway Highlights, #6: High Spots of the Main Stem 152–153
Brooklyn Goes to Las Vegas 165–166
Brooks, Mel 41–42, 51, 128, 144, 147, 191, 211
Brooks, Phyllis 196
Bruce, Carol 197

Caesar, Sid 144, 146, 191–192
Calamari, Antoinette 14; *see also* Ritz, Annette
Cantor, Eddie 86, 130–131, 133–134, 197
Carroll, Madeleine 55, 197
Cinema Circus 153–155
Classic Comedy Teams 183–184
Cocoanuts 29, 150
Cohn, Harry 22, 34
Colgate Comedy Hour 170–171
Collegians 17, 20, 28, 30

Davis, Joan 53, 79
De Carlo, Yvonne 41, 129, 197–198
Dick Cavett Show 177
Don Ameche: Hollywood's Class Act 187–188
Don't Holla 1

Ed Sullivan Show 173; see also *Toast of the Town*

Faye, Alice 31–32, 52, 198
Florida Girl 17, 26–29
Foran, Dick 198
Foster, Phil 166
Frazee, Jane 121, 198–199
From Rags to Ritzes 1
Funny Men see *Hollywood and the Stars: The Funny Men, Part 2*

Galloping Geese 23
Ginger Rogers Show see *Pontiac Star Parade: Ginger Rogers Show*
Goldwyn, Samuel 71–72
Goldwyn Follies 33, 72–78
Gorilla 35–36, 96–103, **_100_**
Great Al Jolson see *Screen Snapshots: The Great Al Jolson*
Greenfield, Charlotte 15

Heath, Betty May 15
Henie, Sonja 31, 47–48, 50–51, 199
Here's Hollywood 173
Hi'Ya Chum 40, 119–122, **_120_**
Hidden Hollywood II: More Treasures from the 20th Century-Fox Vaults 186–187
High Spots of the Main Stem see *Broadway Highlights #6: High Spots of the Main Stem*
Hilarity in Hollywood 206
Hill, Doris 30, 151, 199
Hilliard, Ruth 14
Hollywood and the Stars: the Funny Men, Part 2 179–180
Hollywood Hobbies 159–162

213

Index

Hollywood Hotel 205
Hollywood: The Gift of Laughter 180–183
Hollywood Walk of Fame 8–10
Hollywood's Famous Feet see *Screen Snapshots, Series 29, #11: Hollywood's Famous Feet*
Hollywood's Invisible Man see *Screen Snapshots: Hollywood's Invisible Man*
Hope Deferred 25
Hotel Anchovy 20, 30, 148–152
Hotel Ritz 22
Hovick, Louise see Lee, Gypsy Rose

I and I see *IchundIch*
IchundIch 205

Jackpot Bowling, Starring Milton Berle 172
Jewish Humor: A Serious Study 3
Joachim, Abraham Leib 11
Joachim, George Aaron 11, 33–34
Joachim, Gertrude 12
Joachim, Harry 11
Joachim, Max 12, 16
Joachim, Morris 12
Joachim, Pauline 12–13
Joachim, Samuel 11
Joachim, William 11, 13–14
Joey Bishop Show 174
Jolson, Al 138, 159
Joys see *Texaco Presents Bob Hope in Joys*

Kael, Pauline 1, 37, 84, 191
Kellow, Betty (Roday) 15
Kelly, Patsy 36, 102–103, 199–200
Kentucky Moonshine 33–34, 78–85, **83**

Langford, Frances 40, 123, 200
Lee, Gypsy Rose 61, 133
Lee, Judy 14
Leeds, Andrea 75, 200
Leon, Naomi 15
Let's Make Love 55
Levey, Jules 37
Lewis, Jerry 23, 56, 191–192
Life Begins in College 2, 16, 32–33, 63–70, 156, **66**
Life Can Be Crazy in Balmy Florida 206
Livingston, Bob 126, 129
Lorraine and Ritz 16
Louise, Anita 200

Martin, Tony 60, 68, 81, 201
Marx Brothers 2–4, 23, 28–29, 32, 57, 74, 89, 150, 189–190
Massow, Marjorie 136, 138
Max Liebman Presents 171
Meet the Stars, #6: Stars at Play 162–163
Memories of Famous Hollywood Comedians see *Screen Snapshots, #31: Memories of Famous Hollywood Comedians*
Menjou, Adolphe 43, 75, 201
Meredith, Madge see Massow, Marjorie

Merman, Ethel 1, 86, 89, 201
Merv Griffin Show 140, 174–176
Mike Douglas Show 175
Moore, Pauline 202
Murray, Jan 17, 24, 176
Mussolini, Benito 3

Nelson, Annette 14, 16; see also Ritz, Annette
Never a Dull Moment 40, 122–125

Olympic Fund Telethon 169–170
On the Avenue 31, 52–57
One in a Million 31, 47–52

Pack Up Your Troubles 36, 103–108
Paige, Robert 121, 202
Past Performances 23
Pendleton, Nat 202
Pontiac Star Parade: the Ginger Rogers Show 171
Powell, Dick 52, 56, 202–203
"Puttin' on the Ritz" 11, 19, 22, 51

Rin Tin Tin 63, 139–140, 143
Ritz, Allison 14
Ritz, Annette 14
Ritz, Janna 15
Ritz, Melinda 15
Ritz, Michael 15–16
Ritz, Michelle 15
Ritz, Philip 15
Ritz, Robert 15
Ritz Blitz 23
Ritz Hotel 22

Sawdust Serenade 23
Screen Snapshots 155–159
Screen Snapshots: Hollywood's Invisible Man 158–159
Screen Snapshots, Series 17, #6 156–157
Screen Snapshots, Series 22, #5 157
Screen Snapshots, Series 22, #8: Seeing Hollywood 57
Screen Snapshots, Series 29, #11: Hollywood's Famous Feet 158
Screen Snapshots, Series 31: Memories of Famous Hollywood Comedians 158
Screen Snapshots: The Great Al Jolson 159
Seeing Hollywood see *Screen Snapshots, Series 22, #8: Seeing Hollywood*
Segal, Vivienne 28
Sennett, Mack 23
Show-Business at War 163–165
Siegel, Bugsy (Benjamin) 15, 22
Silent Movie 25, 41–42, 144–148
Sing, Baby, Sing 2, 31, 43–47, 127
Solly Sisters and Jimmy Ritz 16
Sound of Laughter 178–179
Stars at Play see *Meet the Stars #6: Stars at Play*
Straight, Place and Show 24, 34, 85–90
Stuart, Gloria 68, 203, 206

Take It or Leave It 135–139
Texaco Presents Bob Hope in Joys 176
Three Musketeers 35, 90–96, 207–208
Three Vaqueros 23
Tip, Tap and Toe 61
Toast of the Town 22, 167; *see also Ed Sullivan Show*
20th Century-Fox: The First 50 Years 184–186

Walk of Stars (Palm Springs) 9
Weaver, Marjorie 68, 83, 203
What's My Line? 172–173

Withers, Jane 36, 104, 106–107, 192, 203–204
Won Ton Ton, the Dog Who Saved Hollywood 25, 41, 139–144
Wurtzel, Sol 34

Yacht Club Boys 46
You Can't Have Everything **32**, 57–63, **59**

Zanuck, Darryl F. 21, 31, 33, 35–36, 43–44, 48, 52–53, 55, 57–58, 63–64, 67, 79–80, 86–87, 91, 94, 98, 102, 164
Zorina, Vera 71, 75

www.ingramcontent.com/pod-product-compliance
Ingram Content Group UK Ltd.
Pitfield, Milton Keynes, MK11 3LW, UK
UKHW041957140426
5217IPUK00015B/851